Managing
Magazine Publishing

John Wharton

in association with the
Periodicals Training Council

BLUEPRINT
An Imprint of Chapman & Hall

London · Glasgow · New York · Tokyo · Melbourne · Madras

Published by Blueprint, an imprint of Chapman & Hall, 2-6 Boundary Row, London SE1 8HN

Chapman & Hall, 2-6 Boundary Row, London SE1 8HN, UK

Blackie Academic & Professional, Wester Cleddens Road, Bishopbriggs, Glasgow G64 2NZ, UK

Van Nostrand Reinhold Inc., 115 5th Avenue, New York NY10003, USA

Chapman & Hall Japan, Thomson Publishing Japan, Hirakawacho Nemoto Building, 6F, 1-7-11 Hirakawa-cho, Chiyoda-ku, Tokyo 102, Japan

Chapman & Hall Australia, Thomas Nelson Australia, 102 Dodds Street, South Melbourne, Victoria 3205, Australia

Chapman & Hall India, R. Seshadri, 32 Second Main Road, CIT East, Madras 600 035, India

First edition 1992

© 1992 John Wharton

Printed in Great Britain by St Edmundsbury Press, Bury St Edmunds

ISBN 0 948905 80 8

A catalogue record for this book is available from the British Library

Library of Congress Cataloging-in-Publication data available

Managing Magazine Publishing

Acknowledgements

I am indebted to many people for their very kind assistance in the preparation of this book. For their encouragement and support — David Longbottom, Executive Director of the Periodicals Training Council, and the members of the Council; for the original research — Ron Sumption (former Executive Director of the PTC); for patiently answering questions and reading drafts — Brian Cottee, Sandra Nicolson, Gerald Saunders and Phil Baker (International Thomson Business Magazines), David Sheilds (The National Magazine Company Limited), Robin Wood (Morgan-Grampian), Ian Locks, Peter Dear, Jill Simmons and Brian Williamson (PPA), and Brian Rowbotham; for the foreword — Terry Mansfield (The National Magazine Company Limited).

And, of course, warm thanks are due to Vivien James at Blueprint for her help, encouragement and advice.

John Wharton
Autumn 1992

Contents

Foreword

Clearly I am biased, but, for my money, magazine publishing has to be one of the most interesting, varied, demanding, yet rewarding ways of making a living. I have been at it for more than three decades and I don't regret a day of it.

For all of us involved in magazine publishing and, indeed, all those who would like to be, John Wharton's book represents a very valuable and long overdue opportunity. It seems extraordinary that it was not published decades ago — in my case, three decades would have been just about right!

The essence of magazine publishing is not especially complicated. The key thing to remember is that magazines exist first and foremost to satisfy those who read them: fail to get that right and everything else is irrelevant. And yet there is much more to deal with. A good magazine, or even a great magazine, is only the beginning; success requires far more, and continuing success — far, far more.

John Wharton's book gives an invaluable overview of the magazine business from the publisher's standpoint and that overview is complemented by a multiplicity of insights into the various disciplines involved in magazine management and fascinating examples of how they have been applied. Everyone in our business can learn from these pages and I hope that everyone will.

One of the key factors which, it seems to me, makes our business so interesting and inspiring is that it all depends on the people it employs. It goes without saying that the continuing advance of information and printing technologies will change the way we do things, but the what that we do will always depend on the talent, flair, creativity, enthusiasm, energy, commitment and knowledge of the people who use those technologies. The magazine industry can only be as good as the people who work in it and those people can only give of their best when they have the knowledge and training to turn talent into performance. This book is a major contribution in that respect and I am delighted to have been given the opportunity of introducing it to you.

Terry Mansfield
Managing Director
The National Magazine Company Limited

Introduction

When I first became a publisher, my experience was that of a journalist and editor (learnt by looking over someone's shoulder). I had worked in fairly close co-operation with an advertisement manager and I was both reasonably observant of, and interested in, the other aspects of publishing, but really I knew very little of advertising, or of selling, or of circulation, or of budgets and financial control, or anything outside my immediate area.

However, help was at hand. To appreciate the finer points of selling I was sent on a two-day public course run by one Heinz Goldman, a fast-talking American whiz at selling groceries to corner shops. I was introduced to some mnemonics (AIDA has stayed with me — Attention, Interest, Desire, Action), and told how to seduce shopkeepers into stocking more margarine than they actually needed. I had the temerity to ask for specific advice on selling advertising and was told, 'Ah, that's an abstract, but the principle's the same'.

Scarcely enlightened, I went off to tell my advertisement manager how to do it.

Well, times have changed and being thrown in at the deep end or sitting next to Nellie are training methods that have largely been replaced. You can learn to swim if you get pushed in, but with only desperation and intuition for support, life is quite terrifying and more than a little tenuous.

Education and training, the formal and informal acquisition of knowledge and skills, are regarded differently today. We are trained before taking on, or while learning, a particular job (a kind of apprenticeship), we receive further training to help us develop in that job and we also receive training for our next level of skill or responsibility. At least, that's the theory.

I hope this book will be a part of that process. Not a textbook in the sense that it contains precise how-to-do-it instructions, but a source which identifies the various publishing disciplines or activities, the ways in which they work, and how they come together. It will help you get to know and understand what the other person does and the significance of their work to the common objective, profit.

Without profit, a magazine has no point or purpose and the efforts of those involved are wasted. Profit may be interpreted in different ways, of course. First, and most obvious, it is the excess of income over expenditure — Mr Micawber's state of happiness — and is the payback on investment. For some magazine publishers, profit might be the achievement of other goals. The magazine might yield a worthwhile return by spreading a particular gospel to a wider audience or by providing information and news to the members of an organization. Therefore, profit is not necessarily measured in pounds sterling (or even ECUs). Because of the likely interest of the majority of this book's readers, however, I'm going to assume that financial profit is the objective — in any case, the practices and rules are largely the same, whether working to a profit, to break-even or to a loss; it's merely the emphasis that changes.

The same can be said of the differences between the various kinds of magazine. I have been involved, directly or indirectly, in publishing consumer, consumer special interest, business (used to be called trade and technical), scientific, technical and medical (commonly known as STM) and association magazines. The circulation methods have included newstrade, subscription, controlled circulation, free distribution, directed and association membership. It's not any particular talent that has led to this wide experience, but rather the fact that there's a lot more in common between the different types of magazine than most people suppose.

The common factors are financial objectives (i.e. profit, break-even, sometimes even a loss), marketing, editorial, advertising, circulation, production and financial control. What change are the relative importance of those areas and the scale of the operation.

So, most of what this book contains will be of interest to most people holding, or about to hold, the title or role of 'Publisher'. If you have been an editor, an advertisement manager, a circulation manager, a marketing manager or have a financial background, you will know about 20 per cent of what you need to know. And please don't skip the passages relating to your own discipline, for it's as well to know what others are being told about your speciality.

Another issue which obscures the similarity between different magazines is the hairy one of job titles. Most people concur on an editor's role and duties, but the other titles mentioned in this book are capable of different interpretations. So for the purposes of simplification and understanding, let me give you the definitions I am comfortable with.

Publisher: the person to whom the editor, advertisement manager, circulation manager and heads of other of the magazine's activities report, with whom service departments liaise and who is ultimately responsible for the profitability of a magazine. Other titles which might apply are managing director, director, publishing director, general manager.

Advertisement manager: the person responsible to the publisher for the magazine's advertisement sales, both display and classified. Other titles might be advertisement director, sales director, director of advertisement sales, sales manager.

Circulation manager: the person responsible to the publisher for the magazine's circulation. Circulation managers may run a company-wide department and thus report to a number of publishers as head of a service department rather than as a magazine executive. Sometimes the circulation manager is a relatively junior executive within a circulation department who works full-time on a magazine; sometimes the circulation manager is a full member of a magazine's team using the central circulation department as a subcontractor. Other possible titles are circulation director, director of circulation, circulation sales executive, marketing executive.

The publishers of, say, *Woman's Own*, *Radio Times*, *The Grocer*, *The Stage*, *Construction Weekly*, *Illustrated London News*, *Cosmopolitan*, *GQ* and *Brewers' Guardian* have similar objectives (profit) but very different responsibilities. Each of these publications contains editorial and advertising and must achieve and maintain satisfactory levels of circulation and readership, but their quality, volumes, frequency, job titles and job responsibilities, staffing levels, turnover and profit potential vary enormously.

What is it that we produce? The question arises because there are different terms for what appear to be the same thing and the advent of computer technology has changed the shape or appearance of some of what we do.

In my understanding, the essentials of magazine publishing are the seeking out, collation and dissemination of relevant information to an interested audience, the sale of that audience's interest and attention to those wishing to advertise to that audience, and the optimization of the potential which the readers and advertisers offer either separately or together.

These essentials are not altered by the area of interest and whether the aim is primarily to instruct or to entertain, or by the scale, frequency, format or medium in which the information is published. A magazine can be weekly, fortnightly, monthly, quarterly; printed A4, A5, tabloid, portrait, landscape, on glossy paper or newsprint; or published as on-line data, on computer disc, videotape, or by other electronic means.

A rose by any other name . . .
Various terms are used to describe what the industry produces: 'magazines', 'books', 'periodicals', 'newspapers', according to the custom of a particular publishing house or the quirkiness of an individual. A magazine is 'a periodical publication containing articles by various writers'. A periodical is 'a magazine published at fixed intervals'. A newspaper is 'a periodical, esp. daily, publication with the news'. The definitions seem to go in circles. I prefer, and nowadays the industry generally seems to as well, to use the term 'magazine' to describe the great variety of publications produced which are neither a national, regional daily or weekly newspaper containing general news of interest to the community at large. A book (as in novel) is distinctly different and is a misnomer for a magazine, but the variety of other terms is understandable. Just to confuse, of course, some newspapers contain what they call a 'magazine section'.

A publisher today must think laterally — information and/or entertainment which is currently distributed conventionally as print on paper might soon be more profitably disseminated in some other way. There may be opportunities for multi-media publishing (two or more media simultaneously) or for producing new 'magazines' in one of the alternative media. Already many publishers are producing complementary products and services — from conferences and exhibitions, through books and surveys, study tours and videos, industry awards and events, to on-line databases.

Therefore, in thinking of magazine publishing no one should be constrained by a particular format or style, or by ink on paper.

One of the words that is going to crop up fairly frequently in this book is 'sell' or 'sells'. You will find it used not only in the context of advertisement sales, but also with reference to the enticement of readers, whether they are to pay for the magazine or get it free. Don't forget, even if you give your magazine away, you've still got to 'sell' the concept to the readers and get them to peek between the covers.

Please don't be disheartened by thoughts of electronic publishing and vast on-line databases — one of the largest database hosts in the US had to start a magazine for subscribers to the system. There was no more effective way of telling them about the goodies available on-line.

Magazines are very easy for a reader to browse through, picking up pieces of information here and there; data on computer screens is not.

As Joe Hanson, founder of *Folio*, the US 'magazine about magazine publishing', says: 'Each new medium reinforces the need for the medium which preceded it'.

Chapter 1

The magazine market

The first magazine is believed to have been published in Paris in 1665. It was *Journal des Sçavans*, a review of books. The same year saw the publication of *Philosophical Transactions of the Royal Society*. It was not until March 1691 that a magazine appeared with a more general appeal. *The Athenian Gazette*, published at various intervals (weekly to four times weekly), was a question and answer journal; the questions were (allegedly) from readers and were answered by the Society of Gentlemen (the publisher). It closed in 1697. *The Gentleman's Journal* (1692-1694) broadened the scope of magazines by being the first to boast of covering 'News, History, Philosophy, Poetry, Music, Translations, etc.'. Early 18th-century titles included *Tatler* — published three times a week for three years — and *The Spectator*, published daily and selling 4000 copies a day at its peak (1711-1712). Today's *Spectator* was started in 1828 and now has a circulation of almost 40 000.

Another daily title was *The Guardian*, published between March and October 1713 (not related to *The Manchester Guardian*, now *The Guardian*).

Magazines for women developed slowly at first but gathered momentum as female literacy grew, particularly after 1750. In the same period came the first magazines for businessmen, including, for example, *Lloyd's List* (1734).

The evolution continued over the next 100 years, with the style and content of the magazines developing apace, including the introduction of part-works. Considering the standards of education in the country, circulations were high and it was soon realized that magazine publishing could be very profitable.

A major step forward came in the middle of the 19th century, with the publication of *The Illustrated London News*, the first magazine really to make use of illustrations — artists' drawings converted to wood engravings and printed. Published weekly, it covered the world's news and was famed for its war reports. In 1992, *ILN* celebrated 150 years of continuous publication.

Some statistics

It is difficult to estimate the number of magazines now published in the UK, for so much depends on the definition used and there is no complete record of all titles. Indeed, whatever source is used, by the time this book is published the figures will be out of date. Nonetheless, the most authoritative source, *British Rate and Data* (*BRAD*), lists

---

Largest magazine sectors

The ten largest consumer magazine sectors in 1990 were:

	No. of titles
UK and Eire counties	245
Sporting	230
College	96
Entertainment	72
Ethnic	70
Children	64
Women's	63
Music	61
Religious	55
Tourism and travel	54

For business magazines, the ten largest sectors were:

	No. of titles
Medical	383
Sciences	359
Business (general)	253
Social sciences	184
Computing	177
Agriculture and farming	148
Education	153
Engineering	130
Electrical/electronic	104
Legal	94

Source: BRAD, June 1990

more than 7000 magazines which take advertising. How many are there which do not take advertising? No one knows.

Over the ten years 1981 to 1991, the number of titles listed by *BRAD* grew from about 4040 to 7042 (74%). Business magazines went from 2500 to 4608 (84%) and consumer magazines from 1400 to 2434 (74%). The increase in titles from 1990 to 1991 was 11.4% in consumer and 1.5% in business and professional.

Magazine revenue from advertising and copy sales is estimated at £2 billion a year. According to the most recent Department of Trade and Industry figures, magazine publishers receive a further £1 billion plus from associated businesses, such as exhibitions, directories, newsletters and database services.

Statistical information
If you want know the latest figures, a feast of statistics concerning magazine publishing is available from the Periodical Publishers Association (PPA), particularly the Magazine Handbook.
It is the most comprehensive single source and covers:
The Industry — growth, sectors, revenue;
Circulation — growth, sales, cover prices, distribution;
Advertising — revenue, growth, market shares, categories, advertisers, brands, consumer and business;
Readership — sectors, profiles, quality;
Profitability — performance, ratios, profits, costs.
Other information is produced by the Department of Trade and Industry (published in the Business Monitor series), Advertising Association (AA), Audit Bureau of Circulations (ABC), Media Register MEAL, and others. Addresses on page 231.

For business and professional magazines, advertisement revenue is about 82% of the total and circulation revenue 18%. In the consumer field, advertisement revenue is 51% and circulation revenue 49% (PPA Survey, 1991). In the ten years to 1991, magazine circulations rose by 40%. The business and professional magazines' annual circulation is 76% (510 million) free and 24% (163 million) paid.

Subscriptions for consumer magazines represent about 3% of total circulation. By comparison, in the USA over 75% and in Germany close to 30% are sold on subscription. Copy sales revenue of consumer magazines is £800 million. Advertisement revenues in 1991 were £438 million for consumer magazines and £708 million for business and professional titles.

Highest circulations

The highest circulation consumer magazines in 1991 were:

Radio Times	1 591 152	(weekly)
Reader's Digest	1 432 533	(monthly)
TV Times	1 280 505	(weekly)
What's on TV	1 211 686	(weekly)
Viz Comic	1 080 411	(bi-monthly)
Woman's Weekly	905 095	(weekly)
Prima	738 871	(monthly)
Woman's Own	731 348	(weekly)
Woman	716 758	(weekly)
Best	658 441	(weekly)
		Source: ABC, 1992

Types of magazine

The following definitions of magazines are given by the PPA:

Consumer — providing people with leisure-time information and entertainment;

Consumer specialist — specifically aimed at groups of people with particular interests (motor cyclists, stamp collectors, etc.);

Business and professional or business-to-business — providing people with information in connection with their working lives.

Magazines are further classified into interest areas, such as women's interests, engineering, medicine, and so on.

Adapting to change

Magazines as originally conceived cannot go on for ever. Markets, tastes, interests, educational standards, technologies change at an ever-increasing rate and in order to survive a magazine must change as well.

Just consider the changes in society and technology which have taken place in the past 30 years alone. In that time many worthwhile magazines have died or been merged or been re-launched as quite different products. Some titles have continued, but often they are very different in appearance, content, type of readership and even format. Markets change at an alarming rate, and while in one decade there can be a thriving market or interest which will support a number of magazines, a couple of decades later the market may have all but disappeared.

Take, for example, the high street and the many magazines which served retailers a quarter of a century ago. Far fewer magazines are needed today, because retail chains have replaced independent stores and the number of buying points (store buyers) has been reduced.

Industries have also changed — think of coal-mining, steel-making, brewing — the number of establishments and people involved has declined and, again, fewer magazines are able to survive.

Those magazines which have survived have kept abreast of changes in needs, attitudes and taste and have themselves evolved to continue to provide what readers and advertisers want.

Magazines are often described as 'living entities' and, viewed in this way, their survival depends on their ability to adapt to the constant changes with which all living things are faced.

When a magazine does change and thus retains a niche in a viable market, its life can be long and profitable. For example, the leading women's magazines of fifty years ago — *Woman's Weekly, Woman* and *Woman's Own* — are still successful. The style, design and content have changed to reflect the changing taste and lifestyle of women. Like the dinosaur, however, some magazines cannot evolve and for others, sadly, the remedies are applied too late.

Ancillary products

It seems a natural development for magazines to spawn other products and services. Many magazines have some sort of associated or ancillary activity which is marketed to the existing audience (the readership) and some re-use information which is gathered in publishing the magazine either to sell to the readership in a different form or to some other audience. The most common examples of these are:

- enquiry services
- reader offers
- study tours
- books
- conferences
- seminars
- exhibitions
- road shows

- award schemes
- newsletters
- electronic media
- direct mail (using circulation lists)
- special reports
- market information
- dial-up information or entertainment services
- on-line databases
- computer-based bulletin boards.

Not all are suitable activities for all magazines, but they illustrate ventures which can add value to a publication and its brand image and, at the same time, exploit that brand image to generate additional turnover and profit.

Chapter 2

The publisher's role

A publisher is effectively the chief executive of a magazine or group of magazines and is responsible to the top management of the company for the profitability of the activities under his or her control.

Whether the background of the individual lies in advertisement sales or editorial, or, indeed, any of the other publishing disciplines, is not important. The qualities required are an enthusiasm for publishing, management abilities and skills, knowledge of marketing principles and practices, knowledge of the market being served, an understanding of the skills and techniques used in the various aspects of publishing, numeracy, and an open mind.

A magazine publisher's prime responsibility is to meet the publishing and business objectives of the company by:

> Defining the magazine's market niche, expressed in terms of editorial quality, readership, advertising revenue and profit.

> Managing the magazine to meet those objectives.

> Identifying and developing new profit opportunities.

A publisher reports to a more senior manager, perhaps a group publisher, publishing director, or a managing director. Reporting to the publisher as a line manager will be an editor and an advertisement sales manager; there may also be a circulation manager or circulation executive. Reporting to the publisher as a user will be functions or service departments, such as marketing, accounts, circulation, production, personnel, building services, system or data services, etc. External contacts are many, but particularly important are major customers and major suppliers, such as printers.

In some instances, the publisher is also either the editor or sales manager. For example, at the time of writing, the publisher of *UK Press Gazette* is also the editor, while the publisher of *Retail Jeweller* is also the advertisement sales manager. It may be surprising to some, but such dual roles can be extremely effective and seldom give rise to conflicts of interest. After all, they will be carefully considered appointments.

The publisher's role is complex, for in a way he or she has to be all things to all people. A super-salesperson in dealing with worries about the revenue of the publication, a super-editor when dealing with matters relating to the content. Not at all in the sense of how to perform the tasks with which each discipline abounds, but generally in relation to policy and direction.

While the two principal lieutenants have their respective authorities and responsibilities, it is the publisher who is ultimately responsible for the well-being and prosperity of the magazine.

The publisher's role is the complex management task of bringing together diverse talents and skills to achieve a planned common purpose. It requires highly developed skills in dealing with people, along with a sound and sufficient knowledge of marketing, finance, editorial, advertising, circulation, production, personnel and, of course, the market which the magazine serves.

Much of the publisher's authority lies in his or her ability to convince people of the rightness of an approach, 'to take people along' like an evangelist. To be a dictator won't work. Editors, certainly, will not be told what to do or what not to do. Most advertisement managers would probably resist diktats as well.

There will be occasions when there is no time for debate and decisions have to be made on the spot, but discussion and agreement by consensus is a much better way to achieve results.

This is particularly so because the publisher seldom, if ever, will have experience of all the disciplines of editorial, advertising, circulation and so on. In many other industries, a senior manager can work in different areas of a company's activity — such as production, sales, research — but not so in publishing. It is strictly partisan, at times even antagonistic, until general management level is reached. Overnight, the former salesperson is expected to be able to assess the quality and value of editorial and pass judgement on matters which, if journalists are to be believed, no member of a sales department ever understood, especially the complexities of editorial integrity.

An editor has to become highly commercial, and what salesperson would ever accept that a journalist even knew the meaning of the word?

It seems an impasse, and yet there is abundant evidence that the system works. Editors appreciate and understand commercial affairs and the intricacies of selling. Sales managers develop an eye for a well-researched and well-written story and sympathize with journalists' concerns for editorial standards.

Of course, the new publisher has quite a bit of catching up to do to gain the respect of editorial or sales, whichever is the alien field. The important thing is not to feel inhibited by a lack of knowledge or experience, but to admit any ignorance of those matters. Learning is not difficult; much can be learnt from the editor or advertisement manager, much can be learnt from experienced colleagues in circulation, production or marketing, from superiors, or by going on suitable courses, even by reading.

Real problems arise where new – or experienced – publishers refuse to acknowledge their own shortcomings. It is far better to admit ignorance than to try a bluff.

To reiterate: the new publisher cannot have experience of all aspects of publishing and has to learn and take advice. It is not an admission of failure to do so, it is rather a statement of intent. An intent to do the job properly.

What a publisher needs to know

What is the job? Pick out any one of a multitude of words or phrases from a management thesaurus and they will describe a part of the job. Read through the relevant job descriptions in Chapter 9. In any one year a publisher has a great number of tasks and responsibilities. Fortunately, they don't all have to be done at once and many can be delegated.

Remember, the buck stops with the publisher. Even if a task is delegated, the quality and timeliness of the result are the responsibility of the publisher.

To achieve his or her job objectives, a publisher must have some knowledge at least of all the subjects listed on pages 10 and 11.

It is a pretty formidable or pretty impressive list, depending on your point of view, but most people will have encountered a fair number of these subjects by the time they get to the top of either sales or editorial. You can soon identify those subjects on which you have to work up an adequate knowledge:

What a publisher needs to know

Company affairs:
  business objectives
  custom and practice
  history
  structure

Management theory and practice:
  management by objectives
  time management
  leadership
  delegation
  communications
  appraisal and counselling
  motivation
  office administration

Personnel matters:
  policy
  recruitment
  appraisal
  training
  dismissal procedures
  employment law
  trade unions

Marketing principles and practices:
  research
  forecasting
  planning techniques
  promotion

Communications:
  telephone
  telex, fax
  computer-based, Telecom Gold

Financial management principles:
  budgeting
  pricing
  cost control
  credit control

The many aspects of magazine publishing:
    editorial
    design
    advertisement sales
    production
    printing
    circulation and distribution

Product areas allied to magazine publishing:
    exhibitions
    conferences
    newsletters
    package tours
    direct mail
    special offers
    books
    computer-based services
    electronic media — audio, video, CD-ROM

Law:
    libel
    contempt
    the Trade Descriptions Act
    copyright

The magazine:
    policies
    magazine statistics
    markets served
    market share
    strategy and plans
    standing
    history
    managers and people
    competition
    friends and supporters
    enemies
    major customers

Priorities and personalities

Putting it all into practice depends first and foremost on having a plan. In this plan, you prioritize the work and do the important jobs first. As the leader of the team, it is the publisher who must decide what needs to be done, by whom and in what order of priority. In Chapter 3, you will read that in order to plan you have to know where you are, where you want to be and how to get there. Provided the issues are tackled systematically and logically, everything will fall into place quite quickly. After all, the editor, sales manager and other executives are there to help.

The publisher must give the lead, however, and must co-ordinate, guide, support, counsel, coach and inspire the team.

A discussion of the role of the publisher is more than a little open-ended. To start with the objectives is easy enough, but the style and emphasis which one publisher brings to the role are going to be different from that of another. Much comes back to those origins, to personal preferences and the style and abilities of others on the team.

While the publisher is the boss, the public figure-head is the editor. The editor has the final say in many things, and is recognized by the readership and by the advertisers as being of major influence. The editor presents awards, speaks at market events, meets dignitaries, and is the printed voice and the public voice of the magazine.

The publisher is known, by those who need to know, as the power behind the throne, as the business head of the magazine. If the editor cannot carry out the figure-head role, the publisher may have to assume some of the public duties as well. It is not an ideal situation, and will mean the publisher cannot spend as much time on other matters. (The solution, of course, is to train the editor to assume the role more fully.)

Alternatively, if the sales manager is not so hot at writing sales letters, then maybe the publisher should take over that particular task, and so on. It's a juggling act, with many balls to be kept in the air and three pairs of hands to keep them there. A good team can do so very effectively.

Leading the team is the publisher's job. It is about creating an environment in which people can give of their best and then providing the right motivation. Anyone appointed as publisher will have demonstrated some team leadership skills already, but some refinement of those skills is likely to be needed for leading a bigger and more diverse team.

Product development

As the business manager of a magazine, the publisher has to secure its present and future prosperity and is responsible for turning money and other resources into a profit. In other words, product development. Product development can apply to existing or to new products and, apart from the obvious benefit of creating extra profit, may make other valuable contributions to the company. For example, product development can help a company to:

- broaden its base
- reduce its dependency on existing profit-earners
- improve its share of the market sector
- defend itself against predators (other publishers coming into the market, companies on the take-over trail)
- enter more profitable markets.

It may seem easier at first sight to develop an existing product rather than to develop a new one, but there is always a risk in meddling with something which is already working. It is possible that loyal readers and advertisers will be alienated without new ones being attracted. The rule is simple: be very sure before making even minor changes.

Don't change for the sake of it
A 'law', possibly attributable to the prolific Murphy, says, 'If it ain't broke, don't fix it'.
It's a law which every new broom should take to heart — much damage has been done by new managers thinking that they must make their mark by changing things. Change for the sake of change is seldom of any value.

If good management principles and strengths, such as planning, organizing, directing, co-ordinating and the control of projects, are sharply focused, then the risk of failure is reduced.

Here is some empirical wisdom which can be applied to most kinds of product development.

Play to your strengths
Just as the editor made publisher is going to find it easier to make decisions about editorial affairs, so does the company or the publisher find it easier to make decisions about markets of which there is prior knowledge.

If expansion is a priority, first make sure there are no gaps in the markets in which you are already operating and where you have a number of advantages. You and your people have the knowledge, the contacts and, let's hope, the reputation of winning. If you are paying attention to other markets and there is a gap in your base market, then there's a danger someone else may slip in while you're distracted.

Another trap is the belief, held by many, that because of an interest in a particular subject, say aeroplanes, the market surrounding that subject is also understood. Time for a proverb . . . a little knowledge is a dangerous thing!

If new fields have to be found it's worth getting specialist input. Input from people who already have a working knowledge of the market you wish to invade will strengthen considerably the value of your decisions.

Beware of the unknown
'Better the devil you know', 'A cobbler sticks to his last' — proverbs that sum up the importance of not rushing into the unknown. Just so in magazine publishing. Journalists, salespeople and publishers do move around, but it takes some time to get used to a new market environment and sometimes people regret moving out of familiar territory.
It's even more critical if the aim is to invest large sums of money in a market where your inevitable ignorance and few contacts can be little match for the concerted defence efforts by those magazines you are seeking to usurp.
'Look before you leap' and 'Count your chickens', even though 'The grass is greener . . .'

Identify the gap
Contrary to some opinion, desk research is not a cheap, unreliable way of getting information. In the right hands it's an invaluable tool for carrying out the basic research vital to any development project. There is a limit to what can be established, but invariably there is sufficient good information on which to base early decisions. (See Chapter 3 for more on this subject.)

Set a reliable researcher (maybe a member of your team —

a good, investigative journalist, perhaps) to work on an explicit brief and with adequate resources. Ask for a clear report and a recommendation. A thorough job will show you whether to abort or continue.

Research the project
Time, money and a first-class plan. Accurate research, well analysed, will reap great benefits. It will give either the green light and good prospects of further profit or a red light and the possibility of a red balance on the profit and loss account. Having nurtured a project to this stage, and lavished on it energy and company money, it is difficult to call a halt, but a project that is doomed must be stopped. There is always a temptation to ignore the omens and to press ahead regardless because things will get better. They hardly ever do.

The wise thing is to decide the cut-off points when drawing up the plan. If so many readers cannot be identified, stop. If so much advertising value cannot be identified, stop. There are permutations to be played on some of the deci- sions — the revenue from advertising might be augmented by revenue from some other activity, for example — but decision points can be fixed.

The tough thing is to resist the natural desire not to fail (not the same as wanting to win), and actually make the deci- sion when the time comes. Saying no and closing down a project is tough, and people get hurt, but then no one says a publisher doesn't have to make tough decisions.

There is more information on research, planning and budgets in Chapters 3 and 6.

There are always hazards in product development and the real skill is in reducing the level of risk. Good people, good planning, good research, good delegation, good motivation, and good supervision of good ideas is the best way. Having an excellent publisher is a key ingredient.

Publisher's summary

To help keep an eye on things and as an *aide-mémoire*, publishers find it useful to have their private summary of the finances. Small enough to be tucked in a diary or a wallet, such a sheet provides the key information. The headings shown are for a new three-year forecast, but they can be changed to compare actual figures with budget or whatever you choose from the mass of figures available from the management accountant. If you are really lucky, the management accountant will even prepare such a crib sheet for you. It certainly helps when you bump into the MD in the corridor.

Publisher's summary

Title: *Mymag*   **Financial details**

Year 0 £'000		Year 1 £'000	Year 2 £'000	Year 3 £'000
Income				
3181	Advertisements	3836	4305	5404
296	Copy sales	348	414	588
	Other revenue		13	24
3477	**Total Revenue**	4184	4731	6016
Expenditure				
513	Production costs	636	761	1063
76	Distribution costs	89	103	134
33	Editorial costs	43	49	62
	Other costs		8	14
621	**Total Variable Costs**	768	921	1272
221	Advertisement costs	233	261	284
262	Editorial costs	295	339	373
166	Administration costs	175	190	219
111	Promotion costs	129	152	183
760	**Total Fixed Costs**	831	942	1058
2097	**Gross Contribution**	2586	2869	3685
50	Number of issues	50	50	50
23015	Print order	23684	26112	34143
2492	Ad pages	2800	2898	3247
1464	Ed pages	1576	1630	1827
3956	**Total Pages**	4376	4528	5074
1234	Net yield per page	1326	1438	1608
82.1	GM %	81.7	80.5	78.9
60.3	GPP %	61.8	60.6	61.3

See Chapter 7 for more on budgets, accounts and the abbreviations.

Training

Politicians and leaders of industry and trades unions speak at length about training and the need for it. They are right, for the value of good, on-going training is not appreciated sufficiently. Both management and work-force are equally to blame. Some managers won't train because of a fear of losing their people, some because of a fear of personal competition from trained staff. The work-force tends to regard training with a great deal of scepticism. A common view is that much training activity is merely the management paying lip-service to the idea.

Like it or not, training is essential for everyone, whether it is to do the present job better, to use a computer or particular piece of software, to gain or improve skills, to expand understanding or to prepare an individual for promotion. If you are reading this book you are already committed to your own training needs, but how much effort do you put into training others? Should it, could it, be more?

Bearing in mind that the responsibilities of a publisher include developing and improving the product for today and tomorrow, the contribution made by training to developing and improving people at all levels is very much a concern of the publisher.

Further than that, a publisher who fails to equip the staff of a magazine with the skills they need fails to be an effective publisher. Training is a vitally important expense and must feature in all magazine departmental budgets. As much care should be taken in reviewing and selecting training activities as in any other aspect of the magazine.

Training pays. You are likely to know the true value of good training from your own experience — you will either have received it and its benefits, or not received it and be aware of your own shortcomings.

The publisher's direct responsibility is to oversee the training of immediate subordinates, the editor and the sales manager, the publisher's secretary, and so on. A prime source for advice and assistance will be the company's personnel department, or training department (if there is one), as well as the Periodicals Training Council and the PPA (see page 233).

The publisher must ensure that all staff under his or her control are properly trained and that the editor and sales manager set up structured and well-monitored training for their respective departments. The publisher can be involved as a trainer, particularly in talking about the magazine and its market, or as a former journalist or salesperson.

The future

It may be thought that when the team is working well and targets are being met it is time for the publisher to coast a little, to sit back and relax until an emergency comes along. That's a pipe dream. In fact, that is the time for the publisher to look really hard at the future.

Two phrases to bear in mind are:

'the long-term business objectives of the company' and

'identify and develop new profit opportunities'.

A magazine that is successful today may not be successful tomorrow. Many things can happen. Tastes, attitudes, technologies and needs can all change at an alarming rate. It is the publisher's job to watch for any sign of change, and then seize the opportunities it presents, or take defensive action.

It doesn't matter whether the magazine is serving a mass consumer market, an industry, a specialist consumer market, a scientific discipline . . . all are subject to change. If the publisher is in control, then change is not a problem.

Here are just a few examples of change affecting magazines:

Electronics was featured in existing electrical sciences magazines until it became a significant enough subject to need its own magazines.

Advances in communications — from satellites to portable telephones — have brought new subjects for new magazines.

Medical and scientific progress constantly spawns new disciplines and new magazines.

Relaxation of the restrictions broadcasters were able to impose on the use of radio and television programme details has led to real competition between *Radio Times* and *TV Times*. It has also made other programme magazines possible.

The number of independent retailers (each a buying point) is decreasing while chains are extending — each chain of shops has one buying point. Advertising to some retail sectors has lost its value.

Regional consumer magazines are also affected by the decline in independent retailers, because there are fewer potential advertisers.

Shifts in buying power among consumers have brought more magazines for the young.

An ageing UK population has created a special interest readership.

Successful television programmes have introduced magazines, e.g. the BBC's *Good Food* and *Clothes Show.*

The immediacy and entertainment value of television have led to many changes in magazines, from the death of picture news weeklies to the use of more pictures and more colour in all magazines (allied to technological change in printing).

Competition from European publishers has changed the UK women's magazine market (*Elle, Hello, Prima, Best*).

Change in attitudes to sexuality, pornography and obscenity has opened the market for a wide range of magazines.

New lower-cost pre-press and printing technologies have brought a new lease of viability to magazines nearing closure and made new magazines possible.

More travel by more people has brought more travel coverage in existing magazines and some new titles.

Sometimes change is instigated by magazines — for example, there had been much pressure from publishers over the years to break the copyright bar on radio and TV programme details — but most comes from outside, including the activity of other publishers.

So, the publisher has to be on the look-out for challenge and for opportunity. How? Well, there's no quick and easy answer; it is a matter of constantly examining and assessing anything which, however remotely, impinges on your magazine, its market or publishing in general. And that means encouraging and maintaining a flow of ideas from the team — at every level — and from other departments, particularly marketing.

Other trading

Few magazines do not get involved in some form of other trading activity. Normally, it is an activity which is a natural extension of what a magazine is already doing, such as publishing books, special reports, etc., or which is a marketing ploy, e.g. special reader offers, or a mixture of the two — package tours, perhaps.

Such activity is connected with the establishment of the magazine's brand image, where each feeds off the other, and is most certainly connected with generating additional profit. Even where the other trading activity has a high promotional value, the objective should still be to make a profit.

Of all those running a magazine, the publisher is often best suited to oversee the other trading activities. Just as the magazine must have a plan and meet financial projections, so must the other activities. In some instances they are major events requiring a specially employed staff (such as exhibitions, conferences, books); others may be contracted out to specialist suppliers, and a few will be run by the publisher directly.

One feeds off the other...

A magazine's image, its brand, is fashioned from its reputation for authority, integrity, accuracy, coverage of the subject, its style, its standing and the regard in which it is held.

Anything offered by the magazine has its endorsement and assumes the magazine's brand image. Thus, people who have a high regard for the magazine will believe the offer merits a similar high regard. If the offer is good, it will in turn add to the standing of the magazine.

Beware: if the offer is poor, it will have a detrimental effect on the magazine's image.

The viability of other trading activities depends on the nature of the magazine and the interests of the readers, as well as the competition for each likely activity.

It seems not to matter whether a magazine is consumer, business or STM, the range of other trading activities is similar.

Other trading activities might include the following:

- exhibitions
- road shows
- conferences
- seminars
- concerts
- awards schemes
- enquiry services
- newsletters
- special reports
- statistical services

- reprints
- study/package tours
- direct mail
- special offers
- books
- computer-based services — discs, on-line, bulletin boards, transactional services
- telephone-based services — horoscopes, sources of supply, games, market information, etc.
- electronic media — audio tapes, videotapes, CD-ROM.

Other markets — Europe and beyond

For many years, magazines have been extending beyond the UK's borders either to gather information, to sell advertising, or to sell copies.

Gathering editorial from abroad is now second nature for many editors. There is no difficulty in recruiting foreign freelances or sending journalists out from the UK. Some publishers quibble over the costs, but by and large there are not too many problems — apart from language. The Brits do not bother to learn foreign languages, hoping that everyone else speaks English.

Language problems
Common Market or not, there are tides of nationalism sweeping around and it would be well for UK magazines seeking to do much business abroad to look for staff who can speak other languages or be prepared to teach staff suitable languages.

For example, if a magazine is interested in a particular overseas market it is important to be able to read the relevant publications or to communicate with those who do not speak English. Apart from anything else, it is a courtesy.

For selling, a working knowledge of the buyer's language is essential. Many European buyers do speak English, but they do not expect to do so if they are being asked to buy.

Editorial copy and advertising
It is inevitable, with the development of the Common Market, that UK business magazines should look to Europe for editorial material — British companies will need such information more and more, whether or not they are exporting to Europe, because some Conti-

nental firms will certainly be competitors here in the UK. Continental firms seeing the UK as a market will wish to advertise here.

Because of travel, working abroad and the breaking down of borders generally, there will be more editorial emanating from the Continent in consumer magazines and more Continental firms wishing to advertise, although most of these are likely to work through agents or subsidiaries within the UK.

Clearly, the foreign language, foreign editorial and foreign sales issues will vary from magazine to magazine, but they are matters to which publishers should pay close attention.

Joint ventures
In a changing Europe, competition is going to come not only from other UK magazines, but from those published in other European centres as well. As the best form of defence is attack, perhaps UK publishers should take a much more aggressive look at the potential of Europe and make some decisions. A very good move might be to strike up joint publishing arrangements with publishers operating in similar fields. Editorial could be interchanged and advertisers could be offered deals covering very much larger markets.

International magazines
The really successful international magazines seldom start as such. Readership and reputation are built in the originating country; the magazine is then carried by those readers who travel to other countries; nationals of other countries hear of or see the magazine and take out subscriptions, and, when there is sufficient perceived interest, the magazine is actively promoted into those foreign countries and is sold through whatever are the conventional means.

A logical next step is an edition for a particular country or continent (South America, North America, Europe, Southern Africa, etc.) or for a particular language (Spanish, French, English, German). The latter would be circulated within countries speaking that language.

To publish in a foreign language from, say, London, it is better to employ translators and sub-editors whose first language is the one in which you wish to publish.

The logistics of producing different language editions simultaneously are considerable and it is not something which should be entered into lightly. If circulations in other language areas are required, it is much better to consider arrangements with other publishers, such as licensing. For example, there is a monthly edition of

Drapers Record published under licence in Turkey, which arose following an approach from a publisher in that country.

---

23 million copies in 17 languages
A classic among magazines which have developed into many editions serving different languages and cultures is the Reader's Digest. The front cover makes the justifiably proud boast that 23 million copies are printed in 41 editions and 17 languages.

Transplanting magazines

There are pitfalls in cross-border publishing or in transplanting magazines, not the least of which is that the publisher fails to understand the market on the other side. Culture, custom and practice may be different, market sizes and structures may be different, standards of living may be different, a multitude of issues could affect the acceptability of a product. It is far too easy to assume that because there are similarities in one area, everything else will be similar.

The classic example is the assumption by many in the US and some here that because the USA and UK have a similar language (not the same language), American magazines will work here. It goes even further; some Americans equate the Common Market to the United States.

Two very basic differences may serve to illustrate the point. The American population is roughly five times the size of the UK population. Consumer magazines in the States will be sold mainly on subscription and news-stand sales will be low, while in the UK most sales are through newsagents.

In crude and generalized terms, a circulation of 200 000 in the US (0.078% of the population) may be 40 000 in the UK. If both are paid circulations, the 200 000 in the US are likely to be mainly subscriptions (90-95%), paid up-front, and with relatively few returns from news-stands, whereas in the UK the majority are likely to be newstrade sales paid two or three months after publication with quite high returns and few, if any, subscriptions.

Simple arithmetic soon shows up the advantage held by the larger market with the different distribution method. Add in the advertising likely from the larger and more aggressive US market, plus the lower cost structures common there, and the American magazine looks distinctly viable. The UK magazine, on the other hand, may well be borderline. Cross-border publishing or magazine transplanting has to be considered very carefully indeed.

A chastening international experience
An ill-fated transplant was Computer Merchandising International. It was spawned from a highly successful US magazine, Computer Merchandising, which circulated free to computer stores and other PC re-sellers across the United States. The advertising carry was impressive indeed.

The US publisher convinced the British cousin that a similar magazine would work in Europe; not the UK, but Europe. The market was a similar size to that of the US, there were plenty of computer stores, plenty of manufacturers and distributors. Many were the same as in the US and knew the US magazine well. Much advertising could be sold in the US to companies wishing to sell to Europe.

The UK publishers, who had little experience of the computer market or of trans-European publishing, accepted the arguments and went ahead. The sales and editorial staff had limited computer experience.

Computer Merchandising International was published from London in three editions, English, French and German, and was circulated free throughout Europe to personal computer re-sellers. Recipients were invited to nominate their language preference. This was fine for those whose first language was one of the three, but tough on all others.

The three editions each carried exactly the same editorial, and generally the same advertisements, although there was provision to vary advertisement copy and for single edition pages.

Editorial had to be prepared many weeks in advance. The 95% originated in English was sub-edited and sent to translators in France and Germany. Material originally in the other languages was translated into English in London, sub-edited and then sent off to be translated into French and German. Most text, including the translations, was prepared on computers and was provided to the typesetters in this form so double-keying was avoided.

Paid editorial?
A not unnatural concern is that, in growing closer to Europe, British publishers will be encouraged to adopt Continental practices. For example, in some countries it is customary to charge for editorial, or, at least, charge for editorial colour. Companies providing information for editorial purposes are told that if they pay the costs of origination a colour photograph will be used.

This seems a very short step from charging for the text setting as

The English language edition was made up into pages with suitable illustrations and sent to the typesetters. They made up the English edition and followed the same layout for the other editions, squeezing the text typographically (smaller type, less leading, less character- and word-spacing, as necessary) to fit the same space. Those who are familiar with German will realize just how much squeezing had to be done.

Advertising was sold from London with the help (so-called) of agents in Europe. The sales manager spoke only English. All sales material was produced in three languages. Promotion was carried out across Europe and the magazine took stands at all major PC exhibitions directed at re-sellers.

The problems were many. Advertising the US publisher promised to sell never materialized; the big computer internationals' representatives in Europe did not know of the US magazine; they had no European-wide advertising budgets, but had budgets for individual countries controlled from within those countries (to get one page might mean selling to six or more people in as many centres simultaneously − who gets the commission?); the individual country markets were in widely different stages of development; in one or two there were government-imposed market restrictions; there were serious shortages of software in some countries; US or even UK software was of little value in the rest of Europe (for example, apart from language problems, accountancy practice was very different in each country and so accounts programs could not be transported − even the £ sign caused problems); the magazine's production costs were exorbitant; editorial costs were too high because of necessary European and US travel; the editorial was of little value to too many readers.

It was a saddening and chastening experience for all involved.

Within a few months of the closure of the European edition, the US computer market declined and one of the first magazines to feel the pinch was the US version.

and then perhaps adding a charge for the journalist's time. It is possible that control of editorial content would effectively pass out of the hands of the editor and the publisher.

It is not a practice that should be adopted in the UK; indeed, UK publishers should encourage the European publishers concerned to drop it.

Were such charges introduced here, the integrity and authority of British magazines would be seriously undermined.

Bringing it together

The publisher must lead, co-ordinate, guide, support, counsel, coach and inspire the team to publish the market leader, measured in terms of editorial quality, readership, advertising revenue and profit, and by so doing meet the short- and long-term business objectives of the company.

The publisher must develop an excellent working relationship with the two key lieutenants — the editor and the advertisement manager. It is particularly important that the publisher and editor work well together, for it is the editorial content which attracts and retains readers and is thus central to the magazine's success or failure.

The publisher must identify and develop new profit opportunities.

The publisher must think, research, communicate, observe, plan strategically, organize and innovate.

The publisher cannot do it alone.

Chapter 3

Marketing

Textbooks are crammed with snappy definitions of 'marketing', some using the most mind-boggling jargon to justify the subject as a science, the secrets of which are revealed to but a few. For our purposes, the basic theory of 'marketing' is really quite simple: it is to identify, or create, a need common to a number of people and then to meet that need at a profit.

Since trading began, man has been doing just that, and there are plenty of examples through the centuries of people who have done it most successfully. Indeed, the high streets and many of the products we buy are adorned with the names of successful marketeers carried down through generations. So really there is no great mystique; like many other things, it is fundamentally applied common sense.

Yet it's very easy to get it all wrong. There are many magazines which have failed because common sense went out of the window and, wherever the blame is placed, the facts are likely to be that the marketing, in concept or execution, was wrong. Why? Perhaps because many people do not appreciate that the total activity is marketing; it's not something that is added on at the end.

To emphasize the point: the 'marketing' of a magazine is not just for the backroom boys and girls or the sharp-suited folk from an agency, it is the job of each and every executive, whatever their discipline or title.

The marketing plan for a magazine embraces everything to do with its existence; each executive on a magazine is a marketing executive. At the lowest level the marketing objectives are, first, life, and second, survival. Survival in this context is usually more than just keeping a magazine running, although occasionally that may be what is wanted. To survive, a magazine has to make an acceptable level of profit or meet some other corporate objective.

Magazines, along with newspapers and commercial broadcasting, offer a unique marketing challenge — the problem of selling two 'products' to two different markets at the same time. The first 'product' is a magazine created to appeal to specific readers, the second is the 'readership' which is 'sold' to advertisers. The objective is to create the readership that the advertisers need.

In the past it was common for magazines to be founded on an editorial principle or mission. For example, *The Brewer's Guardian* was started in 1871 as the official organ of the Country Brewer's Society to 'protect brewers' interests in licensing, legal, and parliamentary matters'. Many specialist magazines started life because of the passionate interest of the founder-editor in a particular subject or cause.

While campaigning or proselytizing magazines are still launched, either as public relations tools, or as profit-making ventures, most magazines are started with the unabashed intent of making a profit.

Types of magazine
Fuller descriptions are given in Chapter 6, but for the moment, the main categories of magazine are:

Consumer
    General
    Special interest
Business
    General
    Special interest horizontal (across different activities,
        businesses, disciplines, ages, sexes, interests)
    Special interest vertical (particular to an occupation
        or discipline, or interest)
Scientific, technical and medical (STM)
    General
    Society or institution official journals
    Special interest

There are fewer methods of distribution:

Paid
    Newstrade — via distributors and wholesalers
    Other retail outlets — supermarkets, convenience stores,
        petrol stations
    Subscriptions — by post
    Society subscriptions — by post

Free
> Controlled circulation (requested) — by post
> Controlled circulation (non-requested) — by post
> Directed — by post
> Non-controlled — by post
> Direct delivery — by hand to every house or business in
> an area, or given away at railway stations, etc.

Some magazines fall between the two, having paid circulation but needing free circulation in addition to reach the level of readership required by advertisers. Successful controlled circulation publications often offer subscriptions to those who fall outside the terms of control.

The need for planning

Because a successful magazine can be highly profitable, the business has some very large companies with many titles. Equally there are some very small and successful publishing businesses with one or two magazines only. And, as magazines can still be launched on a shoe-string, the number of titles increases almost daily. (See Chapter 1 for some statistics.)

> **The wrong way**
> *'Planning models are an authoritative way of being wrong.'*

Whether having very large circulations, turnovers and profits, or being quite small, each magazine should serve a clearly defined market and each will have a marketing plan. It is true to say that some marketing plans are not formal documents in the style used by the larger publishing companies, but nonetheless the people involved ought to have a very clear idea of where they're going, what they're doing, and why they're doing it.

The key planning areas for any magazine are the same:
- reader market
- editorial policy
- advertising market
- sales policy
- production
- distribution.

On the next page is a ten-step start-up proposal plan.

The ten-step start-up proposal plan

1. Identify a gap in the market, which might be a group of potential readers with common interests, a group of potential advertisers looking for a particular type of customer, or a group of readers or advertisers not well served by existing media.

2. Devise an editorial policy, format and content that will turn potential readers or potential customers into the loyal and regular 'readership' of the magazine.

3. Assess the revenues and costs and determine the sources of revenue, and advertisement and circulation volumes.

4. Devise a circulation policy using one, or a mixture of, fully sold (news-stand sales or subscriptions), free, direct delivery, directed (through the post) or controlled circulation, that will generate the optimum circulation and readership.

5. Devise an advertisement sales policy that demonstrates that the new magazine is better than the proverbial sliced bread in giving the advertiser the required market.

6. Devise a title and logostyle, and design the magazine to appeal to readers and to offer advertisers an appropriate vehicle for their messages.

7. Specify staff required, recruitment policy and training needs.

8. Specify printing and distribution requirements and get estimates.

9. Research and confirm editorial and advertisement markets.

10. Establish objectives, prepare forecasts.

Go through the ten steps (although not necessarily in the order shown here), write a statement describing the magazine's unique qualities and appeal — often called a niche or mission statement — and effectively you have created a publication plan. And the publication plan (by this or any other name) is the key marketing document upon which all subsequent actions are based. Some steps may be taken in parallel with others, and as new facts are amassed some steps will need to be retraced so that the final plan is as accurate and comprehensive as possible.

Step 3 is particularly important. In fact, it's wise to have a spreadsheet running throughout the exercise so that the financial effects of theories and ideas may be tested. The viability of the project can be reviewed continuously as more information is gathered. And please get someone else to cast an eye over the plans and check the figures — it is so easy to miss the obvious.

This sort of procedure applies to any magazine, whether consumer, business-to-business, scientific, technical or medical. With it there is no guarantee of success, but you are less likely to waste money; without it, or something very similar, the chance of success is low.

Missing the obvious

A new magazine, called Furnishing Review, was planned. It was to serve retailers and be published monthly. This was back in the 1960s before the advent of low-cost editorial colour; indeed, trade magazines didn't have colour editorial except on very special occasions. Advertisers in the planned magazine were expected to use colour and, as the subject of furnishing demanded it, the editor was to use colour. It would be an important edge over the competition.

Budgets were prepared. The venture seemed to be viable.

After the first issue actual costs were compared with budgeted costs and there was a very serious overspend — on editorial colour.

Evidently, no one had told the person who prepared the production budget that there was to be editorial full colour throughout the magazine. The assumption was made by one key person that Furnishing Review would be like all the other magazines serving the market and have little or no colour; someone else assumed that everyone knew it was going to be different.

Two conclusions: 1) It is dangerous to make assumptions rather than establish facts; 2) Ideas and plans must be communicated effectively to all who need to know.

Two rules: 1) Always ask questions, even the obvious ones, and never presume you know what is in someone else's mind or plan; 2) Repeat a message as many times as necessary to get confirmation that is has been received and understood.

As for Furnishing Review, it was fortunate the wrong assumptions didn't lead to the magazine's demise, but they so easily might have done.

Of course, as there are exceptions to every rule, there will be magazines which 'on paper' look as though they should work but don't.

The fine language of the publication plan hides the fact that either readers or advertisers, or both, don't **want** the product no matter how much the evidence suggests they **need** it. Also, there will be publishers who do little or no research, and yet achieve success by relying almost totally on gut feeling.

Check your magazine's performance
If a magazine already exists, much the same procedure should be followed from time to time to make sure nothing is being missed. Act out the role of the predatory publisher to check your magazine's performance.

On a day-to-day basis, monitoring of your magazine's vital statistics and comparison with its competition will give an indication of how closely it is meeting the readers' and advertisers' needs.

The vital statistics are:

Circulation statistics
    News-stand sales
    Subscriptions, new and renewals
    Controlled circulation registrations
    Reader enquiries
Advertisement statistics
    Display volume (number of advertisements, number
        of pages) by sector, by size, by colour
    Classified volume (number of advertisements,
        number of pages) by category, size
    Actual/estimated revenues
    Revenue per page
Market share
    Display advertising
    Classified advertising
    Copy sales
Editorial
    Paging
    Coverage

Each of these can be monitored on an issue by issue basis for your own magazine, but for the competition only those statistics which are immediately obvious can be noted, such as advertisement paging and estimates of revenue.

The other statistics will come from ABC (Audit Bureau of Circulations) figures, from information published by the other magazines themselves and from research of one kind or another. Feedback from your own editorial and sales people in the field is most helpful, as is information from advertisers.

Information and its sources

Young soldiers, when given advice about map-reading and getting from A to B, are often told: 'First thing is to find where you are, then where you want to be and then work out the best route between the two'.

Finagle's Law
The information we have is not what we want. The information we want is not what we need. The information we need is not available.

It's exactly the same for any planning exercise: Where are we now, where do we want to be, how do we get there? For the publisher already in a particular market, that advice translates as follows:

'Where are we now?' Review the magazine's current place in the market.

'Where do we want to be?' Assess the market potential as a whole and our magazine in particular; define objectives.

'How do we get there?' Write an action plan.

For the publisher not already in the market-place, it's a question of standing at the threshold and asking virtually the same questions.

The vital ingredient is good information, and that can come from a number of sources.

In-company trading statistics — the performance figures for your own magazine
advertisement paging
revenue
editorial paging
circulation
costs
Desk research — synthesizing and analysing information already available
monitoring competitive media
advertisement paging

revenue
Media Register MEAL
editorial paging
circulation
promotional activities
costs
statistical research using data published by
government
trade associations
special interest groups
Audit Bureau of Circulations (ABC)
National Readership Survey (NRS) and similar bodies
competitors, etc.

Qualitative research — attitudinal, not numerical information
talking with people in the target audience by means of
face-to-face or telephone interview
group discussions
asking pertinent questions about
what they do
what they want to do
what they think about magazines and other media
what they think about key issues
what they think they are going to do and why
what changes they foresee, etc.

Quantitative research — providing numerical information
counting people, organizations or things, according to certain criteria
people reading various magazines
homes with a washing machine
companies using 'widgets', etc.

As the term implies, quantitative research deals with statistical and demographic questions and tells how many, of what and where, which magazines the respondents read and which magazines they purchase (or receive free in the case of many business magazines). It can be accomplished by personal interview, telephone, written questionnaire or, for some information, by desk research into government and other statistics, yearbooks, trade association documents, and so on.

Qualitative research deals more directly with people, probing their opinions and aspirations in depth.

Questions that might be asked include:
        When do you read magazines?
        Why do you read magazines?
        Which articles/advertisements do you remember?
        Which articles/advertisements did you like, and why?
        Did the articles help you in your job/in the home/with
            your hobbies?
        What are your job responsibilities?
        Where do you go for holidays?
        What is your favourite food?
        What is your opinion of . . .?
In fact, you can ask about almost anything.

For the research to be of any value, the people interviewed must be representative of the audience and the sample must be large enough to reduce the likelihood of error to an acceptable level; the questions must be properly constructed to avoid bias in the answers; and the results must be properly analysed. For group discussions, a good, relevant, focused discussion guide is required. It is wise to employ an experienced market research specialist for all such work.

Readership surveys

Readership surveys are invaluable tools for finding out how well you are doing and (it is hoped) for providing advertisers with evidence of your magazine's appeal to its target audience.

There are three options:

1. Research within the target audience by face-to-face or telephone interview or by postal questionnaire.
2. Research within the known readership by face-to-face or telephone interview or by postal questionnaire.
3. Research within the known readership by a questionnaire within the pages of the magazine.

In terms of the quality of results, the best method is the first, but it does have its problems. Defining and identifying the target audience for some magazines is easy — all UK doctors, for example, are well documented, and to identify **women in a particular age band** in a high street is also simple — but for others the task is almost impossible. How do you identify among the population at large those individuals who work in the fashion industry, or those who have a particular interest or hobby?

There are half-way solutions — everyone attending a trade fashion unlikely to be representative of all potential readers. So, research conducted at a fashion show will give part of the answer only. Duplicate the research at other shows, such as those devoted to textiles or furnishings, and more of the answer might be revealed. Indeed, enough of the answer may be obtained to make the exercise worth while and the results a reasonable indication of what people in the industry think about the magazine concerned.

Where such an approach is not practicable — the audience is spread too thinly and/or the costs would be unacceptable — the second technique might be used. Here you need to be able to identify the reader and while this is easy for a magazine distributed by post, for magazines sold over the counter it is impossible. Subscription and controlled or directed magazines can approach current and lapsed readers directly. (Often the latter are the more important people to talk with.) The results will tell you what current and past readers think, but unless you have a pretty large share of the potential readership on your lists, they will not tell you what the target audience thinks — or at least you will not be able to claim that they do.

The third method — the in-magazine questionnaire — may be of less value. Unless a relatively high percentage of readers respond, many people would regard the results as being representative merely of those who responded. Nonetheless, such a survey may be worth doing.

The kind of information which might be obtained in reader surveys is listed on the facing page.

The costs of any programme of research must be evaluated carefully and weighed against the value of the information to be obtained. Remember, too, that there may be a cost if research is not carried out: the cost of a magazine losing its place in the market. So, when making the evaluation, consider not only the positive effects of learning more but also the negative effects of not knowing what's going on. Of course, a major incentive is that in many instances the data, or some of it, can be used when selling to advertisers.

How to approach a plan

One way to approach a planning exercise is to assume that nothing will change and that everything is going to continue along the same path. To project forwards, the planner extrapolates from historical trends.

Well, there's an anonymous quotation which often gets trotted out

Reader survey information

Business magazines	Consumer magazines

Basic information:

type of company	age
size of company	marital status
SIC (Standard Indus-	income
trial Classification)	interests
job function	expenditure patterns
profession	address

Magazine readership:

usefulness overall and	usefulness overall and by
by section of advertis-	section of advertising and
ing and editorial	editorial
frequency of reading	entertainment value
time spent reading	frequency of reading
	time spent reading

The future:

purchasing intentions	purchasing intentions for
of company by	house/flat, furniture,
type of equipment or	decorations, household
service and value	equipment, car,
authority of reader to	holidays,
buy, or specify	clothes, etc.
or influence purchase	types of leisure interest
how will the company	views on marriage
change?	views on sexuality issues
how will products	kind of lifestyle sought
change?	
how will equipment	
and services change?	

Note: NRS, JICMARS, Agridata provide readership information for some business magazines. For larger circulation
consumer magazines normal sources are NRS or similar.
For smaller magazines data may be difficult to obtain.

at marketing seminars for those prepared to listen: 'The future is not what it was'.

It never was and it never will be. The only certain thing about the future is that it will be different.

There is the change beyond our control to which we react:

What if there's a recession?
What if someone else launches a major competitor?
What if party 'A' or party 'B' wins the general election?

and so on.

There is the change for which we can be the instigator:

What if we change editorial policy?
What if we increase the sales effort — by employing more salespeople or spending more on promotion?
What if we change frequency?
What if we start an exhibition?
What if we launch a major circulation campaign?
What if we launch a companion/competitive title?

and so on.

If resources permit and if the potential return merits the investment, it is feasible to build models or scenarios to explore future possibilities, from world influences, through continental and national considerations, to the expectations for a particular section of the population or a particular industry. Arguably, the forecasts which can then be made for each scenario will be more valid.

Such an exercise may be beyond the resources of all except the very largest publishing companies, but it could be valid for groupings of UK or European publishers. One was carried out in the USA a few years ago and it provided much for American magazine publishers to consider.

Of course, there is the danger that with too much information one is so completely bogged down that the trees are obscured by the paper their forebears were used to produce. But, without information, without knowing the starting point or the destination, without knowing something of the hazards that might be encountered, almost any journey is doomed to failure.

You need to know how to obtain, evaluate and use the information effectively. If demographic information or industry statistics are required, there is plenty of data produced by government and by trade associations and so on. Sadly, most of it is out of date by the time it is published, but it's better than nothing. There are reference libraries, both public and private, where a resourceful researcher can obtain a lot of information for no cost except time. Research organizations invariably charge — a low cost to members, a higher cost to non-members.

For example, Pira International, an independent centre for research, consultation, training and information services for the paper, packaging, printing and publishing industries, produces periodic reports on matters of interest to magazine publishers. Often they are multi-client studies in which participants are closely involved in determining the areas of investigation.

An American experience
The US Information Industry Association commissioned the Institute for Alternative Futures to prepare a report describing 'the technologies, applications, social implications and public policy issues emerging from the nascent information age'.
Called The Information Millenium, the report offered four alternative scenarios for the information industry and society in the year 2000; each examined society and the economy, information technology and information applications. The scenarios were:
The High-Tech Information Society — an 'unqualified success' future;
The Creative Society — a 'different kind of success' future based on creativity, learning, and human development;
Things Bog Down — a 'disappointment' future, but not disastrous;
1984 and Beyond — an authoritarian future that occurs as a reaction to hard times.
*Using the report, American publishers were able to plan their role within each of the scenarios, so as to be ready for whichever might come true. Of course, they could opt to plan for one scenario only, but the value was that it was possible to explore strategies across several of the futures and perhaps influence events towards the most beneficial scenario. With such information, decision-makers can 'make more conscious choices about what they **want** the future to be like'.*
An interesting aspect of the report is that the futures described are not the optimistic to pessimistic variants of a 'base case', but are conceptually and structurally different images.

The causal difference between one magazine's success and another's failure is often that one has researched the market and the future a little more thoroughly or more accurately than the other, or drawn more reliable conclusions.

There are specialist freelance researchers who may be employed to do the leg-work, but they need a comprehensive and sensible briefing. For example, the publisher of a magazine about cars, facing the task of planning the magazine's future over the next five years, might tell a researcher

'Go and find out about motor cars' or

'Go and find out about transportation'.

Undoubtedly some useful answers would be obtained, but it would be far better to say something along the lines of:

'Go and find out about public and private transportation, with particular reference to the place of the motor car, motor car design, fuels, road-building . . .'

A foreign place
The past is a foreign country, they do things differently there.
                                    L. P. Hartley, *The Go-Between*

There are research methods and techniques, and systematic planning methods. If you wish to pursue this topic, do your personal research in a good business library or bookshop, or ask your company training officer to find you a suitable course.

The niche statement

A magazine should have its own place in the market and the niche or mission statement describes the magazine's unique qualities and appeal. Broadly, it should cover:

The market:
        Nature
        Extent
        The potential readers' needs
The magazine's role:
        The *raison d'être*, the needs and wants it is to fulfil
        The manner of fulfilment
Editorial:
        The editorial policy
        The nature of editorial content

The relevance of the policy to the readership
The quality of staff
Editorial achievements
Readership:
Who are the readers?
What is the proven circulation?
What buying influence do those readers have?
Revenue:
The magazine's income from advertising, copy sales and
other activities
The size of the market
The magazine's current and optimal share of the market
Other activities which exist or might be developed
Competition:
The magazine's competitors
Their success rating and market share
Why they are more or less successful
Appearance:
The format
Method of production
Paper and print quality
General:
Other strengths and characteristics of the magazine
Editorial, circulation, advertisement sales policies
The magazine's position in the publishing company's
portfolio

Such a statement is really for internal consumption, but an expurgated version (omitting vital commercial information) is often used in promotional material.

Identifying opportunities

With around 7 000 magazines published in the UK, anyone could be forgiven for believing that there's no more room, that the audience for magazines is sated. Take particular areas, such as women's magazines or medical magazines, with scores of titles already and ask if those markets have room for more.

All the evidence suggests that appetites for magazines are not sated and that as long as publishers produce new titles they will be considered by potential readers. This is not to say that all new magazines will succeed, they most certainly will not, but a few will survive the first few weeks of life and go on to success.

Only a very small percentage of those new magazines are covering new ground — say, in new product areas, new medical disciplines or subjects (such as AIDS), or new interests (when the environment became fashionable it spawned a few, as did aerobics) — most are offering merely a different approach.

Some magazines (or quasi-magazines) are not designed to last, but just to satisfy a craze or fad of the moment — a style of pop music, a pop star, skateboarding, Turtles. A short life, but a lusty and profitable one, is perfectly justifiable and should not be denigrated.

And no denigration is intended in the remark that most 'new' magazines are offering merely a different approach. Readers' needs, aspirations and attitudes change and if magazines don't keep pace they soon open up opportunities for others to exploit.

Technologies also change and magazine concepts that would not have been viable a few years ago have become so today.

New markets for British publishers may exist elsewhere and, if the resources are available, may be worth investigating, either for new magazines or other media, or for foreign versions of UK products. English-speaking countries are obvious starting-points and Europe, too, despite the language problems, might be worth considering. Certainly, the continuing and fast developments in communications and computer-based systems may herald new international publishing concepts.

So, the eager publisher looking for new opportunities has to keep watch on a number of fronts and perhaps be prepared to abandon long-established publishing prejudices and prohibitions.

No one person can monitor everything — hence the establishment within the larger companies of 'marketing departments' whose on-going role is to evaluate a number of possible markets at one time. How this is done will depend on a number of factors. Usually there is some relationship between those markets already served and those being evaluated. It is not often that publishing companies move into fields they do not know well to introduce new products, although they may acquire magazines or companies in other areas. Having established a stepping-stone, expansion is then possible.

Normally, the individual publisher's first responsibility in this respect is to monitor activity in the field associated with his or her magazine.

This monitoring involves talking and listening to people in the market-place:

Readers
Non-readers
Advertisers
Non-advertisers
Industry experts
Suppliers
Buyers
Sellers

The first thing is to listen and to hear what is being said. Next, to evaluate what has been said and identify change; to assess the implications of that change; to take or recommend relevant action.

The change could be anything from the fact that a new fad or a new science is evolving (there was a glut of health magazines in the 1980s, for example), through to the consensus that the content of a competitive magazine or even your own magazine is 'tired'.

Defining a reader market
The reader market for a magazine is invariably composed of people with a common need. The need can range from parents wanting tips on child-rearing, to doctors wanting to know about the latest drugs, to engineers wanting to know applications for high tensile plastics, or whatever. Alternatively, those parents, doctors and engineers might all want to know what's on TV or at the cinema, or about a new car.

Essentially there are two types of need: the need which is particular to an occupation or discipline, hobby or special interest, and the need which embraces people across different activities, disciplines, ages, sexes, interests. The first forms what is referred to as a vertical market and the second, a horizontal market.

Defining the reader market for a particular magazine is usually simple enough. If potential advertisers are seeking young women between the ages of 16 and 25 there is little problem. Similarly, there is no problem in saying that the reader market for a magazine is all serious camera-users, all trade fashion buyers, or all doctors specializing in nephrology or obstetrics, or all GPs.

The problems come in creating an editorial content that has the greatest possible appeal to that market sector, in identifying the people concerned and in getting the magazine's message across to them. These issues are discussed in later chapters.

Defining and assessing revenue sources

It depends a little on whether it is the editorial idea or the recognition of a market's advertising potential which comes first, but defining the important revenue sources for a magazine is also reasonably straightforward. If you choose to start with the readers, it's a question of analysing what they buy, either as private individuals (consumers) or as people with some work-related buying responsibility.

Individuals buy washing products, and so manufacturers or sellers of such products are potential advertisers. If the reader market consists of people working in printing companies who buy or influence the purchase of equipment and supplies, then manufacturers of printing machines, paper or ink are potential sources of advertising revenue.

In the consumer magazine markets, it is almost certain that copies will be sold via re-sellers. The issues in assessing circulation revenue, therefore, are to do with the level of sale and the amount of discount given to distributors, wholesalers and retailers.

Most business-to-business magazines are free to readers and only in comparatively few instances does circulation income form any significant part of total revenue. Very few of the top 100 business titles ranked by display revenue have paid-for circulations. The exceptions tend to be magazines of fairly general business appeal (*Campaign, Commercial Motor, Estates Gazette, Personal Computer World*), specialist news magazines of weekly frequency (*Farmer's Weekly, The Grocer, Caterer & Hotelkeeper, Building*), or the more esoteric scientific publications. Most copies of these magazines are sold on subscription, but even so there is a lot of reliance on the retail newstrade. There is more on this subject in Chapter 6.

Another and growing area of revenue for many magazines is that of ancillary activities. These include:

- direct mail (selling circulation lists)
- exhibitions
- road-shows
- books
- videos
- phone-in lines (for pre-recorded information)
- special offers
- on-line bulletin boards (accessed by computers and modems)
- reprint services
- special reports

- awards schemes
- syndication

and so on.

Most of these activities have a useful dual purpose — they promote the magazine and contribute directly to profit. Indeed, there is every reason to suppose that some magazines might not exist were it not for the contribution from 'other' activities. Technology and the future are considered in Chapter 8.

Matching advertiser to reader

Matching the advertiser to the reader involves knowing the sales objectives of the first and the buying interests of the second. On a start-up it's one of the first issues to examine — after all, unless they can be matched there's unlikely to be much revenue — but it should not then be forgotten.

Objectives and tastes change and the publisher with the edge is the one who is fully aware of advertisers' needs and constantly monitors the relationship between those needs and the needs of the reader.

To say that the publisher and the sales team are go-betweens is over-stretching the point, but clearly there is much to be gained from extracting as much information as possible from advertisers about what they want and in feeding back to advertisers the reactions, aims and ambitions of the reader audience.

Part of the latter comes from surveys produced by the magazine and from trends and issues reported in its pages, but a lot can come from a good relationship between the editorial and sales teams. Much worthwhile information about the market can be exchanged between the two.

Branding and positioning

Anyone going into a store to buy, say, a can of baked beans is likely to favour a particular brand. You can probably recall the names of two or three brands and it's likely that one of them will be Heinz. Indeed, there was a campaign which claimed 'beanz meanz Heinz' and few people will be unfamiliar with the brand name.

It is one of the most successfully promoted brands and customers associate it with quality, value and reliability. When someone goes to buy beans or soup or baby foods, that image is highly likely to secure the sale of a Heinz product.

Publishers should strive to emulate the Heinz example in marketing magazines. A magazine should have an image or style which is unique and that in itself is a marketable commodity. It should be used to capture new readers, to reinforce a reader's decision to purchase and become a regular reader, to hold that reader despite inducements from other magazines, and to encourage the reader to buy or make use of the ancillary products and services offered by the magazine.

Just as Heinz or Rolls-Royce are names that mean something to the population generally, so should the name of a magazine mean something to people within its market.

A brand is an identity which, when applied to a magazine or its associated products and services, raises their value beyond that of their intrinsic characteristics. A story in *The Times* will carry far more credibility than the same story in a less highly regarded publication.

David Sheilds, of The National Magazine Company, has drawn up the following series of statements which illustrate how branding works:

> Branding implies identification.
> Identification implies recognition.
> Recognition implies awareness.
> Awareness implies knowledge.
> Knowledge implies confidence.
> Confidence implies esteem.
> Esteem implies value.

The aura of successful brands increases the customer satisfaction which they offer and, in turn, the added value for which they can charge. Brand leaders should always be more profitable than the also-rans.

As the value of brands transcends the value of the products and services they identify, they have an independent existence and have personalities. The personalities reflect three main elements:

- the characteristics of the products they identify
- the promotion of those products and the brand itself
- the values of the parent organization

thus, 'beanz meanz Heinz'.

One other point on the subject of brands and branding: the personalities of brands are affected by their competitors and brand perceptions tend to be more relative than absolute. Frankly, if there is no competition, if there is only one baked bean producer, the term 'baked beans' will serve as well as Heinz or any other term and will convey as much.

The catch-phrase has significance only because Heinz has competition.

And it is when there is competition or the strong likelihood of competition that the positioning of a product becomes important.

Position in the market
Most people can look at a range of motor cars and tell something about the people who own them. At one end of the scale there is the Rolls-Royce, the Jaguar, the Porsche; at the other there are the tiny cars produced by Fiat, Renault, and so on. Each car has its brand image, each is precisely positioned in the market to appeal to a particular sector.

And in each price or style band, one brand of car will be the leader. That, almost invariably, is the optimum position which is sought for any brand.

In the short term, the most significant leadership criterion is profitability. A brand can truly claim to be the market leader when it has the largest share of the total profit generated in its sector. However, branding is inextricably linked with recognition and perceived value and, as these are moving targets, leadership by one brand over its competitors might be short-lived.

Everything connected with a brand, the product itself, its packaging and presentation, its price, its availability, its promotion, what a friend says about it — especially what a friend says — and even the manner of the switchboard operator who takes calls from customers, affects how it is perceived.

It is crucially important that everyone involved in a product understands its brand personality and position. A part of all staff training should be the definition (and understanding) of the innate characteristics of the brand and how they differentiate it from its competitors.

There are the up-market magazines which are in themselves expensive and appeal to those with high incomes (or those who aspire to such), there are magazines for particular lifestyles or age-groups, for men or women, for special interests, and there are mass-market magazines which are read mainly by women. Plus, of course, the multitude of business, scientific, medical and technical magazines.

Before launching a magazine, its position in the market-place must be considered carefully and so must the image it is to create. Readers

The brand leader won

Catering Times was a weekly, newspaper-style magazine serving management in hotels, restaurants and catering establishments generally. It had a sound editorial team; the advertisement sales people were good and diligent. Contributors included leading names in the industry. The publication was well regarded by its readers.

And there lay the problem — not enough people did read it. The paid circulation was less than one sixth of that of the market leader, Caterer & Hotelkeeper.

Many of us worried at the problem. Caterer & Hotelkeeper had been around for a long while, had a strong and loyal readership most of whom bought their copies from local newsagents, carried a lot of display advertising and, very important, published a forest of classified advertising almost every week.

Much of the latter was aimed at management, but an even greater number of the job advertisements were aimed at lower level staff. There seemed to be nothing we could do to break the grip of the brand leader: we couldn't get more display or classified because our circulation was too small, and we couldn't sell more copies because (a) we didn't carry enough advertising to satisfy the readers' needs (a classic Catch 22 scenario) and

(b) there were difficulties in promoting copy sales to such a motley group spread throughout the country.

With hindsight it might be said that we were foolish to tilt against such a well-established market leader, but the pickings looked so good. There were three main chicken-and-egg type problems:

1. Identifying and promoting to the individual members of the target audience.

2. Obtaining sufficient classified to attract readers.

3. Retaining credibility with display advertisers who had expected a high readership.

The market leader fought its corner very strongly. Catering Times was subsequently sold to the company which published Caterer & Hotelkeeper and its policies and approach were changed. It closed after a further two years.

As it happened, some years later I was publishing director of Drapers Record, the undisputed leader in its field. Many sought to usurp DR's position and it was a welcome reversal of roles for me.

Competitors came and went, predators nudged at the door of the market, but by dint of the team's constant vigilance, and by taking care to meet the needs and wants of readers and advertisers, Drapers Record reigned supreme, and still does.

by and large expect a magazine to reflect the image they have of themselves, so if people are to read a magazine they have to see themselves somewhere in its pages.

Also, advertisers are concerned at the environment in which their advertisements are seen. A Rolls-Royce is shown to best advantage in full colour on art paper alongside exquisitely designed editorial. The factors which influence a reader are (in no particular order):

- relevance
- design
- quality
- format
- content
- advertisers.

Yes, many people do read magazines for the advertising content, no matter what journalists might say. If a car, camera or computer buff is leafing through a number of magazines at a bookstall, the advertisements will catch his or her eye as much as the editorial. Generally, the decision about which magazine to buy will be made on the basis of the editorial content, but for some it's the advertising that sells the magazine.

Ask anyone (yourself, perhaps) who has a special interest in, say, photography, why they buy a particular magazine. Alternatively, watch how such magazines are read. The advertisements are important and not least because, bearing in mind paging ratios, they may contain more information than the editorial.

Even the more general interest magazines are bought as a package of which the advertising forms a vital part. It's true that, when asked, many readers discount the importance of the advertisements, yet the measurable reaction to those advertisements suggests that they are read and found of value.

Customer satisfaction
The intangible customer satisfactions of branding and positioning are vitally important to a magazine's success. Magazines are very complex marketing propositions:

They are inessential products.
They serve two markets simultaneously.
They operate under intense competition.
They must maintain consistent quality while constantly changing.

They must respond to customer needs which are complicated, often contradictory and changing.

A positioning statement can help to clarify matters and might contain details of:

- market served
- readership delivered
- the editorial rewards the reader receives
- the reader response the advertiser receives
- the relative values of the characteristics in terms of competitive titles.

To help in the positioning process, here's a three-step plan.

The three-step positioning plan

1. **Define a new or existing market segment.**
   It must be:
   distinctive and identifiable
   attractive to advertisers
   (preferably) growing in importance
   of sufficient size/value
   of sufficient stability to offer long-term
       business prospects.

2. **Define the unique benefit(s) the magazine provides for readers.**
   Look at its:
   relevance
   timeliness
   accuracy
   authority.

3. **Qualify the magazine's readership within the market segment.**
   The characteristics of the readership can be compared with those of competitive magazines to demonstrate its advantages. Points are:
   numbers/coverage
   affluence/buying power
   purchasing patterns
   psychographic characteristics.

Design, format and quality

If you have access to the archives of a magazine that has been around for forty years or more, take time to look through an issue from each year of publication. See how the magazine has evolved in terms of design, format and quality. Consider those changes alongside the other changes which have taken place over that same period and draw some conclusions.

Magazines are very much creatures of fashion and external influences. Technology has played its part with, first, the increased use of black-and-white pictures, and then the move into full colour. Part of the impetus came from reader expectations of visual stimulus created by the advent of television and its move into colour, and part from new techniques that reduced the costs of reproduction and printing.

As time passes, magazines will continue to be influenced by external matters: by educational standards, by the aspirations of new generations, by competition from other media, by technological development. It is up to publishers to keep abreast of each of these developments to secure the future prosperity of their magazines.

The next few years are bound to see an extensive debate concerning the nature of magazine publishing. One school of thought weds the industry to print on paper; the other believes that the product is information or entertainment and that the medium is only the means of delivery. Why shouldn't a magazine be delivered on audio tape, on videotape or on CD-ROM? Why shouldn't it be delivered as a radio signal to be read ultimately on a computer monitor, on a TV set or printed out on an office (or home) laser printer? The possibilities offered by the development of electronics and communications technology will provide publishers with a great challenge.

Product launches

There's quite a bit of blind faith involved in the launch of a new magazine, and not just on the part of the publisher and the team. Much comes from external sources. In all cases a number of advertisers will have been persuaded that it is a good place to put their money. They will have been convinced solely on the projections and promises of readership devised by the publisher. Because of publishing lead times, that commitment is likely to be for a number of issues, so if the new project fails there will be some pretty angry advertisers about. Similarly, if the magazine was to have been sold through the newstrade, there will be disappointed distributors, wholesalers and retailers who will have wasted time and money.

If a magazine fails, it is inevitable that the publisher and publishing company will not only lose money but have their reputations dented as well. The motto is: 'Don't get it wrong and be very sure before embarking on a launch'.

If there is to be a launch, it is essential to allow enough time between the decision to go and the date of the first issue. It is hardly wise to rush what is going to be one of the most sensitive and important periods in a magazine's history.

Clearly there will be occasions when everything must be done quickly — to take advantage of a new fad or fashion or a special event — but as a rule it's worth taking the time to get everything right.

After the decision to launch has been made, there are quite a few jobs that have to be done:

The 12-point pre-launch check-list

1. Recruit, induct and train key executives:
   editor
   advertisement sales manager
   circulation manager
   etc.
2. Recruit, induct and train staff.
3. Set up internal systems and procedures.
4. Finalize editorial and advertisement and circulation sales policies.
5. Devise sales plans.
6. Devise launch plan:
   public relations
   press releases
   advertising
   launch event.
7. Finalize printing and distribution arrangements.
8. Finalize magazine style and design.
9. Create sales and promotional material for advertising and circulation.
10. Create dummy issue to use as sales tool.
11. Make presentations to key advertisers or groups of advertisers and advertising agents.
12. Constantly monitor progress against the launch plan to ensure that all targets, both time and financial, are met.

That is not intended to be a complete list of all the things that have to be done, and it will obviously vary greatly from situation to situation, but it does cover the principal issues. The order in which the various matters are dealt with will vary and will be largely dictated by events.

Increasing market share

The short answer to increasing a magazine's market share might be: 'Be better than, and sell harder, than anyone else'. That's probably a bit too glib, although if everything else is equal that surely is the answer.

First, it's important to know why the market share is not greater than it is. There are many obvious possibilities:

- circulation/readership level/quality
- editorial quality
- production quality
- availability
- sales effort
- resources
- pricing policy
- frequency
- format

and so on.

Having identified the reasons, remedies can be considered and costed, objectives established and plans formulated. It's the planning exercise outlined earlier of 'Where are we now? Where do we want to be? How do we get there?'

Protecting market share

Protecting market share is a somewhat different problem. It is a matter of staying awake and aware and not falling into the very inviting trap of complacency. If your magazine is the market leader, there is always someone wanting and waiting to knock you down.

If your magazine leads by a large margin or if there is no competition it is even worse; there is always the chance of a hungry predator invading the market.

The message is simple: provide readers and advertisers with what they need and want; constantly monitor the magazine's performance; and make sure there is no gap for someone else to come along and fill.

The questions to ask
To illustrate the range of information required before judgements can be made about a particular market, here is an analysis of a number of fictional controlled circulation magazines.

Volume and revenue analysis

Title	Ad pages	Volume share %	Est. rate £*	Est. revenue	Market share %
Amag	350	35.0	115	40250	36.3
Competitor 1	200	20.0	150	30000	27.1
Competitor 2	300	30.0	75	22500	20.3
Competitor 3	150	15.0	120	18000	16.1
Total	1000	100.0		110750	100.0

Title	Circu-lation	Market share %	Est. rate £	Cost (£) per 1000 circ.
Competitor 1	11000	31.9	150	13.6
Amag	10000	29.0	115	11.5
Competitor 2	7500	21.7	75	10.0
Competitor 3	9000	17.4	120	13.3
Total	34500	100.0		

* Estimated rate per page received based on published data.

If it's assumed that we're interested in *Amag*, what questions should we ask?
Copies of the the magazines will establish:
  • style and quality
  • the apparent appeal to market sectors
  • the nature of the content
  • the nature of the advertising.

Questions the resourceful publisher might ask

It is likely there is circulation overlap, what is the incidence?

Who gets what?

Do they read more than one?

Are there some people receiving nothing?

The figures quoted are for circulation, what are the readership figures?

What would the cost/1000 **readers** be?

How long has each magazine been around?

Amag looks to be in a pretty good advertisement revenue position compared with the others, what do trend figures show?

What would happen if *Amag* increased its rates to that of Competitors 1 or 3?

Is it significant that Competitor 1 has a higher circulation than *Amag*?

Is the position of *Amag* improving or declining?

How are the various magazines positioned in the market?

Does one serve top management, another middle management?

Is one for buyers, while the others are for line management?

Is the universe assessment accurate?

Has the cost per thousand any relevance?

What is the advertising market?

How many advertisers are there?

What is their spending pattern?

Are all potential advertisers using the magazines?

Do the readers of these magazines represent the total market for these advertisers?

What is the potential advertising market?

Would the profitability of one or more of the magazines be improved if there were a change in policy (editorial, sales or circulation)?

Is the frequency right?

Clearly, the questions which might be asked will vary according to the type of market and magazine.

The brand leader lost

For many years, the leading magazine for those in the media business was Advertiser's Weekly. Its nearest weekly competitor, World's Press News, dealt with similar issues but from a different standpoint, and was not too successful. Ad Weekly was supreme; it carried more advertising, had a large paid-for circulation and apparently served its market well.

WPN was bought by the young Haymarket Publishing. Within weeks it was closed and replaced by a product which not only caused the speedy demise of a the market leader, but heralded a new approach to business magazine publishing.

The new magazine was Campaign. Bright and easy to read, it was tabloid format on glossy paper, with good photography and a probing editorial style. It was quickly established as the premier media publication. Its 'new look' and style were later emulated by many magazines.

Ad Weekly suffered falling circulation and advertisement revenue and within a few months had closed. There are two points:

The first is that no magazine, however well or long established, has an impregnable position. A market leader survives while it protects its market share, and a pre-emptive policy is more likely to succeed than a reactive one.

The second is that the leading magazine in a market can be dislodged. Accurate identification and interpretation of reader needs and wants, a good, attractive product, plus forceful marketing, can do it.

The dual role

If the theory of marketing is to identify, or create, a need common to a number of people and then to supply that need at a profit, the theory and practice of magazine publishing cannot be separated from it.

To quote from an earlier paragraph in this chapter, 'the "marketing" of a magazine is not just for the backroom boys and girls or the sharp-suited folk from an agency, it is the job of each and every executive, whatever their discipline or title'.

And it is the publisher who must lead and motivate the magazine's team in using the many techniques and tools available.

The publisher's aim must be to:

Identify or create the need for a group of potential advertisers to communicate with a specified group of people.

Identify or create the need for a specified group of people to receive information or entertainment.

Satisfy both the advertiser and reader by creating a magazine or other product which fulfils the needs of each.

Optimize the potential offered to generate a profit.

Apart from the specialist knowledge and experience required to practise market research techniques, 'marketing' as described here is the total activity. It is well within the capabilities of a publisher and his or her lieutenants and should be part of their everyday job.

Chapter 4

Editorial

The importance of the editorial content of a magazine and the policy which guides its creation cannot be overstressed. It is the vital ingredient in the mix. While the policy statement may not be written by the publisher, it is without doubt his or her responsibility to approve it, usually with the participation of more senior management.

Generally speaking, the editor will contribute to the policy formulation and often enough will write it in detail. But, and this is an important distinction, at whatever level it is drawn up or approved, the implementation and interpretation of the editorial policy are the responsibility of the editor. So, in most publishing companies, the publisher, who has overall responsibility for the magazine and is in every respect the editor's line manager, assigns day-to-day control of the editorial to the editor. The exception is where the publisher is also editor-in-chief.

The publisher's editorial responsibility

It is the publisher's responsibility to monitor the editor's performance in relation to the content of the magazine and the supervision of the editorial department, and to seek to rectify any shortcomings using conventional management procedures.

Of course, if the publisher considers the editor is consistently misinterpreting the policy or failing in his or her responsibilities, then the usual disciplinary procedures, including dismissal, are available. More than that, such procedures **must** be invoked, for the publisher is ultimately responsible for the well-being of the magazine and of all those dependent on the magazine for their livelihood.

In turn, the editor is perfectly justified in expressing doubts about the validity of the editorial policy. The editor is, or should be, close to the reader and aware of shifts in opinion and need, and while these can often be accommodated by compensating shifts in emphasis, there may be a need to modify the policy. So, publishers must encourage editors to listen to the readers and they must listen to the editor.

Editorial not wanted

Welling in the breasts of some doughty advertising executives must be the argument that some highly successful magazines have NO EDITORIAL AT ALL. Absolutely true, and editorial would be out of place in them. The magazines or newspapers (for some might dispute the generic relationship), such as Exchange & Mart or Loot for example, are supplying hard information that the reader wants. And in the main, of course, such magazines do not depend on regular readers but on the occasional reader. That is, someone who buys the publication to see the ads when he or she has a purchasing need. Exchange & Mart is based on a sound marketing concept and its success should be well noted by all publishers, particularly those with an editorial background. If with advertising alone a magazine gives readers what they want (or need) then no amount of editorial will make it more successful.

Remember, too, that publications like E & M have disparate readerships, which I doubt could be served by any editorial platform. These magazines are notice-boards or market-places with straightforward offers for sale and the reader is pleased to pay to read them. What could be simpler or more direct?

The policy statement
The editorial policy statement sets out as clearly and as unequivocally as possible the editorial objectives. It might begin with a brief description of the readers, their political or social aspirations, special interests or responsibilities; it will then state the areas of editorial coverage and how the editorial will be matched to the readers' interests or needs; it will describe the type of content, and will perhaps define matters which will be excluded from the content.

The editor's role and responsibilities

Policy statements and job descriptions have a lot to say about the publishing requirement and the editorial role, but the first objective is the creation of a successful editorial content.

At this point, it would be as well to state quite categorically that there is little basic difference between the editorial responsibilities of

the editor of a consumer magazine, of a scientific journal or of a business-to-business magazine. The objective for each is to create a successful editorial content.
There are differences, of course. The commercial pressures may be different, the consequences of error may be different, the physical scale of the operation and the number of staff may be different, the rewards may be different, the frequency, the method of circulation, the printing process, may all be different, but the objective is still to create a successful editorial content.

Get the paper out!
I had spent four days talking with some magazine editors about their role as journalists and as managers. We'd had serious discussion and input from several specialists. One of the group was an editor of long standing, a genuine 'old salt'. He turned to a colleague and muttered: 'This management stuff's all very well, but my job's to get the paper out!'
And, of course, he was absolutely right.

Content
The editorial content is the component that in most instances motivates people to want to buy or read a magazine. To maintain a viable level of interest for readers, the editor must zealously control that content, the individual stories in a given issue and the mix over a number of issues.

Despite the common thread that brings them together, each reader has slightly different needs and interests, so the mix is of fundamental importance. One issue of 40 editorial pages cannot fulfil each reader's information needs any more than each article can be of interest to every reader. Even with twelve times 40 pages it can be difficult to cover the interests of all readers.

The editor has various inputs by which to set the balance of an issue, ranging from personal contacts and research, to statistical analyses of market activity and detailed reader research — there are more comments about this later.

The volume of editorial in an issue, or averaged across a year's issues, usually depends on the volume of advertising. The desired ratio of advertising to editorial, the ad/ed ratio, is set as part of the publication plan and must be adhered to. The ratio will vary according to the objectives of the magazine and the constraints of the format. There is usually a set minimum number of editorial pages or of issue size or a combination of the two, to ensure the reader gets 'value for money'. When advertisement paging is low, it is not always possible to maintain the ratio, hence the common practice of averaging the ratio over a number of issues. See page 145 for more on this topic.

Incidentally, if a magazine cannot cover the interests of its readers with its present editorial volumes and frequency, it's time for the publisher and the editor to take a good, hard look at the publishing policy.

Analyse the figures

There are many things which can emerge from close monitoring by the editor of his or her own magazine. Many years ago I edited a monthly product magazine, Factory Equipment News. As the months went by, we improved the formula, and as reader enquiries increased so did the advertising and my allocation of editorial pages. I viewed the statistics with pleasure, taking delight in the greater volume of enquiries for editorial items compared with those for advertisements, and I was able to attune the content more closely to the interests of the readership.

'Playing' with the figures, I realized that although the number of enquiries continued to increase as issue sizes grew, the average number of enquiries per item was affected by more than the balance of the content. Up to roughly 100 pages the average number of enquiries per item increased, but with larger issues it dropped. It turned out to be an inverse ratio above 100 pages. More detailed investigation soon revealed that there was an optimum issue size for effective response. Too many pages and readers either put the magazine to one side to read at some more convenient time (which never came), or read only part of what was on offer.

The revelation led to a review of the magazine's publishing policy and a change in frequency, but that's another story . . .

The cover and the packaging

If the editorial content is the magnet, then the first point of attraction, for new readers particularly, is the front cover. And this, too, is very much the editor's domain. The front cover must sell everything between it and the back cover. It presents a summary, a taste of what's to come. Whether it's the front page of a tabloid newspaper for butchers or the glossy cover of an up-market women's magazine, it must succeed in seizing the reader's attention and interest.

The editor is responsible for the rest of the packaging as well, for the appearance and appeal of the magazine from the first page to the last (and never forget that some people flick through magazines from the back!).

Of course, the art editor, or the designer (by whatever title), has a most important role to play in interpreting the design brief, but generally the final appearance is the editor's responsibility.

Publication budgets

A major responsibility for the editor lies in contributing to the overall management of the magazine, both in policies, such as marketing objectives and philosophies, and in the preparation of publication budgets. Sadly, some editors choose not to participate, believing that they will be sullied by any kind of involvement in the commercial aspects of a magazine. They are mistaken, for the well-being of the magazine is as important to them as to anyone else and the editor has a lot to offer in terms of product and market knowledge.

The term 'product' is used deliberately. A magazine is a product and is subject to the law of business which states products must make a profit to survive. The editor's full contribution is essential.

Ancillary activities

Another sphere where the editor can have a valuable, even strategic, influence is in the planning and implementation of ancillary activities and services which either enhance the standing of the magazine, improve its profits or, ideally, both. They include such things as:

- enquiry services
- reader offers
- study tours
- books
- conferences
- seminars
- exhibitions
- road shows
- award schemes
- newsletters
- electronic media
- special reports
- market information
- dial-up information or entertainment services
- on-line databases
- computer-based bulletin boards.

The creative force driving such activities might be the publisher or the editor — it depends on the personalities, their experience and enthusiasms.

Managing the department
It must not be forgotten that the editor is also the manager of the editorial department and has the conventional managerial responsibilities, ranging from editorial budgeting and budgetary control, through recruitment, motivation, training (see later paragraphs) and discipline of staff, liaison with other departments, to controlling the editorial diary, dealing with readers, advertisers, suppliers, and contributing generally to company thinking and policy.

Legal responsibilities
A further responsibility which rests with the editor is to ensure the magazine does not offend the laws of libel, defamation, obscenity, copyright, discrimination or trade descriptions, does not infringe the rules of contempt and conforms in all respects to the law as it affects published material. This is a very important matter, for the consequences of error can be most costly and unpleasant. Editorial training teaches journalists the basics they need to know, while for sub-editors and editors there is more detailed training available and a supply of textbooks.

It is generally wise to insure against the possibility of committing an offence; the premiums involved will depend on the type of magazine, its circulation, its history, and so on. Libel insurance is more and more difficult to obtain, except where the magazine agrees to heavy excesses. It is also sensible (and usually a condition of the insurance, if provided) that there is an arrangement with an experienced libel lawyer to advise on matters which may be contentious.

Remember, under the law, the editor (in certain cases with the publisher, printer and distributor) is responsible for the total content of the magazine, including classified and display advertising.

Knowing the market

People read magazines for many different reasons. Initially they do so because of a special interest (and all magazines are specialized in some way, whether women's interests, motoring, do-it-yourself, world affairs, the grocery trade, pop music, and so on), but they are also seeking one or more of the following: information, education,

An editor's responsibilities

An editor's responsibilities will vary between magazines and between companies, but here's a check-list which embraces most if not all the areas in which an editor might expected to contribute.

1. Contribute to editorial policy formulation.
2. Contribute to preparation of publication plan.
3. Prepare editorial plan and budgets.
4. Control costs in accordance with budget provisions.
5. Agree staffing levels and editorial structure with the publisher.
6. Recruit, direct, control, appraise and discipline editorial staff.
7. Ensure staff are properly trained and, in particular, train the deputy editor and other senior staff to run the magazine in the editor's absence.
8. Interpret and implement the editorial policy.
9. Plan issue content.
10. Maintain editorial standards.
11. Ensure the publication conforms to all legal requirements, in particular the laws of libel, contempt and copyright and others relating to published material.
12. Ensure issues are published in accordance with the schedule.
13. Liaise with advertising, marketing, circulation, production and publicity departments.
14. Liaise with government, business and other institutions, organizations and individuals to further the interests of the magazine.
15. Liaise with clients and advertising agencies and help promote the magazine.
16. Help the publisher promote and enhance the magazine in every way.
17. Make media/public appearances.
18. Develop ideas for profitable supplements, special publications and other trading activities.
19. Monitor current events so that changes of mood, needs, tastes, etc., may be reflected in the magazine.
20. Search for new writers, illustrators and photographers and motivate them to produce high-quality work.
21. Through contacts with readers and others, continually monitor and assess the progress of the magazine, and, when necessary, propose changes in policy.

entertainment, ideas, support, encouragement, escapism, advice, reassurance, relaxation.

To meet the readers' needs, the editor needs to know who they are (or should be) and what they are hoping to find in the magazine. This information should be available as part of the publication plan (discussed in Chapter 3).

The sort of information a consumer magazine editor might require would include:

- social grouping
- percentage male/female/adult/teenage/children
- average income
- discretionary expenditure
- jobs
- domicile
- marital status
- magazine purchasing/reading habits
- special interests
- first language
- car ownership

and so on.

For the business-to-business magazine, all or some of the above might be relevant — certainly if the readers are sole traders — plus:

- type, size and location of business
- SIC (Standard Industrial Classification)
- job title
- job function
- products or services for which the reader has buying responsibility or influence.

Market research
If the information isn't already in house, then to get it for an existing magazine is easy enough, if expensive. Market research by postal, telephone or personal survey can provide the answers. For many consumer and some business magazines there are co-operative research projects which measure readership and other statistics on a regular basis.

For new magazines in a new field research can be more difficult because there are no examples to use, but in general the same criteria and methods apply.

However obtained, the editor must have the information to operate effectively. Within reason, the more often the measurement is taken the better. If change is being made to policy or practice, the effects of such change can quickly be evaluated with a regular and frequent programme of research.

Interests, needs and wants
A major pitfall is the confusion between a reader's interests, needs and wants. A reader might express interest in a particular topic but,

---

Editor's check-list of research techniques

Reader panels. A group of randomly selected readers who are used for regular or periodic research. They may be asked to keep diaries, to answer questions every few weeks on the telephone or to attend group meetings.

Group discussions. A manageable number of readers brought together to discuss a particular question in depth. The members of the reader panel might be used.

Questionnaires in issues. A cheap form of research but may have limited value as the response may not be at all representative. Of course, the higher the response rate the more valuable the information.

Editorial monitoring. Otherwise known as 'keeping an eye on the opposition'. If your competitors are covering different issues from you, why? Are they wrong, or are you? The opposition may well do reader research which could be useful, unless, of course, it is research of doubtful quality. Research from a reliable source should be heeded. It may be presented to favour a competitor, but very often there is a message for you.

Editorial advisory boards. Not strictly research, but a useful form of feedback from people within a market sector or industry. People whose views are held in some regard meet at the editor's invitation to discuss matters relating to editorial policy and content. Such boards generally meet at least twice a year, and often more frequently. Of course, editorial advisory panels add kudos and their existence may be used to promote the authority and integrity of the magazine.

The method and manner of research are determined by the information needed, the type and number of people to be interviewed and the available money.

---

when it comes to the crunch, certainly doesn't **need** that information and may not even **want** it. Research must be carried out carefully and with advice from the best research specialists that the magazine can afford.

Questions such as: 'What would you like to read in So-and-So?' may elicit an answer, but it is far more helpful to know about readers' problems, hobbies, ambitions, and so on. It is also possible to find out what readers have read and whether the articles were helpful or not.

Research options
There is more about research in Chapter 3, but there are some methods which an editor can instigate and run if absolutely necessary. In those instances where there is little budgetary provision for publication research, it is the only way to find out. There is one proviso: the editor should never go it alone, but must take advice from a specialist on the techniques to be used, the questions to be asked and the interpretation of the results.

What the reader thinks
Knowing what the reader thinks about a magazine and its competitors is of fundamental importance to securing the future of the magazine.

It can help shape editorial policy and content. For example, readers may not rate one section or subject very highly despite the fact that much space is devoted to it, while another subject, given little space, is considered important. It is a simple matter for the editor to change the balance and thus satisfy the reader's needs. Of course, the readers' views can be used by the sales staff to show advertisers how the magazine is regarded.

Editors are fond of claiming that they know the markets they serve, yet it is surprising how often reader research proves the opposite. No editor should reject the opportunity to research the readership and certainly should not ignore the findings, no matter how unwelcome they may be.

Because of the nature of the job and the natural arrogance of most journalists, it is easy to fall into the trap of believing that one knows and understands the needs of a multifarious readership. Seldom is this true. Properly conducted, regular reader research can avert the disaster of a failed magazine. In addition, the editor personally (and all other members of the team) should be encouraged to talk with readers to establish what they think.

Specialist researchers

Research is best conducted by people who know what they are doing, even if it is expensive. It is far better to invest money in research than to spend much larger sums trying to build up a magazine which has declined. It's important, too, to talk to people who don't read the magazine. Those who answer an in-magazine survey are loyal current readers, but those who have deserted your columns may have a far more valuable contribution to make. Remember, the most expensive kind of reader research is a falling circulation.

The answers from research

So, what can an editor find out from market research? For a new launch, it's a question of discovering what readers think of existing publications, to establish if they are happy with what they are getting and if there is anything else they need or want. There's no prize for realizing that that's what the editor of an existing publication wants to know too.

Most qualitative research centres on issues such as authenticity, credibility, standing; identification with reader needs; vigour, readability and presentation. And it's how a magazine measures up in the eyes of the reader that counts.

There have been instances of magazines which in editorial purists' terms were thought to be excellent, but which failed commercially against 'lesser' magazines which were preferred by readers and, therefore, advertisers.

Editorial balance

Detailed market research can give a clear indication of the appropriate balance of editorial coverage or the editorial mix. Suitable questions can provide information on the perceived relative importance of the possible subjects. Use the answers to plan the magazine's content.

Take, for example, a woman's magazine where research has shown that readers grade the importance of subject areas in the following way:

- General women's affairs 28%
- Fashion 23%
- Beauty 16%

- Personal relations 9%
- Entertainment/arts 7%
- Health 7%
- Business/financial 5%
- Food 2%
- Travel 2%
- Design/home 1%

Whether this is a 'needs' list or a 'wants' list depends on the way the question was phrased. For most purposes it is probably best considered as the latter, in which case, if the editorial content can approximate to this profile over, say, a period of three issues, the readers are likely to be satisfied.

Another approach is to analyse the advertisement content because advertisers, being pretty choosy, tend to put money where they get results, and they get results when readers are interested in what they offer. Thus the breakdown of the main advertising groups might be:

Fashion 30%
Cosmetics/toiletries 30%
Health/fitness 10%

This approach inevitably raises the chicken-and-egg debate, who came first the readers or the advertisers? Nevertheless, when a magazine is up and running, it's not a bad idea to take note of the advertising content. Similarly, with a business magazine covering food manufacturing the analysis might be:

	Reader interests %	Editorial %	Adverts %
Ingredients	22	20	36
Processing	16	15	33
Packaging	15	17	16
Hygiene	12	10	11
Controls	5	4	4
Industry news	20	22	
Marketing	10	12	

In practice, the figures never compare directly, for some editorial subjects attract virtually no advertising — such as industry news or general women's interests — and the advent of major exhibitions or news-related issues — such as a health scare — can distort the pattern.

The point is that the avowed reader interests are closely mirrored by the editorial coverage and that the advertising follows a similar pattern. The advertising is unlikely to have exactly the same percentages, for there will be areas of editorial coverage (news, marketing, people) which are most unlikely to attract advertising support.

If a similar analysis is done for a magazine's competitors and the results compared, much might be learnt about the reasons for one magazine's success and another's failure. For example, one might reflect the readers' interests closely and so be well received, whereas another might balance the content quite differently and thus be of less value to the readers.

A further point for comparison between magazines is the ad/ed ratio. If all else is equal, including total advertising pagination, the magazine with the greater number of editorial pages should be able to give better coverage. The reader would get more editorial from a ratio of 60% than one of 70%.

Editorial programmes

Research enables editors to plan the magazine's content to reflect reader interests. If this planning is done far enough ahead and in co-operation with the publisher and advertisement manager, maximum advantage may be taken of advertiser interests as well.

The editorial programme sets out the skeleton of each issue for a given period ahead. Depending on the frequency of the magazine, this could be for three months, six months or a year.

For most magazines, there are key dates or events which must be observed. For some these might be Easter, Christmas, school holidays, Father's Day, Mother's Day, etc. For others they might be exhibitions, conferences, the crop sowing or harvesting seasons, race meetings, athletics events, concert seasons, and so on. All can be planned into the schedule a year or more ahead.

For many magazines, production schedules are such that issues may go to press several weeks, even months, before an event. A Christmas issue, for example, may be written during August and September and 'passed for press' by the end of October.

Other editorial content is filled in around the 'fixed' features, taking into account expected issue sizes during the period. The peak advertising time for most magazines is from September through to Christmas, which means that editorial activity peaks in the second half of the year.

That this coincides with the major holiday period brings its own problems, for there are inevitable strains in producing the editorial for bumper September to December issues during the summer holiday season.

There has to be some flexibility in the programme to account for sudden increases or falls in advertisement volumes. There needs to be a buffer stock of articles which can be used at the last minute. Because all articles have to be paid for in one way or another — in freelance fees or staff time — a buffer stock often consists of normal feature articles scheduled for use at a later date but prepared early. Plundering the talents of the editorial department to produce a four-page article at a couple of hour's notice, because of a problem elsewhere, is not a desirable course of action.

How many buffer articles to hold depends on the circumstances of a particular magazine.

The editorial programme serves a number of purposes. It enables the editor to commission articles and illustrations from staff writers, freelances or other contributors in good time to ensure the best results. It can be used by the sales department to encourage advertisers. It can be used by the circulation department to plan copy sales promotions around specific issues and to promote generally to potential readers. If published in the magazine itself, it encourages the interest and loyalty of existing readers.

Editorial staffing

Getting the numbers and the quality just right is not easy. And then, just when you think you have a good team, someone decides to leave for perfectly good reasons.

Journalists can have many different skills. They may excel at news-gathering and writing, at sub-editing, at feature writing, at personal interviews; they may be specialists in fashion, in motor-cycling, in hang-gliding, in financial affairs, in civil engineering, and so on. The successful editorial team has the mix of those skills and specialisms which satisfies the demands of the editorial policy and, in turn, the readers.

Given the editorial policy and the reader profile of a new magazine, the editor must decide how the content is to be produced to the budget available.

Whether, for example, to rely on freelances for specialist input on wines, or to employ a wine specialist full time. The decision will depend on the volume of wine stories/features that are planned and the importance of the subject in the overall mix. One consideration may be whether or not the wine writer could cover other subjects as well. For example, wine might be coupled with dining out or food.

Cost and quality
Another consideration might be whether a specialist of sufficient authority could be afforded within the editorial budget. It might be that the best person to write on legal matters would be a practising lawyer who, by nature of that requirement, could not be a full-time member of staff.

Invariably, the specified salary range of a particular job determines the quality of input that might be expected from the ultimate incumbent.

This relates back to the positioning of the journal, the desired reader profile, the level of expertise required (subject knowledge or journalistic skill, or both) and is affected by the market rates for particular skills.

It's very much up to the editor to decide where the editorial money is to be spent, although on the smaller publications there isn't too much scope. If there's only provision for an editor and an assistant, there's no flexibility.

Constantly review staffing
Like most aspects of the publishing process, the staffing of editorial departments must be kept under review — the demands of the readership, the demands of publishing technologies, cost constraints, staff turnover, the personal skills and attributes of those who leave and those who join, all contribute to a state of constant flux. The mixture changes and yet must be controlled to ensure that the demands of the editorial policy and the readers continue to be met.

There are no golden rules about staffing levels; each publication must be judged on its own merits. Clearly, where volumes are low and little money is available, there will be few staff. Where volumes are high then a greater number will be required, although it may be preferable to use a number of freelances on a regular basis and employ only sub-editors full time.

Frequency is another major factor — weekly production schedules exert quite different pressures from monthly schedules. The balance of content between news and features also affects staffing levels, as does the skill level and output capacity of individual members of a team. Highly skilled, highly motivated people are likely to produce more than the other kind.

Covering holidays and sickness

Other matters which particularly influence editorial staffing are holidays, illness and activity peaks. Editorial work cannot be delayed, it has to be done on time as 'the presses won't wait'. Planned absence can very often be accommodated by redeploying existing staff; illness is more difficult to overcome. Freelance back-up, either writers or subs, is a solution to both problems and also to peak period cover.

It could be, for example, that during a two-month peak period the staffing level should be eight people, whereas for the rest of the year only six would be needed. Some might argue for eight people all year, others for seven, while another solution would be to employ six and establish relationships with two or three good freelances.

In the end, it comes down to analysing the volumes over time of the different categories of editorial work and allocating the most resources to the critically important areas. Always, always there is the spectre of costs and the budget limitations within which the job must be done.

Freelance versus full-time staff

There is often a debate over the merits of staffing a magazine with freelances rather than full-time staff. The natural reaction of an editor is to have a close-knit team of permanent people, but the economics of publishing being what they are, there is an opposing argument.

This contends that there is a wide range of competent freelances who can be used as required to perform tasks at which they are particularly adept; that freelance specialists can be found in most subject areas; that because of the high level of competition to which they are subjected, freelances are often more skilled than their full-time counterparts; and, the most telling argument of all, that they are paid only when they produce work that is required and are not a fixed cost on the magazine.

The counters are that while freelances are necessary in some areas and provide a good service, they cannot possibly have the same great loyalty and dedication to a magazine that full-timers have, that they may not be available when wanted, that controls over their work and behaviour would be inadequate, that editorial planning would be more difficult, that there would be a lack of continuity and they could not make a contribution to editorial policy and decision-making.

The truth is that editors must be aware of the costs of creating the editorial content and must be prepared to adopt whichever approach best achieves the publishing objectives to which they are committed.

Editorial budgets

There are several ways editorial budgets come into being: the editor is informed by the publisher of a cash figure which must not be exceeded; an editorial paging forecast is set by the publisher for which the editor is asked to prepare estimates; and some unfortunate editors are not given any information or allowed any input.

Much the better way is for the editor to play a major role in budget preparation and to prepare a cost estimate. This should be based on:

- the magazine's business objectives
- editorial policy
- editorial paging forecasts
- the editorial programme
- market conditions
- special events
- supplements
- advertising features, and so on.

The editor does not control the overall number of editorial pages, because this is based on a ratio set as part of the publication plan (ad/ed ratio). Where the editor does have some flexibility is in the allocation of pages from issue to issue. Issues containing coverage of special events − particularly where the event does not generate advertising − may need to have a disproportionate number of editorial pages. Issues where the advertisement paging is exceptionally low will also have a disproportionate number of editorial pages. It is a matter of swings and roundabouts, for the balance will be restored in those issues which carry high advertisement volumes.

Assessing the resources required

Working with the magazine's management accountant, the editor should assess staffing requirements, freelance/contributor costs, illustration costs, travel, entertaining, training, or whatever range of headings apply to a particular magazine. These are costs falling directly under the control of the editor. Rent, rates, heating, personnel departments and all other such costs are matters for the general management of the company.

The question to be asked is: 'What do I need to spend to achieve my magazine's objectives?' The editor should know how much effort and time are required to cover certain events, say a major exhibition, the time required to research and write in-depth articles, photographic costs, and what effect staff holidays and off-the-job training have on the work-load.

The latter is important. Say, for example, the editorial department needs eight staff, each of whom has three weeks' holiday and is to receive ten days' off-the-job training. Allowing 240 working days a year, the total person-days is 240 x 8 = 1920. Holidays and training take (8 x 15) + (8 x 10) = 200 person-days. That's one person short for ten months.

If sickness (conveniently) takes another 40 days, then the department is operating with one person short for the year. So, maybe the staffing level should be nine.

Useful ratios to measure performance

There are two ratios which can be useful in evaluating the financial performance of an editorial department over time. In some instances the ratios may be used to compare different magazines, although considerable care must be taken to ensure that one is comparing like with like.

The first ratio measures the average number of editorial pages produced per staff journalist per year. It can be valuable for comparing one year's performance with another, or it can be used to calculate the staffing required for a particular level of paging.

The ratio is likely to vary greatly between magazines, unless the content and market are the same or compare closely. With a high level of contributed material the ratio will be high, whereas with a lot of staff-written material the ratio will be low.

It's easy to calculate:

$$\frac{\text{No. of edit pages}}{\text{No. of journalists}} = \text{Editorial pages per journalist}$$

Whether the editor is included depends very much on the way in which a given department works and perhaps on personal preference. Just be consistent.

The second ratio is the average cost per editorial page. Again it's a simple calculation:

$$\frac{\text{Editorial costs}}{\text{No. of editorial pages}} = \text{Average cost per editorial page}$$

It's a quick and easy way of keeping an eye on costs and of comparing performance between one issue and another or year-on-year (after allowing for inflation).

This ratio can be used in comparing the performance of two or more magazines, but be sure that the comparisons are fair. A monthly business magazine and a fishing weekly are very different; even two monthly business magazines, serving similar market needs, carrying similar editorial content and having a similar number of pages might have differences that would distort the ratios. For example, one might be in an area where many people in the market were anxious to provide articles at little or no cost, the subject matter for one might demand hand-drawn illustrations, but the other not, and so on.

There may be a strong correlation between the average number of editorial pages produced per staff journalist per year and the average cost per editorial page since, subject to maintaining editorial quality, the more pages per head the journalists produce, the cheaper the page should be.

Preparing the budget
If the appropriate information is available, preparing a budget is simple. Here's a check-list:

Check-list for preparing editorial budgets

Editorial policy	Entertaining
Paging forecasts	Contributors
Editorial programme	Freelance rates
Training needs	Photography
Systems requirements	Art
Staffing levels	Author's corrections
Staff costs	Any other cost data
Travel	

Why include editorial policy in the list? Well, it might have been decided to change an aspect of policy that will affect costs — for example, to reduce or extend coverage of a particular area. Systems requirements are featured, because the introduction of a new system or changes to an existing system can affect staffing levels, training, productivity and schedules.

A cost area which usually appears in editorial budgets, but which is disappearing from many with the advent of new technologies, is that of author's corrections. This is the cost of correcting errors or making changes to typeset copy.

Sloppy copy preparation, poor casting off (estimating the typeset length of a piece of copy) and indecision lead to considerable expense and much of it is avoidable. With computerized editorial systems, errors are caught at an earlier stage and copy can be edited to length on screen.

Indirect costs
There are indirect editorial costs which should be considered as well which, in some companies, are included within the editorial budget. These are print, typesetting, colour reproduction and paper costs for editorial pages. Certainly, the production department needs to know of editorial plans. If, for example, at least one feature per issue is to use colour photographs, the additional cost involved may appear under several headings in the final magazine budget.

The costs must be phased to suit the budgetary style of the company and presented to the publisher and thereafter to more senior management. If they are not acceptable, the figures will have to be reworked and the cloth cut 'till everything fits. It's not always a pleasant process, but the more accurate and honest the editor, the better.

Neither licence nor strait-jacket
Once the budgets are approved it is up to the editor to spend the money wisely. It is stated elsewhere in this book that budgets should not be rigid structures but a reasonable forecast of what will happen in a given set of circumstances. A budget should not be seen as a licence to spend a certain sum of money, nor should it be a strait-jacket.

Changes in pagination, in world or market economies, in people, in external costs, and so on, can cause actual costs to vary from budgeted costs. The editor should be judged on whether, in given circumstances, costs were wisely and sensibly incurred and controlled.

Editorial integrity

A bone of contention for many years, the integrity of the editorial columns must be defended fiercely. It is founded on the premise that a journalist's work is honest and truthful and that the editorial content of a publication is honest, true and faithful to its avowed editorial policy. The editorial policy of a magazine may have a political bias or champion a particular cause, but that is invariably known and welcomed by the reader.

A dishonest bias is not welcomed by readers and betrays their faith in the magazine. For example, advocating a particular product merely because the manufacturer has taken advertisement space, or because the publicity person is generous with expensive lunches or gifts, is hardly honest. Nor, indeed, is blatant distortion of the truth to gain advantage.

It happens, we know. Most days one can find examples of, say, the restaurant that gets an editorial puff on the same page as its advertisement. To invite the restaurateur to advertise in return for an editorial mention alongside is not acceptable.

To allow, even to encourage, a restaurant to advertise in the same issue in which a review appears is acceptable and makes good commercial sense. It does not affect the writer's choice of restaurant or what the writer says. Any approach to the restaurant is made after the writer has produced the review.

The deliberate distortion of editorial content, or the inclusion of unworthy material for pecuniary advantage, either to the benefit of the individual or the magazine, are not justifiable in any circumstances.

Profit potential
At the same time, editors and journalists must accept that in the tough world of magazine publishing no action should be taken which harms the profit potential of a magazine or a company.

Be honest and truthful about matters which affect the readers, even if it involves revelations which will displease advertisers. If the magazine is respected, authoritative, and has a reputation for honesty and fairness, it will not lose. There is a proviso: care should be taken to ensure that reports and comments are truthful, that the matter is not sensationalized, and that all sides are allowed to express their views. While an advertiser may well dislike what is said, the way in which it is said is often more important.

Keeping the reader in mind
An area which can cause unease among some journalists is the re-stating of previously published information in previews of exhibitions, or in reviews of categories of products, equipment or ser-

vices. The argument is voiced that such-and-such has been featured before and 'we're just giving it a plug'.

Consider the readers. For whatever reason, a percentage of them will not have seen, heard of, or remembered the existence of a particular product, yet will benefit from knowing of it.

Turn the tables; consider what you want in a review of a range of products in which you are personally interested. Do you want to read about all the products available or only those which have never previously been mentioned?

The service offered by the editorial in a magazine is to the readers. The first consideration of the editor and the editorial team is whether the information published is of relevance and value to the readers, not whether it offends some dubious journalistic tenet. If publication encourages an advertiser, so much the better.

Relating readers to advertisers

Editorial integrity when based on honesty and truthfulness must be defended. What cannot be defended is the argument that journalists must not involve themselves with commercial considerations or concern themselves with the consequences of their own actions upon their own magazine. Editors should always relate the reader market to the advertisement market — the one cannot survive without the other. Editors should view the journal's contents, both editorial and advertisements, as a single entity. The reader does.

Management and structures

Managing an editorial department is little different from running any other production orientated department or group of people.

Set aside the editorial skills for a moment and consider the other matters for which an editor might be responsible:

Personal: self-management, training
Personnel: job descriptions, people specification and recruit-
    ment, motivation, discipline, assessment and evaluation,
    training, unions
Departmental structure and delegation
Environment: office conditions, furniture, facilities, equipment
Liaison: senior management, other departments, external and
    internal contacts
Planning

Approving costs and expenses
Public relations.

Whether a department has one person or twenty, these 'general management' responsibilities will exist, but the time and effort demanded by them will vary greatly.

Getting staff to work effectively
First, of course, an editor must self-manage, allocating appropriate time to each part of the job and concentrating on those areas of key importance. There are no hard and fast rules; the balance will depend on the nature and scale of the magazine, on the editor's personal attributes and skills, and on the editor's job description.

Thereafter, it is a question of delegation, supervision and motivation, along with all the other matters involved in getting staff to do their work effectively.

The kinds of staff structure reporting to the editor will vary enormously. The factors affecting the structure will include: volume of editorial, frequency of publication, the balance of news to features, information catchment area (local, UK, Europe, the West, etc.), number of staff, balance of staff to freelances, and systems used.

Systems and techniques
The days when journalists pounded out their stories on battered and bruised manual typewriters of uncertain vintage are disappearing fast. Stand-alone computers or networked systems are now standard equipment in many editorial offices.

The benefits to the writer and sub-editor are considerable, even allowing for the problems some individuals encounter with the learning curve and the early health and safety worries.

Incidentally, it is an editor's responsibility to ensure that editorial staff use computers properly, that furniture and lighting are suitable and that proper breaks are taken. They are not matters that can be ignored or left to personnel or central computer departments.

Training

The editor sets the journalistic standards of a magazine and, as the team leader, knows the strengths and weaknesses of individual journalists. So who better than the editor to have overall responsibility for editorial training within that magazine? This doesn't mean that the editor has to do the training, but it is up to the editor to assess training needs and make sure the appropriate training is carried out by qualified people.

New entrants to journalism come from a variety of sources:

> **Direct from school or university**. The qualification or degree may be relevant or not. These people can go straight on vocational training courses and complete the on-the-job experience necessary for certification.
>
> **From industry or a specialist field**. These would be people with specialist knowledge of a subject, such as electronics, cookery, fashion, construction, etc. They may have writing experience, but will probably need a lot of training in journalistic practice and in writing skills.
>
> **From a full-time magazine journalism pre-entry course**. These people will have an understanding of the way magazines work, can produce reasonable copy and know the theory of libel and contempt. But they have no experience and require careful development.

Existing staff, or those who have joined from another publication, will be assessed and evaluated on their performance as part of normal management procedures. The assessment should identify training needs.

It's a sad fact that people leave schools and universities today without adequate skills in the use of the English language, and this is now a major training requirement for many new entrants. Other training which may be given to new or existing journalists includes:

- news reporting
- feature writing
- sub-editing
- layout
- research
- interviewing techniques
- law for journalists
- shorthand and keyboard skills.

Much of this is covered within the National Vocational Qualification (NVQ) scheme.

The quality of a magazine's content depends on the skills, abilities, knowledge and dedication of the editor and the editorial staff. Good training helps to maintain and improve that quality.

Production

Ensuring that the magazine's publishing schedules are met is a task which is often delegated to a production editor or chief sub-editor. The consequences of schedules not being met can be grave indeed. For a weekly to miss its printing slot has a knock-on effect which can seriously affect distribution and sales, particularly in a highly competitive market-place.

Advertising is often geared to an event — say the launch of a new product, the opening of a new showroom, an exhibition, etc. — and is therefore acutely time-sensitive. Late publication lessens the value of the advertisement to the advertiser. Disappointed advertisers demand compensation, such as price reductions, and lose interest in magazines which are frequently late.

Key dates and times
Print schedules are described in Chapter 8. For the editor, the key dates/times work back from the point at which final pages are passed for press. Last to go should be those pages which contain the material which is most time-sensitive, usually news, or possibly commodity prices, share information and similar information.

The editor must calculate the latest dates at which articles may be commissioned — possibly several months ahead of publication — to allow for sub-editing and any re-writing which may be necessary and for supporting illustrations to be obtained. Different time-scales will be required according to the type of article or feature, the writer, and so on.

The editorial schedule must take account of likely bottle-necks — for example, subbing or layout — particularly when extra large issues are planned.

The packaging

Food is more appetizing if it is nicely presented, on a clean plate, on a suitable table-top and with gleaming cutlery alongside. News and features are more appetizing if they are nicely presented, in a readable typeface, with good illustrations, on a well-designed page and cleanly printed on appropriate paper.

Cover appeal
Of course, your magazine's packaging has to do several jobs. First of

all, the cover must make people want to pick it up. For a magazine lying on a newsagent's counter or rack, it's a tough job. There have to be recognition symbols for regular, committed readers — title, format, cover style — while for new readers there has to be something which captures their initial interest — usually the cover picture — and then entices them to buy.

It's worth studying the effects of different covers on a magazine's appeal to existing and new readers and establishing design criteria. Great care must be taken in getting the cover right for every issue published, if a magazine's circulation potential is to be maximized.

If anyone questions the meticulous attention which is required, or suggests deviating from the magazine's proven rules, tell them to do their own market research. Stand near a railway station bookstall or a supermarket browser bar and watch people looking for a 'good read'. The importance of illustration, captions, teasers, offers, and so on, will soon become apparent. The difficulties to be overcome will be noticed too — maybe just the left-hand edge or the top couple of inches can be seen because a magazine gets tucked behind several others. If so, the designer has to make that part of the cover work on its own and encourage the browser to pull out the magazine for a better look.

The important contents page
Almost as important in this context is the contents page. Browsers often scan the contents and a well-designed, informative page can do a marvellous selling job. It must be easy to find, of course.

If all this seems to refer solely to consumer magazines, it doesn't. All magazines exist to be read and readers must be encouraged to do just that. Magazines are often read in an environment where there is a lot of competition for the reader's attention. It might come from other magazines, from the view out of the train or office window, from radio or television, from sleep induced by creeping boredom. In the work environment, particularly, there are many things to distract the reader, especially the pressure of time.

The magazine that asks to be read
It's the editor's job to create a product which the reader wants to pick up and read.

The writing style, the typography and the layout of a publication have one aim — to make it easy to read. Faced with a page of different typefaces, all at different angles, or vast slabs of tightly set, small type, readers are consciously or unconsciously deterred. A simple, straightforward layout style, using ample illustrations, with clear captions, introductions or summaries, can make even the dullest subject appear more interesting. If illustrations aren't available, sensible use of cross-headings or typographical devices can break long articles into readable chunks.

There is nothing more off-putting to the reader than a magazine which is poorly illustrated, where captions say little more than 'Figure 5', or where there is page after page of solid text. Most people need encouragement to read, so make them think it's going to be easy to follow the layout, easy to absorb the text and won't take up too much valuable time.

Browsing through a magazine, the reader is looking for reasons to stop and enjoy or learn. Headings are essential eye-stoppers, as are pictures. Caught by one or both of those, amplification and further enticement are sought from introductory paragraphs (intros) and from captions. The editor must ensure that each element works.

Personal skills

The editor is invariably the leading spokesperson for a magazine. At exhibitions and meetings, on the radio or TV, at all kinds of public/industry/trade engagements, it is the editor who catches the reader's imagination, not the publisher or advertising salespeople.

Speak up!
The ability to stand up in public and speak clearly, concisely, amusingly, entertainingly — you choose the adjective — is a skill with which few are born, yet have you or any of your colleagues been on a public speaking course?

As a publisher, I sent many people on such courses or arranged them in-house with a specialist tutor brought in. The 'ums' and 'ers' soon disappeared. Personal prestige of the editors was improved and so was the prestige of their magazines.

Internally, the editor has to 'sell' the magazine's concept to the editorial and other staff. If the magazine has a sales conference, the editor should be one of the star turns.

The editor should be available to meet advertisers and should play a part in major presentations to clients and their advertising agents. Being 'on show' is an important part of an editor's duties and can be vital to the success of a magazine.

Editorial check-list

If something is wrong with a magazine's editorial, it takes a little time to show up in the circulation or readership figures, by when, of course, a great deal of damage may have been done. While the reader is the final arbiter, it is possible to run an eye over each issue and examine these four key areas:

Content
Are the prime matters of reader interest covered?
Are the articles/stories properly and adequately researched?
Are arguments for and against given?
Is the content unbiased?
Are there items which are irrelevant to the readership?
Are there items which have been omitted (discovered by scanning other media)?

Balance
Does the content meet the needs of readers right across the market or range of interest?

Quality
Is the content well written?
Do headlines, intros, captions draw the reader into the page and the article?
Does the content conform to the house style?

Visual
Are the layout, graphics, typography and pictures of acceptable standard?
Does the magazine look 'easy to read', or is it going to take a lot of time and effort?
Is there a continuity of style — does the magazine look a complete entity?

Some of these questions overlap from one area to another and there most certainly will be other questions which should be asked. A careful study of each issue as it as published could save much heartache when the circulation figures become available.

The editor also does a selling job on contributors and potential editorial interviewees: if you want to interview a captain of industry or a senior politician you've got to sell the idea to them, or at the very least their publicity officer.

So, the editor is a kind of super-salesperson and it should be highlighted in the job description or list of job objectives. The publisher must ensure the editor has this ability and must provide appropriate training and encouragement to develop such skills.

The editor's persona

A difficult, but important, concept to grasp is that the editor must have a personality to match the attributes which readers and others will ascribe to the post. Most magazine readers would expect the editor of a glossy, up-market women's magazine to have good dress sense, be well groomed and stylish and to speak well (cogently, with good grammar and vocabulary). Similarly, one expects the editor of a business magazine to convey a businesslike and professional image.

The public promotion of the editor through personal appearances and participation in trade events is to enhance the magazine, not the individual who sits in the editor's chair.

Chapter 5

Advertising

An advertisement manager is either a super-salesperson, a super-manager, or a mixture of the two. Proven sales ability is essential for any advertisement manager's job, but, of course, not all such jobs call for a super-manager. Like most other things in magazine publishing, it depends on the demands of a particular situation.

The one-man-band operation doesn't require too much managerial time except to exercise personal disciplines, whereas magazines with high advertisement volumes usually require a great deal of management time and greater management skill to control and motivate the many salespeople involved.

It must be stressed that not all good salespeople make good managers. Be very sure before taking a top sales executive off the road to 'sit behind a desk'; too often good salespeople fail as managers.

If you are contemplating promoting someone just to keep him or her on the team, don't. It's far better to be honest with such individuals and yourself; if they are really good, pay them their worth to stay. If a salesperson is generating high turnover, it really shouldn't matter if he or she earns more than either peers or superiors. Should such a situation cause problems, the solution may be to improve the calibre of the other members of staff rather than lose the one good person, by whatever means. Just think, that may lead to a much more profitable magazine.

The advertisement manager's role

Like the editor, the advertisement manager has a role to play in forging the policy of the magazine. After all, he or she is in constant contact, either directly or through the sales-force, with the people who provide most, if not all, the revenue. The advertisement manager must seek the opinions of advertisers and, particularly perhaps, of non-advertisers as part of normal business contact. The advertisement manager should be the first to identify changes in advertiser needs, fads or fancies or to sense dissatisfaction with the magazine for whatever reason.

The advertisement manager's most obvious role is managing and motivating the sales-force to achieve sales targets, but this is the tip of the iceberg. Here are some of the responsibilities which might be included in a job description:

> Help formulate publication policy
> Help formulate sales policy
> Implement sales policy
> Help prepare sales promotional material
> Specify, recruit, train and discipline sales staff
> Fix sales targets
> Monitor sales staff activity
> Maintain relationships with important clients
> Keep editor and publisher informed of advertiser attitudes and needs
> Maintain a sales area.

Sales policy

A part of the overall publication plan, the sales policy guides the activities of the sales manager and the sales staff just as the editorial policy guides the editor.

The sales policy of a magazine sets out:

- the market(s) to which advertising is to be offered
- the nature of that advertising
- the justification for approaching advertisers
- prices
- the allocation of sales areas by
  type of business or product (cameras, cars, etc.)
  type of advertising (display, classified, supplements) or
  geographical area (North West, London, etc.)
- sales methods — telephone, face-to-face
- promotional expenditure
- the number and type of salespeople
- training requirements.

The advertiser's needs

An understanding of the requirements and expectations of advertisers and advertising agencies is the key to successful advertisement sales and is the major influence when setting the sales policy. An advertiser's prime objective is to obtain a reaction to an advertisement. The desired reaction might be:

- retail sales
- direct sales
- customer/reader enquiries
- attendance at an event
- awareness
- creation of a mood or opinion, etc.

Whatever the objective, success in achieving that reaction depends upon the advertiser and the magazine working together to get at least eight factors right:

Eight factors for success

1. Market/audience identification
2. The message
3. Market coverage of the magazine
4. The environment created by the magazine
5. Quality of reproduction
6. Position in the magazine
7. Advertisement frequency
8. Timing

It's really up to the advertiser to get the first two factors right, although magazine salespeople are often able to help refine an approach. Indeed, many advertisers lean quite heavily on the salesperson for advice and assistance.

It sometimes happens that a direct request is made for help, but more often than not it's a gradual process, with the salesperson winning the confidence of the advertiser. In this dual-role situation, the salesperson becomes a kind of marketing adviser, planning a campaign and writing and designing copy.

There are risks in such a close relationship for both advertiser and magazine. It's possible for the advertiser to be persuaded to spend money unwisely, which can cause disaffection and be detrimental to the magazine in the longer term; it's possible that the close affinity which develops between the advertiser and the salesperson is such that if the salesperson moves job then the advertising follows.

What most advertisers expect is that the salesperson will know and understand the market in question, and can relate the needs of the advertiser to that market and to the coverage and services provided by the magazine.

The salesperson must demonstrate to the potential advertiser that:
- the market the advertiser wishes to reach is that served by the magazine
- the coverage of that market is of an appropriate level and at a reasonable or competitive cost
- the magazine's content, style and presentation will enhance the advertiser's product
- appropriate positions (in a particular part of the magazine, on a specified page) are available
- the frequency and timing are right.

The market and the advertising

The publication plan specifies the market in which the magazine is operating and the type of advertising to be carried, i.e. the various categories of product or service and whether display or classified. It's very much up to the advertisement sales manager to take this specification further.

The first step is to classify the sectors of the given advertising market, to estimate their respective importance (in advertisement volume and revenue terms) and then to identify potential advertisers and assess their relative importance.

This is desk research into the statistics of the market, and can be carried out using sources similar to those described in Chapter 3. The assessment is made, using published information or by monitoring other publications, of the amount of money spent by advertisers, in groupings and singly. The groupings will indicate sector importance.

With this information it is possible to prioritize the sectors and individual advertisers, often into three groups termed primary, secondary and tertiary, and to set sales objectives and targets.

Advertisement rates

The rates charged for advertising grow out of a number of factors:
- the costs of producing the magazine
- the advertising potential
- competitors' rates
- the perceived value of an advertisement to an advertiser (what the market will bear)
- the profit required.

The base rate (full page, single insertion) is normally fixed early in the planning process.

Constructing the rate card
Construction of the rate card, or schedule of advertising charges, depends on another set of factors:
- the format of the magazine
- the ratio of colour to mono advertising
- the ratio of display to classified, full pages to smaller sizes, etc.
- the ratio of single insertions to series bookings
- the frequency of publication.

There are extra charges for:
- special positions (cover or back cover, facing editorial, facing specified pages)
- bleeds
- special effects (metallic ink, gatefolds)
- origination
- colour proofs.

Classified rates vary by size and by classification (situations vacant often having the highest rates).

The objective is to achieve the highest possible yield (income after discounts) per page.

On the next page is a typical display advertisement rate card for an A4 business magazine (a consumer magazine rate card would look much the same).

There is a discount for series bookings. This is to encourage the advertiser to place the maximum amount of business at one time, although most publishers allow retrospective discounts within a twelve-month period.

The discount is valid because it helps secure business and also because it is much more cost efficient to sell a contract of 12 insertions than to sell 12 single insertions.

In the example given, the steps are at 4% of the base rate for a given size, to a maximum of 12%. Some publishers give a further discount based on the overall value of business in the period to encourage the big spenders to spend even more.

There is a premium for smaller sizes. Two half pages yield 8% more than a full page and four quarter pages yield 28% more.

Special positions are not subject to series discounts and the front

Display advertisement rates

No. of insertions	1	3	6	12
	£	£	£	£
Mono				
Page	900	864	828	792
Half	486	467	447	428
Quarter	288	276	265	253
Four colour				
DPS*	3500	3360	3220	3080
Page	1900	1824	1748	1672
Half	1026	985	944	903

* (double page spread)

Special or spot colours
Extra charge per colour per insertion

Metallic inks	550
One process colour	350
Other single colours	450

Special positions

Per insertion	*Colour*	*Mono*
Front cover	3000	n.a.
Inside front cover	2000	1000
Outside back cover	2250	1100
Facing matter	2050	1100
1st right-hand page	2050	1100
Bleed pages	+100	+100
Solus	+200	+200

Loose inserts   from 1500 (single sheet A4)

Origination charges

1 transparency	350
Additional transparencies each	130

Agency commission	10%

and back covers are at a very high premium. Front covers are invariably subject to the advance approval of the editor.

An accredited advertising agent placing business on behalf of a client is allowed a discount, usually 10 or 15 per cent, depending on whether it is a business or consumer magazine.

Classified advertisement rates might look like this:

Classified advertisement rates

£ per single
column centimetre (scc)

Appointments		18.00
Minimum 4 centimetres		
Discount: 2nd insertion	10%	
Discount: 3rd insertion	15%	
Non-recruitment		16.00
Minimum 3 centimetres		
Discount: 4 insertions	5%	
Discount: 7 insertions	7%	
Discount: 12 insertions	10%	
Discount: 26 insertions	13%	
Discount: 52 insertions	15%	

Directory
Minimum 3 centimetres and minimum 13 insertions

13 insertions, per insertion	11.60
26 insertions, per insertion	11.55
52 insertions, per insertion	11.40

Insertions must be consecutive

A rate card states the dates between which the rates are effective, e.g. September 1992 to October 1993, or the date on which the rates come into effect. The rate card often contains other vital information:

Mechanical data — the sizes for each standard advertisement, specifications for colour separations, specifications for black and white materials.

Copy dates — the latest times by which copy must be delivered to the publisher.

Cancellation dates — the dates up to which cancellations will be accepted without charge. After the cancellation date the full cost of the advertisement or a percentage thereof will be charged.

Terms and conditions — specifying the rules under which advertising is accepted, warranties and exclusions, payment terms, etc.

The terms and conditions may vary in their scope, but there are a number of matters which are usually common to all:

The publisher's right to refuse or amend an advertisement.

Compliance by the advertiser with the British Code of Advertising Practice.

Terms of payment.

Liabilities or otherwise for late copy, late publication or failure to publish.

Indemnification of the publisher against any damage or expense as a direct or indirect consequence of the advertisement.

The advertiser's warranty that the advertisement conforms to the law.

The last two points are most important in the context of the legal obligations of the advertiser under various laws and regulations, from consumer protection through to libel.

Sales areas

It is usual to split a display advertising market into geographic and/or category sales areas. The number of clients and their location are the principal determinant factors. The most common split for the UK is:

London and the South East
The Midlands
Wales and the West
The North of England
Scotland
Northern Ireland

Much depends on where the centres of activity for a particular market are to be found, and there may be more or fewer divisions.

To split by market sectors is less common in the magazine world, although it does happen. In such instances a specialist salesperson might cover the country or work in a particular area (usually London and the South East), with support from a more general salesperson in the other locations. Specialisms might be cars, property, financial services, etc. Classified advertising is almost always sold over the telephone nowadays.

Sales methods

Any sales manager will want the salespeople to operate according to particular standards and to adopt particular methods. For example, in order to contact the maximum number of potential clients, it may be that display salespeople will be encouraged to use the telephone. Alternatively, face-to-face selling may be preferred, as it is likely to establish a firmer relationship with clients.

There may be a preferred way of presenting facts and information in a sales interview, or of discussing competitive publications. There will be quality standards for the data presented to clients. There will be a required frequency of contact with each client.

The sales team
The number and level of salespeople depends on

- the size of the market (numerical)
- the physical location of clients
- the prime selling method (face-to-face or telephone)
- the optimum amount of time required in selling to each client
- the incidence of advertising agencies
- whether much advertising comes from overseas
- the number and strength of competitors
- the need for 'strength in the field'.

Unfortunately, there are no hard and fast rules about the number of staff required. It can only be fixed by assessing the work involved in a given situation.

Similar criteria apply to classified sales, with the exception that much depends on the source of the advertisements. In most cases the advertiser will approach the magazine and emphasis must be placed on facilitating the approach. An obvious example is to offer telephone access at local call rates.

The level of clerical support within a sales department depends on the number of salespeople and matters such as the amount of direct mail used, the amount of monitoring and the ways in which sales leads are found.

Getting the message across

It is not enough for a potential advertiser to know that a magazine exists; its benefits have to be sold dynamically to ensure genuine understanding. With a two-way exchange, the feedback can be used to control and progress sales.

While employing full-time salespeople to sell face-to-face with clients is the most expensive option, it does offer the greatest level of success and control and is the method favoured by most publishers.

It goes almost without saying that the contribution of the salespeople to any magazine's success is vital, and it follows, therefore, that the most critical aspect of advertisement sales management is the selection, training, motivation and control of sales staff.

Clear objectives
Irrespective of how good the salespeople are, they will always need help, guidance and the appropriate motivation to produce improved results on a consistent basis.

To be effective in creating the right environment, managers must have clear objectives, be able to fix similarly clear objectives for the salespeople, and have an effective system for measuring performance against the standards desired. This system of measurement or assessment will

- establish an on-going dialogue related to performance
- identify individual strengths and weaknesses
- establish training needs and any other assistance required
- determine the individual's career path.

Apart from sales results, there are three key areas for assessment — product knowledge, market knowledge, and personal skills and attitudes.

Equipping the salesperson
Advertising is about concepts and ideas, abstractions, intangibles, analysis and statistics. To discuss such matters effectively the salesperson must have a comprehensive knowledge and understanding of the market, the magazine and the advertiser's needs. The greater the knowledge, the more effective the sales staff. Knowledge implies credibility, creates confidence and gains the respect of the buyer.

The key topics which should be instilled into the salespeople are:
Advertising — what it is, why it is needed, how it works.

The market — the products or services involved, the trends, changes in ownership, company results, people and events, etc.

The magazine — history, editorial, circulation, research, promotion, advertising, production.

The competition — strengths and weaknesses in circulation, editorial, research, rates.

The advertiser or prospect — the prospect's background, products, markets, sales and marketing departments, advertising agency; the contact's personality, interests, likes and dislikes, etc.

To be used effectively, the knowledge must be backed up by a number of skills or attributes which can be categorized into three areas: preparation, action and administration.

Preparation is the work that should be done before meeting the client:
- researching the client company
  the products
  the current advertising
  standing in the market
  the key executives
  the competitors
- setting an objective for the sales call, along with getting the interview and planning how the sales call is to be conducted.

Action is the call itself:
- conducting the meeting
  the presentation
  handling objections
  closing
- personal attributes and attitudes
  appearance
  punctuality
  manners.

Administration is the post-call activity
- call report
- updating records
- follow-up activity
  correspondence
  call-back date.

High on any list of personal needs for a salesperson (or any other member of staff for that matter) is job satisfaction. Consistently good

sales results are impossible to achieve unless there is a high level of
job satisfaction within the sales force which, in turn, demands good
motivation. Staff motivation must feature high on any manager's list
of priorities.

Factors which contribute to good motivation and which may be
directly controlled or influenced by the sales manager include:

- the parameters of the job, the particular areas of activity,
  territory, product category, etc.
- the chain of command
- personal objectives
- training
- recognition
- rewards
- sales support.

Monthly sales report

A sales department's monthly report might look something like the
specimen on the facing page.

There are two sets of figures:

Booked revenue shows the net value of orders taken in the
month and the value of orders taken so far in the year. Both
figures are compared with the same time last year.

Published revenue shows the net value of business published
in the month and for the year to date. Both figures are
compared with target and with the same time in the previous year.

Looking at the published revenue performance of Rep 1: target has
been missed by £2000 for the month, but £3000 more business has
been published than in the previous year. For the year to date Rep 1
is £8000 below target, but £6000 better than last year. Rep 2 has beaten
the month's target by £1000 and is £3000 up on the previous year. For
the year to date Rep 2 is £2000 ahead of target and £12 000 better than
the previous year.

The first question to ask about Rep 1's performance is whether the
target was fairly set. If it was, then the performance is over nine per
cent below target. There may be some special reason for the variance,
such as an advertiser going out of business or the cancellation of an
expected event, but it is the sales manager's responsibility to establish its cause.

Sales report		March 1992	
Booked revenue £'000	Rep 1	Rep 2	Total
Total for month 1992	24	18	42
Total for month 1991	18	12	30
Cumulative 1992	76	69	145
Cumulative 1991	65	66	131
Published revenue £'000			
Actual revenue			
this month	32	30	62
Target revenue			
this month	34	29	63
Variance	(2)	1	(1)
Actual revenue			
this month 1991	29	27	56
Variance 1992 to 1991	3	3	6
1992 actual to date	79	84	163
1992 target to date	87	82	169
Variance	(8)	2	(6)
Actual to date 1991	73	72	145
Variance 1992 to 1991	6	12	18

Of course, if a team or individual goes wildly over target, then the cause should be established also.

Training

Intelligence and education plus aptitude are what most people bring to a job. The skills and knowledge they need to do that job effectively are the result of training provided directly or indirectly by an employer. It is given either by the example of colleagues in the workplace, or by formal on-the-job or off-the-job training. Those given formal training are generally the ones who will make the best sales contribution.

Yes, there are those who appear to be natural salespeople, but they are going to be much better salespeople when the natural ability is shaped and directed.

The sales manager should devote considerable attention to identifying the training needs of the sales team and to ensuring that those needs are met.

And although not necessarily expected to be the trainer, it obviously helps if the manager has training skills, certainly for the on-the-job part of the programme. A sales manager should be measured on the effectiveness of the training he or she provides. Most companies have training officers who are able to give plenty of support in assessing the need and in arranging suitable training. If there's no training officer, there are many organizations offering sound sales training.

To be clear on the point, the purpose of sales training is to ensure that the magazine has a professional, well-motivated team capable of generating the maximum possible advertisement revenue and of increasing, or at least maintaining, its market share.

It is an expensive process, in both the actual cost of the training and the possible loss of revenue caused by taking the sales executive 'off the road' for the duration. It is essential, therefore, that training be planned, monitored and controlled as thoroughly as any other part of the publishing operation.

The first stage in developing a sales training programme is to define the knowledge of the magazine and of the market and the skills needed by the salespeople.

Regular appraisal and assessment of sales performance will help to identify agreed areas where training can improve a weakness. In fact, training should always be related to assessment and have a defined objective — it can be highly demoralizing to an experienced salesperson to be sent, without explanation, on a training course. It follows that anyone sent on a training course should be properly debriefed afterwards, or the value of the training is likely to be reduced.

New recruits expect to be trained, and should be shown exactly what is required of them and given the sales material, information and support they need to carry it out.

Successful training usually involves both off-the-job and on-the-job techniques.

Formal classroom teaching or practice away from the day-to-day work pressures is an invaluable preparation and speeds up the learning process, but it has its limitations. Real proficiency will only come about through on-the-job guidance and experience. The on-the-job training should be provided by the manager or a senior sales executive.

Sales aids

To be effective, a salesperson must be able to demonstrate the relevance and advantages of the magazine. Much can be done by word of mouth, but spoken words are soon forgotten or easily mis-remembered. The same message offered in some other form can augment and reinforce the salesperson's efforts. In some situations — where direct mail is used, for example — the message in non-verbal form replaces the spoken word.

Until comparatively recently, the alternative form would always have been printed, but it is now possible to present a sales message on audio tape, video or computer disc, etc. Whatever the physical form of the sales aid, it should present a range of information.

The nature and quality of sales material are very much influenced by the market and the magazine itself. An up-market magazine certainly requires promotional material of at least a similar quality. But there is no rule that says magazines of a lower quality can make do with lower quality promotional material. It happens, of course, but it is not really to be desired.

Clearly, the expense involved in producing promotional material is controlled by the likely return — the profit potential of a given magazine — but publishers and advertisement managers should always strive for the highest standards.

Remember, promotional material represents the magazine talking about itself. Poor quality research, bad writing, or poor design are hardly good advertisements for the magazine.

Magazine promotion can take a number of forms:

- advertising, in other media (newspapers, televison, posters)
- direct mail, to existing and potential advertisers
- brochures, leaflets, features lists
- rate cards
- media packs
- exhibitions
- research
- industry involvement.

The familiar article is the 'media pack', meaning a brochure or package containing a variety of information about a magazine. It can be used by a salesperson during a presentation to help tell the story, it can be left with a prospective client to mull over, and it can be used as part of a mailshot.

As the number one, and very often the sole, sales aid, it should be well written and presented and be easily understood by all levels of client. It presents to a potential advertiser a picture of the magazine and its environment and should reflect the image that the publisher seeks for the magazine.

The content of the media pack will vary according to the needs of the magazine and its market, the unique selling proposition the magazine offers, and the data available to support it.

A comprehensive media pack might describe:

- the importance of the market to which the magazine circulates; its size and buying power in relation to specific products and services
- the structure of the market and its relationship with other markets (where appropriate)
- the magazine's niche or mission statement
- the magazine's coverage of the market; how the circulation and readership relates to the market structure and to its buying power
- the editorial content and its relevance to the readership; the prestige, authority, integrity of the editorial; the standing and stature of the editor
- the editorial programme, features and events due to be covered editorially
- the researched evidence of reader loyalty, respect and dependence on the magazine, (what they like about it and what they say about it)
- proof of effectiveness, comparative reader research, reader profiles and reader enquiry data
- value for money; cost comparisons with competitive media
- industry/market involvement, exhibition sponsorship, conferences, seminars, study tours, workshops, educational services, awards, or other commitments to the market, a sector of the market or to the industry concerned
- other services and activities offered by the magazine
- the advertisers, who else uses the magazine and unsolicited testimonials
- enquiry services offered by the magazine and analysis of reader response
- advertisement rates and sizes
- terms and conditions.

The manner of presentation for all this may vary from a bound volume, to a ring-binder, to a series of single sheets published simultaneously or separately. Most publishers go for a snappy, eye-catching and colourful style, but some still undervalue the importance of such material and either duplicate or photocopy poorly typed originals. Well-written, pertinent, well-designed material will win every time.

Analysing the competition

There are three stages in persuading someone to advertise. The first is to persuade the potential advertiser that there will be some benefit to be obtained — increased sales, enquiries, etc. — from advertising to a particular market. The second is to persuade them that a magazine is the best place to get results, as opposed to TV, radio, cinema, direct mail, newspapers, posters, exhibitions, etc., or that a magazine complements promotion through other media. The third is to put a convincing case for the benefits to be gained from using a particular magazine.

The points of comparison for each magazine involved are:

- market coverage or readership by interest or geographical area
- relevance of individual readerships to the advertiser's needs
- editorial coverage and standing
- research findings
- frequency — the relative merits of weekly versus monthly, perhaps
- format — tabloid or A4, which is the best show-case
- cost, and cost per thousand readers
- relative costs for a particular type of reader.

The object of the exercise is to present your publication in the best light. Play up your strengths and play down your weaknesses, play up the opposition's weaknesses and play down its strengths.

There are rules to the business of talking about competitors and there is an expression which is trotted out when everyone is feeling benign about the subject: 'Dog doesn't eat dog'. Knocking the competition to the extent of spreading rumour and falsehood is frowned upon by most magazine executives. If you have a good magazine, backed by good research, it shouldn't be necessary to resort to dirty tricks and, in any case, such selling methods seldom present more than a short-term advantage.

Sales leads

All the sales management and all the sales training in the world are of little value without someone to whom to sell. Finding potential customers is easy for some magazines, but a lot more difficult for others.

If you are selling to motor dealers, there are names galore in telephone books, other magazines and newspapers. Selling to people who sell to motor dealers is a little more complex, and there aren't nearly as many names of prime prospects to be found. There's a lot more winkling out to be done.

The first step is to identify what motor dealers buy and then locate the suppliers of such equipment and services. There will be lists in various sources for each type of equipment or service, but not all of those firms listed will see motor dealers as prime targets, whatever a magazine publisher may think. Through diligent desk research, the lists can be edited to provide primary, secondary and tertiary prospects.

With such sales leads, the members of the team can plan their work effectively, giving most attention to those prospects who are most likely to buy, the primaries. This group merits a lot of attention, direct mail, telephone calls and personal visits.

The secondary prospects receive direct mail and are alerted about special features. The occasional telephone call might probe to determine any change in needs, but they are seldom called on unless the salesperson is in the district with half an hour to spare.

Tertiary prospects are included in some mailshots and may be contacted by telephone or at an exhibition. Often little effort is made to pursue them unless a salesperson has exhausted all other possibilities.

On some magazines, cold-calling on secondary and tertiary prospects to ascertain any interest may be done by a suitably trained telesales canvasser. If positive, the contact would be passed to a display salesperson to follow up personally. It's more cost effective than using a display salesperson to make the first contact.

Sales administration

However well trained and motivated the advertisement sales force, it cannot operate effectively without the support of a sound administrative system. It should be simple in concept, helping the salesperson to be more effective, rather than a burden which hampers their efforts.

It needs to have a number of elements:

- prospect/client records
- call reports
- order acknowledgement and processing
- call-back diary.

Some sales departments may generate invoices or invoicing data and most will have some system which interfaces with bad debtor lists.

The ways in which an administrative system might assist a salesperson are in providing general information about the client, data on past advertising in the magazine and its competitors (monitoring), and details of products and of the contact person. A really sophisticated system might also include information about an individual client's competitors.

Call reports, always considered a chore by salespeople, can be simplified, perhaps by means of multiple choice questions about the meeting. Automatic generation of call-back dates (the next contact with the client) can help to improve the effectiveness of a sales department.

A basic call report may look like this:

Magazine:	**Date:**	**Area:**	**Rep:**

Client:
Address:
Contact: Telephone:

Advertising agent:
Address:
Contact: Telephone:

Meeting with: client/agent

Purpose of meeting:

Outcome:

Further action:

Value of business expected: £

CALL-BACK DATE   Visit/Phone/Letter

Classified sales

Advertisements in the classified pages of magazines generally include those seeking to recruit staff, either permanent or part-time, and those from individuals or small businesses seeking to sell products or services. There may also be sections devoted to messages, births, marriages and deaths, plus a directory or buyer's guide of some kind.

There are some major differences between classified and display advertising. Those who use classified, particularly for situations vacant, messages or births, marriages and deaths, are likely to be readers of the magazine who advertise in it only occasionally. They are seldom approached by the magazine, except if they advertised first in another magazine or they are being invited to repeat an advertisement. They will have contacted the magazine themselves.

It is important for these people that details of how to contact the classified sales department are prominently displayed in the magazine, along with the costs of advertising.

Such advertisers are not generally worthwhile prospects to chase at random, for their need to advertise cannot be predicted by the magazine. There are exceptions, of course, such as companies which have a high staff turnover and which therefore advertise regularly. Telephone sales canvassers would be expected to contact these advertisers on a regular basis.

The main function of the telesales canvasser is to receive advertisements over the telephone, help the infrequent advertiser compose the advertisement and encourage the caller to take an advertisement of appropriate size and design. The latter technique is often termed 'selling up' and the purpose is to increase the revenue per advertisement.

Again, it's one of those areas which is open to abuse — an advertiser meeting an over-zealous canvasser may be sold an unnecessarily large space. Fortunately, most magazines train the canvassers well and such incidents are few.

Display advertisers will often use the directory or buyer's guide sections of the classified and some will use the situations vacant columns when seeking staff. Obviously, such usage depends very much on the nature of the readership.

The small businesses which use classified to offer goods and services may blossom and grow into display advertisers, so they are well worth watching.

Classified sales training has been highly refined and is a continuing activity in most magazines. It is very much geared around the premise of making life easy for the advertiser, making sure that the message is correct (what make of car, model, year, colour, engine size, mileage, special features or fittings, price, where it can be seen, who to contact, where and when, etc.) and, of course, obtaining the optimum revenue from each advertisement.

Canvassers usually have check-lists for each type of advertisement and product category. Those for cars, for example, would highlight among other things the alternative specifications for a given model, so that the advertiser could be reminded to include the relevant detail.

Administrative support is important, too, for the advertisement traffic can be high and many of the advertisements may be time sensitive. As copy is frequently taken over the telephone, accuracy is essential.

Classified statistics
Statistical reports will generally be similar to those for display, with the exception that the figures will be broken down to show performance by category. Classified can give short-term indicators of the state of a market. An increase or decline in the volume of situations vacant advertising gives a pretty strong message about business confidence.

Financial incentives

Although the payment of commission to salespeople is widespread, some managements doubt whether it really results in higher revenues. On the other hand, others are certain that it does.

The arguments for commission payments are:

- payments are linked directly to sales revenue
- maximum financial incentive to hard workers
- a personal and direct reward based on performance.

The arguments against are:

- unsettling effect of fluctuating earnings
- incomes may exceed those of higher grade employees
- can undermine team spirit
- difficulties in coping with booms and depressions in the market.

There are other forms of incentive which may be used and for which great success is claimed:

- a bonus paid on team results
- better company car for consistently good performers
- competitions, awards, vouchers, merchandise.

Remuneration packages

Any remuneration package must be simple to operate, clearly understood by the sales force and seen to be fair to all. It must also be flexible and offer a strong incentive for the right people to stay.

In magazine publishing, the commission structure is likely to be either:

- straight percentage of sales
- percentage over a base line, or
- straight percentage and an enhanced percentage over the base line.

It is said that, to be really effective, commission should always be significant and should provide a potential of about 20-30% of basic salary.

Sales forecasting, targets and controls

A sales forecast is an estimate of future sales based on the best information available at a given point in time. As has been said elsewhere, forecasts are necessary in any business to plan the flow of work and money and to ensure that the activity will generate a profit.

A secondary use for forecasts is to set sales targets for each person on the sales team.

Sadly, there is no known technique for predicting future sales accurately, so companies and individuals use their own pet formulae in an attempt to get it right. There are certainly two important rules:

Any forecast is only as good as the assumptions on which it is based; such assumptions must always be clearly stated.

The more information available from all sources, the better the chances of making an accurate forecast.

On the next two pages is a check-list of possible data sources and matters which should be considered when making forecasts. It is not comprehensive, but may stimulate those making forecasts to look far and wide for information.

Forecasts: data sources and considerations

1. **Forecasts of general business prospects**
   To be found in trade association reports, economic forecasts, etc. Factors affecting the economy:
   Employment trends
   Investment levels
   Wage settlements
   Domestic consumption
   Output/productivity levels.
2. **Individual industry or market sector trends**
   A similar approach to that described in 1.
3. **Detailed forecasts by salespeople**
   This is a client-by-client assessment by the salespeople concerned of the level of business expected from each client or prospect. Each estimate should be discussed with the sales manager and a forecast agreed.
   It is important to take account of the natural optimism or pessimism of individuals and to temper the forecasts accordingly.
4. **Trends and cycles**
   An assessment of the current state of the market and the market shares held by the magazine and its competitors. In particular consider:
   Previous years' activities
   Trading cycles
   Special events affecting the pattern
   Total market trend
   Strength of actual and potential competition.
5. **Forward bookings**
   A comparison of forward bookings at the same time in previous years with the final results for those years will establish any relationship between forward bookings and final published business. If there is a constant, this may be used to calculate for the period immediately ahead.
6. **Other factors which influence forecasts**
   Changes to the magazine which may influence sales, and known market or magazine events :
   Circulation changes
   Rate increases
   Research, surveys
   Staffing levels
   Supplements
   Features

Promotions.

Exhibitions

The activities of competing magazines should also be considered.

7. **The consolidated magazine forecast**

In setting the final forecast, the publisher must compare the general and specific forecasts and the various influencing factors. For example, if overall market forecasts indicate a 5% increase in business, it might be expected that the sales team forecast would reflect a similar percentage increase. If there is a difference, further research may be required, or it might be that historically one of the forecasts is more likely to be accurate. In some circumstances it might be advisable to take an average across the various forecasts. The influencing factors (Point 6) may cause the magazine or its competitors to go against the market trend.

Targets

A salesperson's prime objective is to achieve a certain level of sales. The figure is agreed with the sales manager and publisher and is described as the 'target'. Different companies and managers view the target in different ways. Most believe the target must be a challenge and, as the budget is a 'reasonable forecast', the target must be higher than the budget. A few use the same figures; some set the target below the budget figure.

The reasons for the different approaches are really to do with commission or incentive payments and management control over the amount of commission which may be earned. With the first approach, high commission earnings on sales over a target figure are unlikely. They are more likely with the second and third approaches.

A target should be achievable, but if it is to produce worthwhile additional income — the gilt on the gingerbread for both the magazine and the salesperson — it should not be too easily reached. Much depends on the individual salesperson and his or her response to targets and incentives.

It probably should be either just under or just over the achievable sales figure. Don't be over-optimistic, and don't play it too safe.

Controls

There are many areas of display and classified advertising where the sales effort can be directly measured; for example, the number of calls per day or week. But there are calls and calls. A good sales call would be one where the client contact has time to listen, is prepared to discuss the proposition and has the authority to buy. A bad sales call would be too short, wouldn't get down to the nitty gritty and would be with the wrong person anyway.

The time spent by display sales executives in face-to-face selling can be a small percentage of their working day — in some cases as low as 10%. The rest of the time is spent travelling, preparing for calls, following up and on administration. To produce good and consistent results, salespeople must maintain a high level of face-to-face contact with clients and those contacts must be fruitful.

The most elementary and vital control statistic is the number of pages sold or, for classified, the number of column centimetres sold. This figure can be converted easily to a value and allocated to the issues for which the advertising is booked. When orders are received and acknowledged, the sales manager should check to ensure the correct rate is being charged. Deviation from the rate card prices will cause page yields to drop and profitability to fall.

It's useful to measure the amount of new business compared with repeat business. Certainly, in an expanding market, the volume of new business is a key indicator of the success of the magazine and its sales-force.

Here is an 18-point sales check-list.

Advertisement sales 18-point check-list

What an advertisement salesperson needs to know or to do.

The market:
1. Industry or sector. Statistics, problems, trends, forecasts/prospects, company reports, unions, closures, start-ups, take-overs, growth points, blue chip companies, research reports, people, events, technical advances.
2. Structure. Who needs whom, buying/selling patterns, product distribution, international links, competitive tensions.
3. Prospect contact. Knowing the right person in the company, personal details.
4. Prospect company. General background, size, national reputation, take-overs/mergers, products, markets, subsidiaries, main competitors, growth success record, main thrust of sales effort, new product development,

publicity department, advertising planning schedule, advertisement spend, basis of spend (e.g. percentage of sales or turnover), media record over previous two years, chain of decision, major objective for advertising (e.g. target market, leads), style/design, slogans, special characteristics, demands (e.g. cover, bleed, facing matter, inserts, four-colour, etc.), main copy line, corporate policy, new product launches, other media used (e.g. brochures, posters, exhibitions, conferences, demos, TV, etc.).

5. Advertisement agency (if used). Planning schedule, contacts, decision-making hierarchy, relationship with client, length of service with client, client's previous agency, overall billing, relative status of client, agency strengths (e.g. marketing or creative).

6. Prospect company sales. Organization, structure, distributors, exports, turnover, product hierarchy.

The magazine:

7. History. When launched, when acquired, major updates, relaunches.

8. Editorial. Policy, relevance, authority, service to readers, comparison with competitors, position in the market, nature of content, editorial balance, style, design, editor and staff, standing and integrity. There is no substitute for reading and understanding the product. Liaison with the editorial team should be routine.

9. Circulation. Policy, sales, registrations, audit. Reader profile compared with universe, quantitative and qualitative data. Promotion: list building, response rate, renewal rate (subscriptions).

10. Research. Comparative readership, syndicated company research, industry research. Market trends.

11. Promotion. Media pack, brochures, direct mail shots and exhibitions, receptions, special events, features, supplements, awards.

12. Reader response. Enquiry services: nature, procedures and statistics.

13. Advertising. Analysis by product group, size, colour, frequency, major advertisers. Success stories, testimonials. Volume: trends. Market share. Special advertising opportunities, features, supplements, special positions.

14. Production. Origination, printing method, paper. Copy dates. Handling complaints: corrections not made, wrong

copy, wrong colour, poor registration, wrong position, poor quality; compensation.
15. Rates. Price per unit, frequency discounts, special discounts, colour, bleed, special positions, volume discounts, last price increase, next price increase. Comparisons with competitors, cost per 1000 (often written as: '000 or M).

Competitors:
16. Play down strengths, emphasize weaknesses in:
Circulation and readership: comparative profile. For controlled circulation magazines: registration level, selection criteria, reader data, reverification period. For paid circulation magazines: net sale, trade and subscription.
Editorial: policy differences, coverage, comparative balance, quality of team, design, writing.
Reader research: comparative results and explanatory critique of proprietary research, if any.
Claims: counter-claims and objections, contradictions; disparities between reader/editorial profiles.
Rates: comparative, absolute cost, cost per 1000, discounts.

Sales techniques:
17. Skills. Pre-call: journey planning, call planning, use of telephone, getting appointments, telephone investigating, desk research; handling client secretaries, receptionists; sales kit. Face-to-face: seeing the right person, call objectives, establish rapport, control meeting, asking questions, establishing needs, future plans, listening, the sales pitch, using sales aids, handling objections, reading 'signals', closing the sale. Post-call: call reports, records, action required, follow-up, correspondence.
18. Personal attributes. Appearance, speech, courtesy, consideration, punctuality, table manners, personal habits, drinking, smoking.
Organization: use of diary, time management, record-keeping, procrastination, preparation, planning, coverage of territory, expenses.

Chapter 6

Circulation

The circulation policy, defined as part of the overall publication plan, is implemented by the circulation manager or circulation executive (depending on the company structure) or may be subcontracted to an external specialist. The responsible person reports to the publisher of the magazine on all matters to do with the magazine's circulation and allied matters, but in other respects may report to a circulation department line manager.

Falling within the ambit of circulation are:

- trade sales
- subscription sales
- controlled circulation reader registrations
- circulation profile maintenance
- distribution of copies
- circulation prospect list building
- promotional campaigns
- participation in exhibitions
- reader service card processing
- direct mail services (based on circulation lists)
- reader research
- production of circulation statistics.

The circulation policy specifies:

- the target reader profile(s)
- how many there are
- where they are
- target circulation figures by reader type
- whether the magazine is to be sold
  - newstrade or subscription
- or distributed free
  - controlled circulation, directed, doorstep delivery, handed out at railway stations

- cover price, subscription rate
- distribution arrangements
- returns policy
- registration policy (controlled)

and so on.

In essence, the circulation manager's job is to get copies in front of a sufficient number of the right people. Whereas there are similarities in the way advertising is sold and editorial is produced for the different magazine types, free and paid circulation methods involve distinctly different approaches.

Types of circulation

The descriptions applied to the various types of circulation emanate from rules established by The Audit Bureau of Circulations Ltd (ABC), the body which provides standards for the measurement of circulations, oversees the auditing involved and gives independent certification of a magazine's past circulation.

> **Consumer magazine distribution**
> *The PPA's Magazine Handbook, quoting Harvest '87, gives the distribution of UK consumer magazines as:*
> *Confectioners, tobacconists, newsagents (CTN) — 60%*
> *Subscriptions — 3%*
> *Supermarkets — 4%*
> *Others (booksellers, street vendors) - 33%.*
> *This compares with the United States breakdown for the same year (Veronis, Suhler and Associates) of:*
> *Subscriptions — 76%*
> *CTN/other — 24%.*
> *Just think of all that subscription money up front!*

The audit for a magazine is conducted by an auditor appointed by the ABC and it covers a period of either six or 12 months. For new magazines, the first two audit periods may be for three months. The prime purpose of an ABC certificate is to prove to advertisers that the circulation claimed is genuine. When certificates are issued, the details are also sent to *British Rate and Data (BRAD)* for publication.

Most consumer magazines copies are either sold direct (subscriptions), through the newstrade (newsagents and bookstalls) or through other outlets (supermarkets, corner shops, etc.). Audited paid sale figures are based on returns and receipts from distributors and wholesalers and, for subscriptions, on cheques and other monies received direct from readers or subscription agents. Copies of consumer magazines that are free will either be sent to members of a club or organization, distributed to addresses in a specified area and conforming to certain criteria, or handed to potential readers at railway stations or in the street. The distributors concerned must provide evidence that copies have actually been delivered and it is from such information that audits are completed.

Supermarket sales
In the past few years supermarkets, along with the retail newstrade, have woken up to the fact that a supermarket is a sensible place to sell newspapers and magazines. For years there was argument and refusal to compromise. Two magazines, *Family Circle* and *Living*, developed specially for the check-out, were sold by supermarkets and only after many years were they sold by the newstrade.

Now, after looking at what happens elsewhere in the world, and following a few trials, the larger supermarkets stock appropriate magazines and the newstrade has realized that increased opportunities for the public to buy magazines are good for all. It should be stressed that while supermarkets are important outlets for mass-circulation women's magazines, they are not really suitable for specialist titles.

Business magazines
Business and STM magazine circulations are far more complex. There are many classifications and some magazines might fall into more than one. The principal descriptions are:

Paid circulation
> Newstrade and single copy sales — copies supplied normally through the wholesale newstrade.
> Single paid subscriptions — individual subscriptions to either a private or company address.
> Multiple sales other than newstrade through accepted outlets — airlines, hotels, clubs, dealers (e.g. model shops), etc.

Society/association circulation
> Paid optional — where members pay a sum in addition to the membership fee to receive the magazine.
> Unpaid requested — there is no charge for copies but they must have been requested by individual recipients.

Non-requested — copies are sent to members without the individuals making any special payment or requesting copies.

Controlled circulation

Individually requested — copies requested by individuals by completed request card, other written document or tele-communication.

Company requested — copies requested by companies by completed request card, other written document or tele-communication.

Note: to be valid a request must be no more than three years old, but many publishers are asking readers to register every two years to keep demographics up to date.

Non-requested by name — personally addressed copies to individuals falling within the terms of control.

Non-requested by job title/function — copies addressed to job titles/functions within companies or organizations fall-ing within the terms of control.

Non-controlled free circulation — this must be to an indi-vidual or company interested in the field covered by the magazine.

Terms used to describe readers of controlled circulation magazines
Registered reader — the reader of a controlled circulation magazine who has completed, signed and returned a regis-tration card and where the reader's details meet the terms of control.

Non-registered reader — individuals who are being encour-aged to register, or people who appear to conform to the readership criteria and are being circulated to make up the numbers.

Subscribers — people who wish to receive such a publica-tion and who do not fall within the terms of control, but who are prepared to buy it.

Directed circulation

To people identified by job title or buying power (business), or by address, socio-economic category, etc., and usually addressed personally;

The 'terms of control' for a free magazine are set by the publisher but must be registered with the ABC.

They define the criteria used to decide whether a potential reader is eligible to receive the magazine.

For example:
'This magazine is distributed to executives interested in personal computers.'
Job titles or functions may be included in the terms. Not all recipients of a controlled circulation magazine will necessarily be registered, any more than all free magazines have a controlled circulation. It should be noted that the word 'reader' is used in this context to denote the recipient of a magazine or one who has asked to receive it.

Readership v. circulation

Not all copies of magazines will be read by all those who receive them. And all magazines, whether consumer or business, paid or free, will have an element of pass-on readership. Thus, the circulation of a magazine and its actual readership will not be the same.

The number of recipients not reading a magazine is likely to be higher among those magazines issued free without any form of registration. Understandably, the figures, even if known to the publishers concerned, are not made available.

The average number of pass-on readers per copy is published if known. The figure varies with the type of magazine and its content, but is generally between two and ten readers per copy, with some magazines having over 20 readers per copy.

In assessing a magazine, therefore, advertisers are considering not just the number of copies sold or distributed but also the number of readers per copy. For magazine 'A' which sells 1 000 000 copies with four readers per copy, the readership is 4 000 000 people; for magazine 'B' which sells 500 000 copies with eight readers per copy, the readership is also 4 000 000 people.

Cost per thousand
In the consumer markets and in some business markets, the readership figure is crucial in deciding where to place advertising. The measure used is the cost of reaching one thousand readers, or cost per thousand. That is the cost of one standard page divided by the number of readers in thousands.

Take the two examples above. A page in magazine 'A' costs £5000 because of high production and distribution costs (more copies are printed and circulated) and perhaps also because of better editorial coverage. The cost per thousand is £1.25. Magazine 'B', with the lower circulation, has lower costs and charges £4000 for a similar page. The cost per thousand is £1.00. Thus it appears to be cheaper in cost per thousand terms to take advertising space in magazine 'B'.

However, it might be that a proportion of readers retain magazine 'A' as a source of reference and will therefore be exposed to an advertisement several times, whereas magazine 'B' is passed on quickly. Such a fact, if established, might influence an advertiser. The process is further complicated when sex, age, social grade, geographical region and TV viewing habits are taken into account.

Magazine 'A' might offer many more readers in a particular sector than magazine 'B' and be the 'best buy' in cost per thousand terms for advertisers wishing to reach that sector. Say, for example that magazine 'A' has 850 000 readers in the sector concerned. If an advertiser were solely interested in those people, the cost per thousand would be £5000/850, or £5.88. Magazine 'B' might have 600 000 such readers at a comparable cost of £4000/600, or £6.67.

So, in highly competitive markets it is essential to know the number and type of readers per copy and how they use the magazine to assess the true cost of advertising.

Market surveys
The only way to obtain the readership figures is by market research. Fortunately, in those markets where the figures matter most, there are joint on-going surveys which provide the information. For consumer magazines it is the National Readership Survey and for business magazines there are a number of separate surveys (of which the PPA can provide details).

Magazines not party to any of the surveys often include pass-on readership questions in other market research investigations.

For some magazines, pass-on readership is of little value and it doesn't help the case with advertisers to say there are so many readers per copy. The publisher, and the advertiser in some instances, would prefer that each eligible person had their own copy of the magazine and kept it for future reference. This is particularly so in magazines where there is a high level of advertising attached to features which can be used for reference. It is often better for a magazine to sell additional copies (provided the revenue per copy is greater than the cost of printing and distribution) and reduce the pass-on readership, or, of course, increase the number of copies available for passing-on. This is sometimes achieved by promotion drives that suggest being a pass-on reader is only second best.

Targeting the reader

Whatever the magazine, getting it to the reader is the prime task. Without them no one goes any further. The target reader is described in the publication plan. People matching the description have to be identified, addressed and persuaded.

When a new TV listings magazine is being launched, it is easy to identify potential readers — it's anyone who watches TV. Most people watch TV at some point, and therefore any promotion in any medium (newspapers, magazines, TV, cinemas, posters) is going to reach a percentage of the desired audience. The objective is to reach the largest possible number of potential readers of the new magazine at the lowest cost. Trailing through *BRAD* and the equivalent listings for TV, cinemas and posters, it would be possible to come up with a relatively low-cost schedule. This would then be modified to suit the amount of money available and the circulation criteria in broader terms, i.e. social group, region, age, sex, etc.

A magazine on a more esoteric topic presents the more difficult problem of finding a few thousand potential readers scattered at random through a population of many millions. Some groups are well documented and easy to find (e.g. members of organizations or professions) but many are not — such as those who like chocolate enough to buy a specialist magazine about it.

In the business magazines field, the problems are no different. All managing directors of all companies are easy to identify, as are companies buying office furniture (every company at some point), but not so individuals in industry buying enough office furniture to merit their receiving a specialist magazine on the subject each month. Maybe the companies can be identified, but who in those companies makes the decision? Is it the managing director, the personnel director, the accountant, the data processing manager, the office manager, the buyer, or is it all of them?

To put this issue in some kind of perspective, it might be worth considering how purchasing decisions are made in the companies which you know well, especially the one by which you are employed. On anything major it is rare that one person makes the decision. Usually a number of people contribute to the decision, whoever signs the purchase order or negotiates the deal.

Each of them, of course, is looking at the transaction from a different perspective. One might consider cost only, another the working environment and the decor, another only ergonomic factors and productivity, another the effects on the morale of the work-force, and so on. Such issues should be considered when the target reader is defined, but they serve to illustrate the complexities of identifying the reader, whatever the market.

The next stage involves persuading the reader to buy or willingly receive the magazine. For clarity, it is best to consider that there are three circulation options, whether the magazine is consumer, consumer specialist, business or STM. These are: newstrade sales, subscriptions and free.

Depending on the company and its magazines, a circulation department may be operating all three types of circulation, or only one or two. There may also be one or both of two secondary services: reader enquiry processing and direct mail services. In some companies the circulation department may also handle book distribution, special offers, or some other service.

Newstrade sales

The UK newstrade operates through about 200 wholesale depots supplying around 40 000 newsagents and other sales points throughout the country. The largest wholesaler is W.H. Smith, which handles about 45% of sales by volume, through 69 depots. The next largest group, John Menzies, handles 25% of sales.

Only about 35 000 newsagents are significant in the sale of magazines. Sixty per cent are independently owned, but retail multiples control most of the prime sites and account for about 35% of magazine sales.

Clearly, it is important that the two major wholesalers do handle a magazine, or otherwise its prospects for success are limited. Of course, none of the wholesalers or retailers is obliged to handle all magazines on offer. There is no legislation in the UK compelling wholesalers to stock a magazine, as there is in some other countries.

Some large magazine publishers negotiate with and distribute directly to wholesalers, but the majority work through a distributor. Working for a number of magazines and publishers, a distributor can usually offer the benefits of scale and well-established links with the wholesalers and newsagents, and can relieve the publisher of the more tedious aspects of distribution, such as negotiating terms, invoicing and crediting.

Whether the publisher subcontracts or not, the steps involved in distribution are:

1. **Sell to the wholesaler**. Persuade the wholesaler that the magazine has an audience and that it will sell a certain number, that the cover price is right and that the magazine will be backed by promotion to potential readers. Negotiate terms, e.g. discount.
2. **Sell to the newsagent**. This can be done through a field sales-force, direct mail, or advertising in the newstrade press. Persuade the newsagent that the magazine is going to sell to the public and that it will be well supported by promotion. The retailer will order through the wholesaler, although the distributors' representatives may take and pass on such orders.
3. **Receive and collate orders**. Orders must be obtained from wholesalers, totalled and passed to the publisher as the quantity required for distribution.
4. **Distribute copies**. Copies, received direct from the printers, are parcelled for individual wholesale depots and delivered in good time for the on-sale date. Copies are usually required by the carrier one week before the on-sale date, but for topical magazines a shorter lead time is possible.
5. **Ensure wholesale distribution**. Monitor wholesale depots to ensure copies are distributed to retailers as ordered.
6. **Ensure retail sale**. Make sure that retailers display copies prominently, that shelves are re-stocked, and that top-up copies are ordered if sales go well. Monitor sales.
7. **Receive returns**. Unsold copies (or evidence of unsolds) must be returned to the distributor via the wholesaler within a specified period.
8. **Invoice for copies sold**. The distributor invoices the wholesaler for all copies as soon as distribution is complete and credits the returns at the end of the on-sale period. (Payment is usually staged, allowing for an agreed percentage of returns which is adjusted at the end of the on-sale period.)
9. **Report to publisher**. Periodic reports are given to the publisher based on the sales monitoring (see point 6). Full sales statistics are given for each issue, down to type of outlet and type of area, including the number of copies ordered and returned.
10. **Payment to publisher**. The distributor makes staged payments on an anticipated level of sale, adjusting for returns at the end of the on-sale period.

It is usual for the distributor to agree terms based on a percentage of the cover price. The actual figure will vary according to frequency and sales levels, but includes the distributor's costs, plus the discount for the wholesaler and the newsagent. Some costs will be in addition and will be charged to the publisher separately, such as advertising in the trade press and in-store promotions or displays.

Not all distributors work in exactly the same way, and not all distributors handle the entire circulation of a magazine. It may be that there are specialist outlets required which will be handled by a specialist distributor — theatre bookstalls, for example. Overseas trade circulation is likely to be handled by the main distributor — most have special departments for the purpose — but may be placed separately.

In day-to-day operation, it is vital to work closely with the distributor to achieve additional sales. These may be as the result of promotions, special issues or special events. It may be that the magazine is growing in stature and more people are wanting to buy it — information that should be coming through in the field reports and statistical analyses.

A sale can happen only if the magazine is available. The magazine will be available only if the retailer knows about it and believes it will sell. With the exception of the multiples (which thankfully have the best sites), retail newsagents are notoriously poor at marketing and in the main are merely stockists, not sellers, of magazines.

It is a sobering thought that there are something like 4000 magazines (consumer and business) competing for space on the retailers' shelves. Keep your distributors on their toes.

Sale or return
Mention has been made of returns. These are copies not sold by the retailer and which are returned via the wholesaler and distributor to the publisher. They are called SOR (sale or return) copies and are necessary if a magazine is to maximize every sales opportunity — be on the shelf and available to a casual purchaser. The alternative — a rare practice nowadays and certainly not for launches — is to supply to the trade on firm order only. It reduces the number of copies ordered and eliminates returns, but means that newsagents take copies to fulfil firm orders only. A casual purchaser is most unlikely to find a copy on display, although newsagents will usually obtain a copy if pressed to do so.

Where copies are supplied sale or return, the level of returns should be monitored closely. A profitable relationship between the cost of producing additional copies and the revenue from increased sales must be maintained. For example, consider a situation where the additional production cost (the run-on cost — the cost of printing and paper after all set-up costs have been met) is 17p per copy and the cover price is £1.60 which, after a discount of 50% to the distributor, makes the revenue per copy sold 80p. An additional 1000 copies will cost £170. To break even, 213 copies must be sold (213 x 80p = £170.40), or the returns must not exceed 787 out of every 1000 (78.7%). Of course, any promotion cost of getting extra sales must also be considered.

The benefits of increased sales and readership are great indeed. The magazine's revenue and standing are improved and, most important, increased circulation gives the advertisement sales staff a much stronger story.

Subscription sales

There are many advantages to be obtained from having a subscription circulation:
- very significantly, subscriptions are paid in advance
- readers are identifiable and the demographic data which can be provided are more accurate and more detailed
- advertisers and potential advertisers can be given 'proof positive' of the reader profile, and buying and influencing power
- the subscribers form a viable database which may be offered for direct mail purposes
- the print order need include no wasted copies.

Consumer magazines
Subscriptions are actively encouraged by consumer magazines. And this is despite the long-standing and satisfactory method of distribution via the newstrade, where readers pay on or after delivery, at the cover price. It was felt by many readers that to pay for a year's copies, in advance, was just not as attractive.

Indeed, at one time, publishers encouraged this situation by charging subscriptions at a higher rate per copy to cover wrapping and postage costs and to keep retailers sweet. If the newsagent objected to subscriptions, then the publisher could say that they were discouraged through this higher pricing.

The publishers' change of attitude has been influenced by the US experience (most magazines there are sold on subscription) and by the success of *The Reader's Digest* and other publications in obtaining subscriptions in the UK.

Where consumer magazines are offering subscriptions, targeting the audience is relatively straightforward, the first place to advertise being the magazine itself. Sometimes this is the only place where subscriptions are promoted but, increasingly, clean, up-to-date lists of prospective subscribers are being mailed or contacted by telephone. Sources are those attending exhibitions, ACORN listings, magazines' own lists of lapsed subscribers and the many list brokers who now operate.

Business and STM magazines
Many paid-for business and STM magazines are available through the newstrade, but for these there is a greater dependence on the subscriber. Some magazines rely totally on subscription sales.

While businesses and businesspeople are more attuned to paying in advance, there are still some problems, but none is insurmountable. First and foremost is the fact that people are reluctant to pay for information, although this resistance diminishes when the potential reader can see a measurable benefit in subscribing (e.g. where there is fast-moving price information). It's up to the magazine to prove that the content is of value. Secondly, while £1.75 a week for a magazine may be acceptable, to pay £89.25 for 51 issues seems expensive.

This latter problem is compounded where more than one copy is going into a company and the central purchasing office identifies that ten people are getting the same magazine, at a total cost of nearly £900. One of the cost-cutting blitzes that is undertaken all too frequently by most companies (even magazine publishers!) is to reduce the money spent on subscriptions. If one copy is taken and circulated to the ten, £800 could be saved, runs the argument.

These facts point up the need for publishers to prove that their magazines do give measurable value for money, that the price is right, and that individual executives need a personal copy. If all else fails, special discounts can be introduced for bulk supplies. (ABC rules allow for this.)

It is a question of identifying the issues and prioritizing them correctly. Take, for example, the company which cuts the number of copies purchased from ten to one. The more important issue may be that because the number of copies sold is reduced by nine, the magazine becomes less attractive to advertisers. Proving that those nine people still see and read the magazine is difficult, and perhaps they don't, for the magazine itself may be pretty tattered by the time it gets even half-way round, always provided it isn't mislaid.

It's probably better to keep up the level of copies to bolster the case to advertisers and lose most of the subscription revenue. A deal where a company pays for one full subscription and the others are heavily discounted might be sensible.

As already implied, this is a compromise, for it would be much better for the publisher if every subscriber paid the full rate.

Free circulation

Readers are not charged to receive copies of free publications, although a payment in kind is often demanded. All the revenue comes from advertisers, but, in theory at least, they know exactly to whom copies of the magazine are being despatched.

There are several types of free circulation, as described earlier in this chapter. However, this section will centre on controlled circulation, as it is the most complex and probably the most desirable.

A fully controlled circulation exists when each recipient of a magazine conforms to the terms of control and has registered to receive the magazine within the past three years. It is an idyllic state and is not easy to achieve, although many publishers do.

With any free publication it is up to the publisher to fix the number of copies to be circulated. Setting this figure depends on:

- competitive circulations
- size of the market and level of coverage required
- costs of production and distribution
- what the advertiser expects
- advertising cost per thousand 'readers'
- quality of readership.

Occasionally, and particularly for fields where no norms have been established, a figure is virtually plucked out of the air. There is no formula and no 'right' figure. What the advertiser is prepared to pay for advertising ultimately imposes a ceiling and this will more than likely be quite arbitrary. Remember, market penetration is what most advertisers seek and they will usually favour the magazine which gives the optimum mix of market coverage and cost.

Ultimately, there are upper and lower limits, and it may be a question of 'putting a toe in the water to test the temperature'. Research can help by establishing market sizes and numbers.

The payment in kind comes at the time of registration, when the reader is asked to provide information about his or her job, its responsibilities and authority, and the employing company. It takes only a few minutes to give, but its value to the magazine is considerable for it strengthens the case which can be presented to advertisers.

Apart from name, company, address and job title, the kind of multiple-choice questions asked by a computer magazine include (the number of choices is shown in brackets):

What is your job function? (20)
What is the company's main business activity? (14)
How many people are employed full time? (7)
What is the turnover? (9)
What is the computer equipment budget for the year? (7)
Which computer systems are used? (4)
Which equipment is used? (15)
Which software is used? (11)
Which equipment does the company intend purchasing? (18)
Which services does the company provide? (12)
Which services does the company intend providing? (12)
Which external services does the company use? (12)
Which financial services would you consider using? (4)
What is your role in purchasing decisions? (5)
Which items do you have the personal authority to purchase? (8)
Will your budget increase, decrease or stay the same in the next two years? (3)
Which system do you use personally? (4)
Which magazines do you read? (6)
How many other people in your company do you expect to read your copy of this magazine? (6)

Each answer is coded. When entered on a database, the circulation can be analysed in detail to provide information of value to the editor in preparing editorial content and a wealth of information for advertisers about interests and intentions.

A secondary use is to identify readers for special mailings. All of those people with a specific buying intention for, say, imagesetters, can be offered to imagesetter producers for special attention and at a special price.

Similarly, if the magazine markets books it is possible to target them exactly to those people most likely to be interested.

It should be noted, of course, that any information held on a computer is subject to the provisions of the Data Protection Act and it is essential that they be observed.

Promoting to the potential reader

Whichever method of circulation is used, the magazine has to be brought to the attention of the reader, so that he or she can either order from a newsagent, place a subscription, or register.

Identifying the potential reader and putting the message across is the key. The ways in which magazines become known are:

- advertising
  newspapers
  other magazines
  radio
  television
  posters
- direct mail
- telephone sales
- exhibition promotions
- pass-on readers
  in the home
  in the office
  in waiting-rooms
  found on a train, etc.
- word-of-mouth recommendation.

Decisions about promotion come back to an assessment of the likely return. For high circulations and high advertising stakes, it is undoubtedly worth heavyweight promotion involving advertising in one or several of the media listed. Direct mail would be an unlikely choice for a mass market product, although exhibitions might be used.

Coming down the scale in market size, the more expensive advertising media would be rejected and direct mail used. This would be strongly supported by attendance at specialist exhibitions.

Telephone sales is an option that more magazines are using. It works well for selling subscriptions and encouraging lapsed subscribers to renew, and for obtaining controlled circulation registrations.

Whichever method of promotion is used, it must be carefully targeted at the potential reader. It would be usual to involve advertising agents for their specialist skills and, similarly, specialists should be used for direct mail campaigns. Writing a good sales letter is not as easy as it might look and the packaging is very important.

Alongside the message to buy or register, an incentive can work well — anything from free pens to free entry in prize draws and reduced rates ('£10 off for new subscribers — the normal rate is £60 but you pay only £50!').

Promotion is expensive and must be most carefully evaluated. A balance must be maintained between the investment and the potential return and a publisher must be very sure, therefore, of the reasons for seeking extra readers. Is it to get more revenue from circulation? Is it to present a better story to advertisers? Is it a combination of the two?

Where new launches are concerned, subscribers can be offered 'founder' or 'charter' subscriptions. It is as if they have been invited to join a club and and they will be given special treatment and concessions as long as they remain subscribers.

To summarize, successful direct promotion demands that these criteria are met.

The criteria for successful direct promotion

A magazine with a clear, succinct policy; it must be well written, well designed, well produced and meet the needs and wants of the desired readership.

The right subscription rate (if a paid-for magazine).

A clean, up-to-date list of prospective, accurately-targeted readers.

Promotional material that is bright, well written, well designed and targeted, or expertly trained telesales canvassers, or both.

Testing.

Accurate costings.

Close monitoring of results.

It cannot be overstressed that costings and likely response must be accurately assessed. Before embarking on major expenditure, it is wise to carry out some small-scale test promotions to determine the best package to achieve the best response. In some cases, depending on the package cost and the subscription rate, a response of 2-3% will be worth while. Some add into the calculation the subscription income from years two, three and beyond.

For example, if the mailing package costs £1, the subscription rate is £75, some 5000 are mailed and the response is 2%, the result will be:

Subscribers 5000 x 2% = 100	
Subscription income 100 x £75	£7500
Mailing cost 5000 x £1p	£5000
Net revenue	£2500

Assuming 70% of these readers renew their subscriptions each year, over the next two years (at constant prices) there is a further revenue of £8925 (£7500 x 70% = £5250 in year 1, plus £5250 x 70% = £3675 in year 2) to be obtained.

Obviously, controlled circulation magazine publishers cannot take subscription revenue into account, but in other respects the criteria must be the same.

Renewals

Most subscriptions are of a year's duration and must be renewed annually. With a good product and a loyal readership, it might be expected that readers will respond with a cheque as soon as they are asked. Unfortunately, this is not so. Too many people are forgetful or resist paying until the last possible moment, or matters get delayed in company accounts departments.

It may take many reminders over a period of several months to secure a renewal. There may be a pattern for a given magazine, in which case a renewal routine can be designed to suit. If there is no pattern, the publisher will have to institute arbitrary rules.

For example, a monthly magazine might send out the following packages according to this timetable:

Two months before expiry: letter explaining some of the benefits of the magazine and of the subscription, renewal notice and invoice.

One month before expiry: reminder reiterating and expanding on the benefits of the magazine and of the subscription, and copy invoice.

Month of expiry: reminder reiterating the benefits and discussing the forthcoming editorial programme, and copy invoice.

Month after expiry: letter again discussing the benefits of the magazine and its forthcoming editorial programme, regretting that further copies will not be sent if renewal is not received, and copy invoice.

Two months after expiry: letter from editor expressing regret that no renewal has been received and reiterating benefits. Asks readers determined not to renew to complete a questionnaire establishing reasons.

Such a routine can be stretched or reduced in time and other factors introduced.

If there is a record of enquiries from the reader or if the reader has participated in offers or activities, such facts might be used to illustrate the benefits of subscribing. Membership of a reader club or special concessions available only to those who renew might be offered.

The renewal rate for a magazine is a good indicator of reader satisfaction, and if it falls below the norm (for the particular magazine) the reasons should be quickly determined so that remedial action may be taken. There will always be some fall-off — people die, move away, retire, lose interest in a subject, change jobs, or whatever — but it should be a relatively small percentage.

Subscription agents
Subscription agents operate throughout the world, selling mainly to libraries, universities and other institutions. Generally, they do not deal with consumer magazines, although there are exceptions, but with academic and learned journals. Orders received are processed by the agent, who charges publishers a commission.

Prospect lists
Some categories of individual or company are well documented and lists are easy to find in directories or to buy from list broking companies. These will be the same lists that everyone else uses and that is inevitable, but over time a magazine can build its own lists.

These may be culled from various sources:

- advertisers' lists of customers
- editorial mentions in magazines
- people attending events such as
  exhibitions
  conferences
  trade dinners
- directories.

From whatever source obtained, the lists must be de-duplicated and checked to ensure relevance. In most markets, in order to achieve a quality readership only some individuals or establishments will be wanted — those who have the real spending power. Those companies and people must be identified by appropriate criteria. For companies, this might be:

- SIC (standard industrial classification)
- turnover
- number of employees
- sales figures
- product range
- advertising spend
- number of locations
- equipment and materials purchased
- buying intentions.

For individual people, it's likely to be:

- job title
- job function
- buying responsibility
- influencing responsibility
- buying intentions
- equipment/materials used/controlled.

Various sources of reference will include some or all of such information. Those companies that do slip through can be eliminated at a later stage when registrations are received.

Prospect lists should be prioritized to match the profile requirement of the magazine, with perhaps several categories:

'A' — those who **must** read the magazine to give it the 'quality' demanded by advertisers

'B' — those who would benefit from the magazine and would put cream on the cake for advertisers

'C' — those who would benefit from the magazine but don't buy enough to interest the advertisers

'D' — fringe interests.

It makes deciding where and how to spend promotion money a little easier.

Any magazine which sells direct depends on good list building for its future, and the time and effort put into the activity should not be minimized.

Distribution

For trade sales, the distribution of copies is generally handled by the distributor — indeed, it's one of the reasons for employing such a company. Copies are delivered by the printer to a carrier or directly to the distributor to meet a predetermined schedule. The distributor will pack and label the copies according to wholesalers' requirements and will monitor the rest of the operation to ensure copies arrive in the newsagents in good time and are actually placed on sale. Monitoring a high sale magazine may mean having a number of staff people on the road as well; for smaller circulations the job may be left to the distributor, the publisher being involved only when readers complain.

Personal advertisements
An extension of the inkjetting facility to print the address details on the cover of the magazine is to use the same process to personalize advertisements or other messages. It's a facility that has been available in the USA for some years.
Fancy opening your favourite magazine and reading an advertisement aimed personally at you — just like a high-cost direct mail letter!

For copies distributed by post (Royal Mail or other carriers), there is the additional operation of wrapping, usually in film, and labelling. The film may carry a paid advertisement or promotion for the magazine. The address label can be on a carrier sheet inserted under the film, can be stuck on the film or can be inkjetted on to the film or the carrier sheet. The latter system can also inkjet directly on to the magazine cover if required.

No monopoly
Magazines are not part of the Royal Mail monopoly and an increasing number of alternative methods of postal distribution are becoming available. The PPA publishes a list of approved couriers.

Whichever system is used, the label or inkjet output is pre-sorted to comply with Royal Mail or other carrier requirements to achieve the lowest postal cost for the desired level of service.

Postage costs are high, and the publisher, working with the circulation manager, must ensure that the magazine makes the best possible use of special rates and services. The company's circulation department will have information about the various options available for UK and overseas postings, and up-to-date details of special schemes are available from the PPA and The Royal Mail.

Nowadays, circulation fulfilment, and all the other activities of list building, mailing and so on, demand the services of first-class computer systems and software.

Reader enquiry service

A feature of many magazines, whether paid or free, is the reader service card. The reader is invited to indicate on the card, usually by circling a reference number, the products or services featured in editorial or advertising about which more information is required. The card is completed with the reader's name and address and posted to the magazine.

A section of the circulation department is often responsible for processing the enquiries or a specialist subcontractor is used. The enquirer's details are recorded and are passed to the advertiser to follow up.

The service is of benefit to the reader — it's an easy way to get more information; to the advertiser — it's a genuine sales lead; to the magazine — it gives another indication of the value and relevance of the content, and provides ammunition to persuade advertisers and prospects to use the magazine.

A secondary virtue is that it provides a means of getting re-registrations and new registrations. A condition of providing the details requested by the reader is that the card, which contains questions similar to those on a reader registration form, is completed fully. It then becomes the most recent request from that reader to receive copies. Much simpler and certainly cheaper than mounting a separate operation to register readers.

Of course, if a magazine designed to generate enquiries doesn't do so, the fact will be evident within days of publication.

Chapter 7

Finance and accounts

To magazine executives not trained as an accountant, the word 'budget' invariably starts a little tremor of apprehension — even fear — in their hearts and minds. Possibly this is because it is an exercise which some people mistakenly consider detracts from the main point of a line executive's life, although just possibly it's a genuine fear of accounts and accountants.

True meaning?

Any budgetary exercise depends very much on assumptions being made about all of those matters which influence revenues and costs, everything from basic assumptions about the market to printing costs. I remember learning at Henley Management College a different way to write that important word: *ASS-U-ME.*

Yet, without the yardstick of a budget, how can managers measure the performance of their departments? Sales might be higher or lower than last month or last year, but performance should be related to potential not just to history, and a company **needs to know what is likely to happen**.

That foreknowledge is vitally necessary to plan the use of resources — money, people, equipment — for investment in the future.

With plans and budgets, a company can allocate resources to achieve the best return or take action to avoid or alleviate shortfalls in profits or to reduce losses.

It should be a required part of any manager's role to participate fully in the planning and budgeting exercise. After all, the plan sets the parameters against which the manager is to be judged or measured in the future.

Most companies have taken some of the fear out of the subject, by asking line executives to do only the planning part of the exercise, not the 'number crunching'. Of course, there is still apprehension about committing a forecast to paper, but with experience that becomes less worrying.

The budget itself is the financial interpretation of the publication plan. As discussed in Chapter 3, the plan sets out the magazine's policy and the various parameters which must be considered in the budget — magazine frequency, number of staff, quality of production, and so on. It also includes the reasoned estimates produced by the sales and circulation managers of revenues and costs of sales, and the editor's estimates of costs.

The point at which these inputs are pulled together will vary according to custom and practice, but it will be up to the executives concerned to set the figures or the basis for the figures. For example, the editorial plan may well include a series of specially commissioned features; the editor will know the costs for writing and photography. Similarly, staffing levels in the various departments, as dictated by the requirements of the plan, will attract a calculable cost.

Budgeting

Once the plan for a magazine has been established, the budget, falls into place quite easily.

When the calculations are complete, there will be a profit or loss figure which will be acceptable to senior management, or not. If not, it is a question of modifying the plan to suit the required financial objectives. This is where the 'what if' facilities of a good spreadsheet come into play and where the abilities of a publisher to 'cut the cloth' are tested.

Of course, there is sometimes a limit to how far a publisher can accede to a request to generate more profit (or less loss). If the company demands a level of profit which cannot be achieved, it would be quite wrong for the publisher to agree to an unattainable budget. A difficult position to defend, but better to do so at budget time than when the 'promised' figures do not materialize.

Paramount considerations
In planning and budgeting, the paramount considerations are the overall company objectives, as perceived by the board of directors, and a magazine's objectives, as perceived by its publisher. Sadly, the two don't always fit neatly together. For example, investment money wanted by one publisher might yield a better return for the company if used elsewhere for a new project or to bolster a loss-making magazine.

The publisher faced with such a dilemma must go back to the plan and re-draft it to give the company what is required. It should never be just a question of slashing expenditure plans or of increasing revenue forecasts unrealistically to present the figures which are wanted. It must be a thorough re-evaluation of the plan. Sometimes a publisher may have to fight his or her corner on the grounds that irreparable harm will be caused to the magazine if planned investment is not made or if, in an attempt to get more revenue, rates are pushed too high. But that is what the publisher is expected to do. A publisher must fight to secure the future for the magazine under his or her control.

If there is no alternative and cuts must be made, then the publisher must strive to ensure that those cuts do not harm the magazine. It may appear to be an impossible task, but sometimes that's the job.

The accountant's role
Somewhere in the accounts department is an executive — often called a management accountant — who spends a good deal of time looking after the affairs of individual magazines. This may be a newly qualified accountant, a trainee accountant or a senior clerk. Whichever, the role is to bring together the income and expenditure transactions which relate to a magazine and to present them in a form which line and senior management can understand.

In well-ordered companies, the publisher and the management accountant are encouraged to work closely together at all times. Thus, the management accountant is involved early in the planning stage and is able to contribute a finance department view, to calculate revenues and costs (the 'number crunching') based on projections, generally to participate in the management of the magazine, and to produce the monthly management accounts which are compared with the budget.

The management accountant does not take decisions, but is able to advise the publisher on all matters to do with budgets and cost allocation. If equipped with a computer then so much the better, for it's possible to calculate quickly the 'what if' questions. For example: 'What if advertisement rates are increased by 10%?'
'What if editorial paging is increased or reduced?'

A budget document

There are no hard and fast rules about the physical appearance of a budget document or about the headings and descriptions used. Not surprisingly, there are differences of opinion about whether particular costs fall under one heading or another, and about the use of terms such as variable, fixed, direct and indirect to describe them. However, there is sufficient similarity between the various formats used for a particular layout to be described here. If your company's format is different and you require some clarification, ask your management accountant.

Usually, there is a top sheet which summarizes all activities for a given period, generally a year, followed by a page or two for each department or activity. A top sheet might include:

Budget top sheet headings

Revenue
  — advertisement
  — circulation
  — other trading (or ancillary activities)

Variable costs
  — production
  — distribution
  — editorial
  — sales
  — other trading

Gross margin (sometimes called gross profit)
  GM %

Fixed costs
  — sales
  — editorial
  — administration
  — promotion
  — circulation
  — other trading

Gross publication profit (sometimes called net publication profit or contribution)
  GPP %

The top sheet will probably include total figures from previous years, together with the year-on-year percentage change.

Each revenue or cost line on the top sheet has a corresponding section on the backing sheets which shows how the totals are calculated.

Activities are phased through the year into convenient measurement periods, usually a calendar month. One month's figures would therefore include one issue for a monthly, but four or five for a weekly (most people work on a constant of two months at four issues and one at five and so on to give 52 issues in a year, i.e. 4, 4, 5, 4, 4, 5, 4, 4, 5, 4, 4, 5).

Revenue

Advertisement revenue
It is usual to start with revenue figures and the first part of the advertising information, which sets out the expected volumes, might have the following headings:

Volume headings

Display
 — Inserts
 — Mono
 — 2 colour
 — 4 colour
 Other display
 Total display
Classified
 — Recruitment
 — Non-recruitment
 — Buyer's guide
 Total classified
Total advertising pages
Ad/ed ratio
No. of issues

Advertisement volumes are normally expressed in pages, but some magazines of newspaper format use column centimetres (col. cm.). Again, some magazines use page units for display but col. cm. for classified.

Display is split into categories because each yields a different rate per page and incurs a different production cost. Inserts may be loose or bound in. Other display is likely to include special advertisements such as gatefolds, ads in special colours or those with special effects, such as stuck-on coupons or samples, or scratch and sniff areas. Classified is split up to differentiate between rate categories and one-off or series advertisements, such as buyer's guide or directory entries.

Advertisement yields and revenue
An advertisement rate card has different rates for different sections and facilities. A four-colour advertisement is more expensive than two-colour, which is more expensive than black and white. Full pages are cheaper per sq. cm. than half pages, which are cheaper than quarter pages. A classified col. cm. is the most expensive advertisement, size for size. (A specimen rate card is shown in Chapter 5.) Accordingly, there is a separate net advertising 'yield' (the net revenue generated) per page for each kind of advertisement. In some instances there may be some overriding discount, either for volume or value, or spread across a number of magazines in the same publishing house.

A further factor is the effect of series discounts on average yields. Most, if not all, magazines offer such a discount to advertisers who take a number of advertisements during a period. For a monthly, the maximum discount would be based on 12 insertions, then nine, six and three insertions.

Actual discount percentages vary from magazine to magazine. Advertising agents placing business on behalf of their clients are also eligible for a discount (usually 10% for business magazines and 15% for consumer magazines).

The yield is calculated by dividing the net revenue for the category concerned by the number of pages or column centimetres.

For existing magazines, there is a historical yield for each category which takes all the discounts into account. When there is a rate increase, the effect over time can be calculated and added to the average yield figures.

For new magazines, estimated yield figures will be calculated from the rate card, making allowances for series and other discounts.

In forecasts, average yield estimates are multiplied by the anticipated number of pages to give the estimated revenue for each category in turn. Ultimately, there are likely to be variations between actual and estimated yields, but such variations should not be great.

Ad/ed ratio
Ad/ed ratio expressed as a percentage is the relationship between advertisement and editorial paging. For most magazines there is an optimum ratio, which is based on issue sizes which give optimum profit to the publisher and optimum value to the reader and adver-

Ad/ed ratio

This is a table of ratios for an A4 magazine which must have a minimum of 20 pages of editorial in each issue and has a target ratio of 60:40 (advertisement pages : editorial pages). The total number of pages must be divisible by four — the smallest section that may be printed and bound. A further constraint is that it is not possible to perfect bind an issue of less than 44 pages (including cover) and so the minimum issue size is 44 pages.

Month	Advert pages	Edit pages	Total pages	Ad/ed ratio %
Jan	20	24	44	45.5
Feb	24	20	44	54.6
Mar	30	26	56	53.6
Apr	40	28	68	58.8
May	60	40	100	60.0
Jun	50	34	84	59.5
Jul	30	26	56	53.6
Aug	24	20	44	54.6
Sep	40	28	68	58.8
Oct	120	48	168	71.4
Nov	100	48	148	67.6
Dec	30	22	52	57.7
Total	568	364	932	60.9

In March and July a higher ratio could have been achieved but additional editorial pages were provided to cover special events and the target ratio for the year was achieved.
It is common practice to juggle ratios between issues to provide readers with 'value for money' in all issues.

tiser. It is calculated by dividing advertisement paging by total paging and multiplying by 100.

The common approach when preparing an issue for press is to use the total advertisement paging and the ad/ed ratio to calculate total paging; this figure is then corrected to the nearest four pages (the usual minimum number of pages that may be added or deducted because of printing constraints).

At the extremes of issue sizes, there will be minimum/maximum levels. For example, management policy may be that the optimum ad/ed ratio should be 60% but that issues must not fall below a minimum number of pages overall (say 44 pages) and a minimum number of editorial pages (say 20 pages). The smallest number of advertisement pages to sustain the optimum ratio of 60% and 20 pages of editorial would be 32 pages, giving a total issue size of 52 pages. However, if only 20 pages of advertising were sold there would have to be 24 pages of editorial to meet the minimum issue size requirement and the ratio would be 45.5%. At the other end of the scale, there may be a maximum number of editorial pages which might push the ratio up to 70% or more. The target would be to average at 60% over the year.

Other companies may set a minimum number of editorial pages and have an advertisement target. Once the target is reached, and as more advertisements are sold, pages are added in a ratio of, say, three advertisements to one editorial page.

Number of issues
The number of issues published in the accounting period by cover date.

Circulation revenue
The second major revenue category for paid-for magazines is circulation. It's the same process as for advertising — volume of sales, average yields per copy and the calculated revenue. The volume headings are likely to be:

Circulation volumes
    — Newstrade
    — Subscriptions
    — Frees
    — Returns
Print order

The yield and revenue sections would have similar headings. For a controlled circulation magazine, headings are likely to be:

Circulation volumes
  − Registered
  − Non-registered
  − Subscriptions
  − Frees
Print order

Trade sales refer to copies sold via a re-seller. The normal chain is distributor-wholesaler-retailer. Overseas sales will follow a similar chain, but there are variations depending on the country concerned. The average yield figure which is used to calculate revenue is net of all discounts given to re-sellers.

Subscriptions are copies supplied direct to readers by the publisher (or the publisher's agent) and the revenue is collected in advance. An average yield per copy figure is again used to calculate revenues.

Frees are any copies distributed free of charge to advertisers and others, copies used in promotional mailings or copies used internally and which go to make up the balance of the print order.

Returns are copies which are provided to the newstrade for sale, but which are returned unsold (sale or return, SOR). It is possible, in given circumstances, to calculate the number of copies which must be distributed to gain a particular level of sale and therefore the level of returns.

Levels of sale may fluctuate during the year according to the market concerned and promotional activities, and so the print order is not a constant.

Controlled circulation or free magazines have no circulation revenue, except occasionally from a small number of subscribers and the value is seldom significant. For such publications the print order is invariably fixed at a constant level, although there may be variations for publicity and special issue purposes where more copies may be required.

Other trading revenue
Other trading is any business activity (special offers, exhibitions, books, study tours, list selling, etc.) ancillary to the core business (the magazine). There will be suitable headings for each category and income will be allocated to particular months or allocated over the year as appropriate.

Variable costs

Variable costs are those which are incurred as a direct result of publishing a particular issue (if there were no issue published there would be no variable costs). In a busy publishing month they will be high, at other times low. They are likely to include production, distribution, editorial and sales costs, plus other trading variables.

Production costs
Production costs include typesetting, origination, printing, binding and paper. For some magazines, typesetting no longer features here as it is carried out within the editorial department as a part of the copy generation process. These costs are usually calculated by a production manager, using the issue size and circulation forecasts to produce an estimate for each issue.

Some companies use price constants to facilitate estimating, such as:

Setting CPP — the cost of setting an average page
Print MCP — the cost of printing and binding 1000 copies of one average page
Paper MCP — the cost of paper for 1000 copies of one page.

Beware: the terms used do not neccessarily mean the same thing to all production managers, and the figures are accurate only within a fairly narrow band of variances (i.e. the print and paper constants calculated on 25 000 copies would be reasonably accurate between 20 000 and 30 000 but would be unsafe for estimates of 5000 or 50 000). However, provided the limits are understood, they are a quick and easy way to calculate likely costs.

The run-on cost of a magazine is an important factor in planning and assessing promotion expenditure, because an 'extra' copy will cost less than an 'average' copy. The run-on cost (for the 'extra' copy) is the cost of paper, printing machine time and binding time. An 'average' issue costs include setting, origination, plates, and machine make-ready charges, as well as paper, printing machine time and binding time. For example, the cost per 'average' copy of a 64-page magazine with a 22 000 print order might be 48p, whereas an 'extra' copy could cost only 17p.

Distribution costs
A magazine might be distributed by post or via distributors and wholesalers. Costs depend ultimately on the size (weight) of issues

and the number of copies. The costs of wrappering or enveloping and addressing/labelling are also allocated here.

Editorial costs
The two costs which generally appear are Contributors (payment to any external source for editorial material used in the issue(s) concerned) and Art (photographic fees, illustrations, etc.). Where magazines are typeset externally, the author's corrections charge sometimes appears here as well.

Sales costs
This would be commissions paid to advertisement sales agents acting on behalf of the magazine, particluarly those abroad.

Other trading costs
The way these costs are formulated will vary according to the nature of the other trading activity. Books or any articles which are held in stock and sold, for example, are likely to be charged on a unit cost basis. For events such as exhibitions, the costs might be accrued over a number of weeks or months and charged in the month in which the corresponding revenue is shown.

Gross margin

This is the difference between total revenue and total variable costs for a given issue or period. It will be a gross profit or a gross loss. Often two figures are given: gross margin without other trading, gross margin with other trading. A loss figure is signified either by a minus sign or by placing the number in brackets: -1000 or (1000).

Gross margin % is the ratio of gross margin to revenue expressed as a percentage. Again, two figures are often given.

Fixed costs

Fixed costs are incurred whether or not an issue is published. Under the departments Advertising, Editorial and Administration there will be headings for:
Salaries, NI and pensions
Travel
Entertaining
Motor expenses and motor depreciation

Recruitment
Training.
Under Administration, there are also likely to be headings for:
Stationery
Newspapers/magazines
Telephones
Computer costs
Bad debts.
It is common for the recruitment and training and other employ-
ment costs to be allocated to individual departments — the needs of
individual magazines may vary greatly — and there must be provi-
sion for them in the budget. Similarly, computer costs are often
charged directly to a magazine.

Gross publication profit

Gross publication profit (GPP) is calculated by subtracting the fixed
costs from the gross margin. It may, of course, be a loss figure (GPL).
It is the point to which most companies take individual magazine
budgets and trading accounts, at least as far as the publisher is
concerned.

Subsequent charges, such as those for centralized departments —
marketing, accounts, circulation — and rent and rates are often left
as 'central overheads'.

It may be that the publisher is told what those charges are, but
seldom does the publisher have any influence over the method of
allocation. Nevertheless, more and more companies now allocate
these overheads back to magazines, even if it is only a notional figure,
so that it may be determined whether the magazine actually makes
a net profit.

A satisfactory GPP
Generally, the objective for the publisher is to achieve a satisfactory
level of publication profit. That success will be measured in two
ways: the actual GPP or contribution and its movement in real terms
year-on-year; and the GPP as a percentage of turnover and its movement year-on-year.

The percentage figures are important, for they give a good measure
of performance. If a magazine's revenue increases, the gross margin
and publication profit figures should increase. A decline in the percentages occurs either when costs increase disproportionately to the

increase in revenue, or when costs increase while revenue is static or declining.

So, the objective is to increase the profit figures and also improve the percentages.

Disproportionate increases
Often when a magazine is expanding there will be points where costs do increase disproportionately, but provided these are controlled increases there is no problem. One example is where an increase in advertisement paging results in a need to increase advertising and editorial staff; there is likely to be a blip before the full effect of their work contribution is seen.

To illustrate, look at these simple figures based on constant prices (no inflation):

	Year 1	Year 2	Year 3	Year 4
Revenue	100	110	120	140
Variable costs	25	27.5	30	35
GM	75	82.5	90	105
GM%	**75**	**75**	**75**	**75**
Fixed costs	25	25	32	32
GPP	50	57.5	58	73
GPP%	**50**	**52**	**48.3**	**52**

The 10% revenue increase in Year 2 could be accommodated within the same cost ratio as Year 1, but the Year 3 increase (20% up on Year 1) required additional resources (people) and the costs rose disproportionately. In Year 4 the increased work could be absorbed and the GPP% was back to 52%.

Budgets are not always accepted first time and may have to be recast several times before everyone is satisfied. The use of spreadsheets with 'what if?' facilities speeds this process considerably.

Measurement against budget

Once the budget is accepted, copies should be distributed to the editor and advertisement manager. (They should control and monitor their own expenditure and the ad manager must also be responsible for revenue.) The budget is then the document against which achievement can be measured, because it is **a reasonable forecast, at a given point of time, of what is likely to happen**.

The way in which companies regard a budget varies. Some believe it to be a rigid document which cannot be varied; others believe it to be only a guide that sets parameters and relationships between revenues, costs and profit.

The rigid approach seldom holds good. Should advertising be turned away because it exceeds the budgeted level? Should editorial staff not be recruited because the recruitment budget has been exhausted? Should additional and necessary equipment not be purchased because it did not appear in the budget?

Most people would say 'No' to each of those questions. The fact is that some things are not possible to predict or control, and some revenue forecasts will prove to be wrong. Equally, if when the time comes to make budgeted expenditure the expense is not actually justified, then the money should not be spent.

Accurate predictions
The publisher, advertisement manager and editor should be close enough to the market to predict ahead reasonably accurately. Problems begin when salespeople are over-confident or more senior management is over-demanding. For a budget to work it must be an honest forecast of what can be achieved, taking account of the state and size of the market and the possible market share, and of incentives and motivation.

Sales targets are a different matter and while they should not be widely at variance with budgeted sales — there's little point in having an unachievable target, or one too easily reached — they should produce the gilt on the gingerbread.

That is a matter for the publisher and the sales manager, and the differential between budget and target will vary according to the nature of the magazine, the market, the needs and abilities of the salespeople, and the incentive formula — the carrot and the stick.

Variances are important
When it comes to the event, and actual performance is being judged against budget, it is the variance which often gets the most attention. It shows just how accurate the forecasts were, or how good or bad the performance has been. And just as management gets pretty shirty about shortfalls, it has every right to be perturbed at excessive budget beating. Either way, the publisher and the team have got something wrong. Either way, the overall performance of the company will be affected.

Why should making a considerably greater GPP perturb management? Simply because, if management had known that money was to be available, it would have been better able to plan its use. There may be compensations in that other magazines in the group haven't fared too well against budget, and the monies balance out, but nonetheless it does imply that the publisher is not in control.

So, the message is: 'Be honest and accurate in forecasting'.

Monthly accounts

Most companies look on a calendar month as a standard trading period, and so budgets are prepared in that way and trading accounts are produced at the end of each month.

The monthly account (called trading account, or publication profit and loss account, or something similar) is like a budget document, but with a few extra columns. Running across the page, the headings are likely to be:

For the month
    Actual
    Budget
    Variance
    Variance %.

And for the year
    Year to date
    Actual
    Budget
    Variance
    Variance %
    Last year
    Variance
    Variance %.

    Full year
    Latest estimate (LE)
    Budget
    Variance
    Variance %
    Last year
    Variance to LE
    Variance to LE %.

Most of these headings are self-explanatory. Some need a few words of clarification. The monthly account, as well as showing what has happened, is comparing the actual results with the budget. The end-of-year figure is updated by including actual results for past months and the budget figures for months to come and is called the latest estimate (LE).

For example, at the end of March the year-to-date figures show what has happened compared with budget and with last year at the same time. The full-year figures show the budget for the year compared with the latest estimate (the actual for January to March plus the budget for April to December) and compare the LE with the previous year's final figures.

Revised budgets
If the variances become significant and it is established that the trend is going to continue, management may call for a revised budget. The purpose is to obtain a more accurate estimate of what is actually going to happen. It is a simpler exercise than preparing a full budget, but it does involve reassessing the plan and perhaps making some pretty hard decisions.

If things are going badly, for example, it may be prudent to cut costs by axing pet projects or, in an extreme situation, by cutting staff numbers.

If things are going particularly well an increase in staff may be indicated, with the resulting costs and problems. Remember there are dangers in increasing staff numbers without adequate consideration of the need. Staff are a fixed cost and, while it is comparatively easy to increase the number of jobs, it is not so easy, and can be expensive, to reduce jobs. It may be better at times of surging revenues to cover the work by means of freelances — journalists, artists or salespeople — or temporary clerical staff.

Cost control
One use to which line managers put the monthly accounts is in monitoring their effectiveness in cost control. Of course, the process begins before the cost is incurred by making sure that those who spend money in whatever way — from personal expenses through to ordering promotional material or commissioning freelances and photography — are fully aware of the budgets beforehand.

There is a little point in complaining that someone has spent too much if they didn't know in advance how much they were allowed to spend.

Each line manager should have a copy of the budget over which he or she has control and must exercise that control by keeping a personal record or by working with the management accountant on a day-to-day basis.

If a manager knows that costs are going to be exceeded, alarm bells should be rung and the line manager above should be informed. In that way, the monthly accounts don't come as a nasty shock.

Another problem which occurs is that costs can be allocated to the wrong month (and sometimes to the wrong department). It is part of the liaison process to ensure that the accounts department allocates costs correctly. For example, an article may be commissioned and paid for several weeks or months before it is used, but the cost should be charged to the issue in which it ultimately appears.

Reading accounts
Even the most numerate person can be overawed when first faced with a set of management accounts, although if they've had a hand in formulating the budget it shouldn't be too bad. Really, of course, they are not as difficult to read and understand as they may look. If they do present problems, ask the management accountant for explanations.

As with the budget, the logic is simple: start with income, take off the costs which relate directly to the income, then take off the other costs of the magazine and end up with the GPP.

Although a fearsome sounding term, gross publication profit is the contribution which the magazine makes to the company before central overheads are deducted.

Variances
Where monthly accounts are sometimes a little confusing is in the way variances are calculated. Here are some examples:

	Actual	Budget	Variance	Var. %
Advertising revenue	1000	800	200	+25
Circulation revenue	80	100	-20	-20
Production costs	225	250	-25	-10
Editorial costs	200	180	+20	+11

The variance is calculated by subtracting the budget figure from the actual figure. The result is expressed also as a percentage of the budget figure.

At first glance it might be assumed the two 'plus' variances were good and the two 'minus' variances were bad. Not so. It is good that advertising revenue is up 25%, it's bad that circulation revenue is down 20%, bad that editorial costs are up 11% and good that production costs are down 10%. In this instance the variances show whether the actual figure is 'greater than' or 'less than' the budgeted figure, but whether it is a good or bad variance depends on the nature of the item. Generally, it must be good when revenues show a plus variance, and when costs show a minus variance.

Cause of variance

The publisher of this magazine may be saying, 'This result is excellent, but it would have been better if circulation revenue and editorial costs had been on budget'. The next step would be to find out the cause of the variances and take appropriate action. The increase in costs may be directly attributable to the increase in revenue and that would be acceptable.

The circulation revenue drop and the drop in production costs may be directly related also. In real terms, the former is £20 and the latter is £25; does it really mean that if we take £20 less in sales we save £25 in costs? What happens if we take £20 more in sales? Do we spend £25 more in production, giving a net loss of £5? Is it a disparity that merits examination?

Incidentally, when comparing two percentages the actual difference between the figures is a difference of percentage points, not of percentage.

Bad debts

A *bête noire* of all sales managers is the bad debt list or blacklist. It shows those accounts which are overdue for payment and from which no further advertising should be accepted until settlement is received.

In this context, a bad debtor is a company, advertising agency or individual who has failed to pay within the payment period set down in the magazine's terms and conditions. Failure to pay in time could impose undue expense on the company in two ways:

- in the payment of interest on a bank overdraft to fund the business while awaiting payment
- in the cost of collecting the debt.

Each and every slow-paying customer causes the costs of a business to rise.

In many instances, advertisers or their agents attempt to use the magazine publishing company as a money-lender; they advertise and reap the benefits, but deliberately delay payment until the last possible moment. It is important that the publisher and the sales team play a part in controlling debtors. Indeed, it might be sensible to adopt the attitude that a sale is not completed until the invoice is paid. Part of a salesperson's job should be to ensure the bona fides of an advertiser and to help collect the money when payment is late. It is not something that can be ignored or just left to the credit controller.

Long-term planning

Long-term plan budgets are really no more complicated than annual budgets. In fact, in some senses they are simpler, for figures tend to be rounded to the nearest thousand or higher and the detail is not as great.

Think of a number . . .
I was first introduced to the FIVE-YEAR PLAN many years ago, long before personal computers, even before pocket calculators. It was a major exercise taking several weeks and was imposed on a bunch of managers who had enough problems doing an annual budget. For calculations most people used scraps of paper or slide-rules, while the very fortunate among us had mechanical calculators. The projections were extrapolations from two or three years' records and were calculated to at least two decimals places five years ahead! Changes to rates and costs were based on long-term economic forecasts handed down from on high; narratives told what the extrapolations revealed, rather than giving any reasoned assessment of what might happen.
At the time, the magazines were doing well and in consequence some mighty profits were forecast for future years. These looked so ridiculous, even to this untrained forecaster's eyes, that thousands were lopped off here and there so that one didn't appear too foolish. The plans went up the line to be accepted or amended by various levels of management and were then filed away. At least I presume this is what happened, as, thankfully, I heard no more of them. That first time was a fearsome experience.
Come to think of it, long-term plans still are pretty fearsome, but we do at least try to gauge what is going to happen before working out the figures. It makes a lot more sense.

The principle is the same. A plan narrative outlines what may happen, the budget presents the resulting figures. The trap to avoid is making the document an extrapolation — it should be a forecast based on a scenario of market conditions.

In any budgeting exercise it is not the actual figure work, the 'number crunching', which is the problem, it's the market and product knowledge, the research, the assumptions and the conclusions which are the key to getting it right.

Specimen budgets and trading accounts

On the following pages are an annual budget, a three-year plan summary and one month's trading account for a fictitious magazine. It is an A4 magazine, published weekly and has an average circulation of about 23 500 copies. The basic advertisement rates for single insertions are:

Mono page	£1375.00
Colour page	£2020.00
Classified	£18 per scc
Directory	£12 per scc

Annual budget

Sheet 1 shows a summary of revenues and costs, the gross margin and gross publication profit figures and the key ratios (GM% and GPP%). The ensuing five pages show:

Sheet 2: Advertisement volumes, yields (net average income per page) and revenue for each type of advertising. For this budget it is assumed that yields will be at a constant level through the year, although in reality they may vary as a result of discounts, special arrangements, features, etc. When a rate increase is introduced, it is usual to honour existing contracts, which means that yields do not rise to the new level immediately. Depending on the way in which advertising space is sold, the proportion and length of series bookings, it may take several months — even a year — for an increase to be fully effective.

Sheet 3: Circulation volumes, yields and revenues. Note that the volume figures show the average number of copies per issue and not the total number of copies in the period. The revenue figure is calculated by multiplying the average number of copies per issue by the number of issues in the period and then by the average yield. Any cover price increase would have an immediate effect on trade sales but only a gradual effect on subscriptions, as it would apply only to renewals and new subscriptions. It would take a year for the increase to be fully effective on annual subscriptions and pro rata for longer periods.

Sheet 4:   Variable costs for production, distribution and editorial. This publication does not have a reader service card and there are no separate charges for author's corrections. The typesetter's cost per page for setting includes corrections.

Sheet 5:   Fixed costs for advertising and editorial. Similar headings are used for each department, although 'bonus' is normally not applicable for editorial.

Sheet 6:   Administration fixed costs and promotion costs. The former include a number of additional costs for materials and services used by all the magazine's departments (stationery, telephones, subscriptions, etc.), and the cost of bad debts. It will be noted that some costs are spread across the year in equal monthly amounts. Promotion costs include mailings and other costs involved in developing circulation. (It is clear from the number of copies produced — Sheet 3 — that the mailings do not include copies of the magazine, or otherwise the number of 'frees' would be higher.) Exhibitions at which the magazine is exhibited occur in March, April, September and October. Increased trade copy sales (Sheet 3) at these times include copies sold from the exhibition stands. Rate cards, etc., includes brochures and other printed material to promote advertisement sales. Two research projects are planned: the first will be a quantitative analysis of the circulation and the second will be a follow-up qualitative survey. Miscellaneous is a safety net provision to cover participation in events and activities which may occur at any time during the year.

The final section gives staff numbers.

Three-year plan

This is what the first or summary page of a three-year plan might look like. The headings show the latest estimate for current year (Year 0), and the budget for next year and the forecast for the following two years, together with the year-on-year variances (sterling and percentage). All the figures are shown at current values; in other words no allowance is made for inflation in either revenues or costs.

The GPP increases from £2 055 489 in the current year to £3 685 914 in Year 3. Year-on-year increases are 23.8%, 12.8% and 28.5%. The GPP percentage remains remarkably close at 59.8%, 61.5%, 60.6% and

61.3%. Variable costs have increased to match page volume increases, additional investment in editorial colour and circulation increases.

There is investment in editorial staffing in Year 1 and again in Year 2. Sales staff is increased in Year 2 and administrative staff in Year 3. Other fixed cost increases reflect the increased activity in support of the considerable increases in revenue.

In Year 2, other trading activities have been introduced and make a GM contribution of £4103. In Year 3, the contribution is £9683.

If it can be achieved, the GPP growth of over £1.63 million (or 79.3%) in three years will earn the publisher many plaudits!

Trading account
Trading accounts usually follow the same layout as the budget for comparison purposes. The horizontal headings are quite different, however, and usually are in three sections: this month, year to date, the full year — latest estimate. Actual figures are compared with budget and with the same month/period in the previous year.

Variances are shown, together with percentage variance. In each case, the variance is the actual figure minus the budget figure (or last year's figure). The result is expressed also as a percentage of the budget figure (or last year). A positive variance means the actual figure is greater, a minus figure means it is smaller. Whether or not it is a desirable variance depends on the nature of the item — an increase in a revenue figure is good, but an increase in a cost is bad.

Consider the results for the month. The gross margin is 7.8% below budget but is 24% better than the same month last year. The year to date (Jan, Feb, Mar) is 13.5% below budget and 4.6% below last year. Turn to Sheet 2 and the reason for the shortfall in revenue is soon evident.

Inserts are down two in number and £194 in yield	-£4664
Colour is down 7 pages but yield is up £45	-£8900
Classified is down 7 pages and yield is down £166	-£25 864
Mono is up 5 pages and yield is up £28	+£8940
Total shortfall	-£29 554

Mono and colour almost cancelled each other out (+£40). Inserts and classified were together down £30 528.

Because the total number of advertising pages did not fall materially (down 8) and the ratio had to be maintained, the total number of pages published (472 pages) was down only 12. Production costs did not fall; indeed the print MCP figure indicates an increase of just under 8%.

Savings in fixed costs amounted to £2030, or 2.7%. Promotion was over budget by £1715, or 12%. This was mainly due to an overspend on exhibition activity.

The year-to-date figures show a drop of 13.7% in advertising revenue, but the increase in circulation revenue of 5.8% means that the total revenue figure is down 11.8%. There are small savings in variable costs of 4.3%, and the gross margin is down 13.5%. With the exception of promotion, fixed costs show savings, the net being 3.6%. The GPP is well down − 17%. The percentage GPP has dropped 6.8 points, or 10.7%

The full-year estimate gives an idea of what effect the first three months will have, provided issues meet budgets for the rest of the year. GPP will be down 3.8%, or £95 827, and GM% down just less than half a percentage point. But will the rest of the year perform as budget? As the GM is down 13.5% on budget already, it would be sensible to carry out a budget revision, starting with revenue forecasts and looking carefully at fixed costs which, although close to budget, are well up on the previous year at this time.

Budget Layout

	JAN	FEB	MAR	APR	MAY
Revenue					
Display	130136	154176	283140	253240	256762
Classified	62712	75452	139464	125424	126724
Total ad revenue	192848	229628	422604	378664	383486
Circulation	26424	˙26680	36380	29232	28421
Total publishing revenue	219272	256308	458984	407896	411907
Other trading					
TOTAL	219272	256308	458984	407896	411907
Variable Costs					
Production	30209	36549	73081	65141	64776
Distribution	6994	6956	8747	7096	7088
Editorial	2000	2400	4400	3900	4000
Total publishing	39202	45905	86228	76137	75864
Other trading					
TOTAL	39202	45905	86228	76137	75864
Publishing GM	180070	210404	372757	331759	336043
Other trading GM					
GROSS MARGIN	180070	210404	372757	331759	336043
Fixed Costs					
Advertising	16998	17741	21449	20550	20709
Editorial	23186	23609	25724	25211	25301
Administration	13744	13977	15143	14860	14910
Promotion	4692	8048	14215	17324	11075
TOTAL	58620	63375	76531	77945	71995
GROSS PUBLICATION PROFIT	121450	147029	296226	253814	264048
Publishing GM %	82.1	82.1	81.2	81.3	81.6
Total GM %	82.1	82.1	81.2	81.3	81.6
GPP %	55.4	57.4	64.5	62.2	64.1

	Sheet 1						
JUN	**JUL**	**AUG**	**SEP**	**OCT**	**NOV**	**DEC**	**TOTAL**
206344	154176	102586	359348	307180	230972	102586	2540646
101244	75452	49972	176696	152204	113984	49972	1249300
307588	229628	152558	536044	459384	344956	152558	3789946
33435	26771	26554	37537	30005	28418	19238	349095
341023	256399	179112	573581	489389	373374	171796	4139041
341023	256399	179112	573581	489389	373374	171796	4139041
48713	36403	24060	94985	81214	57969	22671	635770
8900	7251	7130	8908	7235	7174	5316	88796
3200	2400	1600	5575	4775	3600	1600	39450
60813	46054	32790	109468	93224	68744	29587	764016
60813	46054	32790	109468	93224	68744	29587	764016
280210	210344	146322	464113	396164	304631	142209	3375026
280210	210344	146322	464113	396164	304631	142209	3375026
19223	17741	16231	23649	22191	19966	16231	232679
24455	23609	22748	26978	26147	24878	22748	294594
14444	13977	13503	15834	15376	14677	13503	173948
4835	4727	8798	22557	20942	7046	4633	128890
62957	60054	61280	89018	84656	66567	57115	830111
217253	150290	85042	375095	311508	238064	85094	2544915
82.2	82.0	81.7	80.9	81.0	81.6	82.8	81.5
82.27	82.0	81.7	80.9	81.0	81.6	82.8	81.5
63.7	58.6	47.5	65.4	63.7	63.8	49.5	61.5

Budget Layout

	JAN	FEB	MAR	APR	MAY
Advertisement Volumes					
Inserts	4	4	8	8	7
Ad pages: mono	48	58	105	90	96
Ad pages: colour	38	45	83	76	75
Ad pages: classified	30	36	67	60	61
Ad pages: directory	24	29	53	48	48
Ad pages: TOTAL	140	168	308	274	280
Ad/ed ratio	63.6	63.6	63.6	63.7	63.6
Editorial pages	80	96	176	156	160
TOTAL PAGES	220	264	484	430	440
NO. OF ISSUES	4	4	5	4	4
Advertisement Yields					
Inserts	1750	1750	1750	1750	1750
Mono	1172	1172	1172	1172	1172
Colour	1760	1760	1760	1760	1760
Classified	1300	1300	1300	1300	1300
Directory	988	988	988	988	988
Average (ex inserts)	1327	1325	1327	1331	1326
Advertisement Revenue					
Inserts	7000	7000	14000	14000	12250
Mono	56256	67976	123060	105480	112512
Colour	66880	79200	146080	133760	132000
TOTAL DISPLAY (ex ins)	123136	147176	269140	239240	244512
Classified	39000	46800	87100	78000	79300
Directory	23712	28652	52364	47424	47424
TOTAL	192848	229628	422604	378664	383486

			Sheet 2				
JUN	**JUL**	**AUG**	**SEP**	**OCT**	**NOV**	**DEC**	**TOTAL**
6	4	3	10	8	6	3	71
77	58	38	134	115	86	38	943
60	45	30	105	90	68	30	745
49	36	24	85	73	55	24	600
38	29	19	67	58	43	19	475
224	168	111	391	336	252	111	2763
63.6	63.6	63.4	63.7	63.8	63.6	63.4	63.6
128	96	64	223	191	144	64	1578
352	264	175	614	527	396	175	4341
5	4	4	5	4	4	3	50
1750	1750	1750	1750	1750	1750	1750	1750
1172	1172	1172	1172	1172	1172	1172	1172
1760	1760	1760	1760	1760	1760	1760	1760
1300	1300	1300	1300	1300	1300	1300	1300
988	988	988	988	988	988	988	988
1326	1325	1327	1326	1326	1327	1327	1327
10500	7000	5250	17500	14000	10500	5250	124250
90244	67976	44536	157048	134780	100792	44536	1105196
105600	79200	52800	184800	158400	119680	52800	1311200
195844	147176	97336	341848	293180	220472	97336	2416396
63700	46800	31200	110500	94900	71500	31200	780000
37544	28652	18772	66196	57304	42484	18772	469300
307588	229628	152558	536044	459384	344956	152558	3789946

Budget Layout

	JAN	FEB	MAR	APR	MAY
Circulation Volumes					
Trade	17304	17600	19876	19870	19100
Subscriptions	4900	4870	4903	4981	4975
Frees	168	186	258	234	247
Returns					
Print order	22372	22656	25037	25085	24322
Circulation Yields					
Trade	.26	.26	.26	.26	.26
Subscriptions	.43	.43	.43	.43	.43
Circulation Revenue					
Trade	17996	18304	25839	20665	19864
Subscriptions	8428	8376	10541	8567	8557
TOTAL	26424	26680	36380	29232	28421

Sheet 3							
JUN	JUL	AUG	SEP	OCT	NOV	DEC	TOTAL
17450	17300	17250	20597	20431	18985	16436	18517
5000	5104	5008	5005	5091	5043	4975	4988
140	145	146	160	160	150	150	179
22549	22404	25762	25682	24178	21561	23684	
.26	.26	.26	.26	.26	.26	.26	.26
.43	.43	.43	.43	.43	.43	.43	.43
22685	17992	17940	26776	21248	19744	12820	241874
10750	8779	8614	10761	8757	8674	6418	107222
33435	26771	26554	37537	30005	28418	19238	349095

Budget Layout

	JAN	FEB	MAR	APR	MAY
Production Variable Costs					
Setting	2860	3432	6318	5616	5746
Other origination	1800	2160	3960	3510	3600
Printing	12600	15312	31022	27614	27396
Paper	12501	15192	30779	27398	27182
Inserts	447	453	1001	1003	851
Reader service cards					
TOTAL	30209	36549	73081	65141	64776
Distribution Variable Costs					
Carriage	800	800	1000	800	800
Postage	5096	5065	6374	5180	5174
Wrapping	1098	1091	1373	1116	1114
TOTAL	6994	6956	8747	7096	7088
Editorial Variable Costs					
Author's corrections					
TOTAL	2000	2400	4400	3900	4000
Statistics					
Print MCP	2.56	2.56	2.56	2.56	2.56
Paper MCP	2.54	2.54	2.54	2.54	2.54

						Sheet 4	
JUN	JUL	AUG	SEP	OCT	NOV	DEC	TOTAL
4602	3432	2288	8008	6864	5174	1664	56004
2880	2160	1440	5018	4298	3240	1440	35505
20356	15240	10037	40494	34648	24511	9659	268888
20197	15120	9959	40177	34377	24319	9584	266787
678	451	336	1288	1027	725	323	8586
48713	36403	24060	94985	81214	57969	22671	635770
1000	800	800	1000	800	800	600	10000
6500	5308	5208	6507	5295	5245	3881	64832
1400	1143	1122	1401	1140	1130	836	13964
8900	7251	7130	8908	7235	7174	5316	88796
3200	2400	1600	5575	4775	3600	1600	39450
2.56	2.56	2.56	2.56	2.56	2.56	2.56	2.60
2.54	2.54	2.54	2.54	2.54	2.54	2.54	2.57

Budget Layout

	JAN	FEB	MAR	APR	MAY
Advertising Fixed Costs					
Salaries	11555	11555	11555	11555	11555
Pensions	1733	1733	1733	1733	1733
Bonus	703	843	1546	1375	1405
Travel	760	912	1672	1488	1520
Entertaining	289	347	635	565	578
Motor expenses	553	664	1217	1083	1107
Recruitment	351	422	773	688	703
Training	1054	1265	2318	2063	2108
TOTAL	16998	17741	21449	20550	20709
Editorial Fixed Costs					
Salaries	15888	15888	15888	15888	15888
Pensions	1589	1589	1589	1589	1589
Bonus					
Travel	1672	2007	3679	3273	3344
Entertaining	443	531	974	867	886
Motor expenses	417	417	417	417	417
Recruitment	794	794	794	794	794
Training	2383	2383	2383	2383	2383
TOTAL	23186	23609	25724	25211	25301

Sheet 5							
JUN	JUL	AUG	SEP	OCT	NOV	DEC	TOTAL
11555	11555	11555	11555	11555	11555	11555	138660
1733	1733	1733	1733	1733	1733	1733	20796
1124	843	557	1962	1686	1265	557	13866
1216	912	603	2123	1824	1368	603	15001
462	347	229	807	693	520	229	5701 513
885	664	439	1545	1328	996	439	10920
562	422	279	981	843	632	279	6935
1686	1265	836	2943	2529	1897	836	20800
19223	17741	16231	23649	22191	19966	16231	232679
15888	15888	15888	15888	15888	15888	15888	190656
1589	1589	1589	1589	1589	1589	1589	19068
2675	2007	1326	4670	4013	3010	1326	33002
709	531	351	1237	1063	797	351	8740
417	417	417	417	417	417	417	5004
794	794	794	794	794	794	794	9528
2383	2383	2383	2383	2383	2383	2383	28596
24455	23609	22748	26978	26147	24878	22748	294594

Budget Layout

	JAN	FEB	MAR	APR	MAY
Administration Fixed Costs					
Salaries	5333	5333	5333	5333	5333
Pensions	533	533	533	533	533
Bonus					
Travel	405	486	892	793	811
Entertaining	608	730	1338	1190	1216
Motor expenses	152	182	334	298	304
Recruitment	208	208	208	208	208
Training	742	742	742	742	742
Sundries	125	125	125	125	125
Stationery	192	192	192	192	192
Subscriptions	42	42	42	42	42
Telephones	667	667	667	667	667
Computers					
Bad debts	4737	4737	4737	4737	4737
TOTAL	13744	13977	15143	14860	14910
Promotion Costs					
Circulation	4392	4448	4915	4924	4775
Exhibitions			9000	12000	
Rate cards, etc.		3200			
Research					6000
Miscellaneous	300	400	300	400	300
TOTAL	4692	8048	14215	17324	11075
FIXED COSTS TOTAL	58620	63375	76531	77945	71995
Editorial staff no.	11	11	11	11	11
Advert sales staff no.	8	8	8	8	8
Administration staff no.	3	3	3	3	3
TOTAL STAFF NO.	22	22	22	22	22

						Sheet 6	
JUN	JUL	AUG	SEP	OCT	NOV	DEC	TOTAL
5333	5333	5333	5333	5333	5333	5333	63996
533	533	533	533	533	533	533	6396
649	486	321	1132	973	730	321	7999
973	730	482	1698	1459	1094	482	12000
243	182	121	425	365	274	121	3001
208	208	208	208	208	208	208	2496
742	742	742	742	742	742	742	8904
125	125	125	125	125	125	125	1500
192	192	192	192	192	192	192	2304
42	42	42	42	42	42	42	504
667	667	667	667	667	667	667	8004
4737	4737	4737	4737	4737	4737	4737	56844
14444	13977	13503	15834	15376	14677	13503	173948
4435	4427	4398	5057	5042	4746	4233	55790
			10000	15500			46500
		4000			2000		9200
			7200				13200
400	300	400	300	400	300	400	4200
4835	4727	8798	22557	20942	7046	4633	128890
62957	60054	61280	89018	84656	66567	57115	830111
11	11	11	11	11	11	11	11
8	8	8	8	8	8	8	8
3	3	3	3	3	3	3	3
22	22	22	22	22	22	22	22

Three year plan

	Year 0	Year 1	Variance	Variance %
Revenue				
Display	2111295	2540646	429351	20.3
Classified	1030317	1249300	218983	21.3
Total advert	3141611	3789946	648335	20.6
Circulation	295855	349095	53240	18.0
Total publishing	3437466	4139041	701575	20.4
Other trading				
TOTAL	3437466	4139041	701575	20.4
Variable costs				
Production	513826	635770	121944	23.7
Distribution	75610	88796	13186	17.4
Editorial	33681	39450	5769	17.1
Total Publishing	623116	764016	140899	22.6
Other trading				
TOTAL	623116	764016	140899	22.6
Publishing GM	2814350	3375026	560675	19.9
Other trading GM				
GROSS MARGIN	2814350	3375026	560675	19.9
Fixed Costs				
Advertising	221045	232679	11634	5.3
Editorial	261749	294594	32845	12.5
Administration	165251	173948	8697	5.3
Promotion	110817	128890	18073	16.3
TOTAL	758862	830111	71249	9.4
GPP	2055489	2544915	489426	23.8
Publishing GM %	81.9	81.5	-0.3	-0.4
Total GM %	81.9	81.5	-0.3	-0.4
GPP %	59.8	61.5	1.7	2.8

Year 2	Variance	Variance %	Year 3	Variance	Variance %
2886652	346006	13.6	3582719	696066	24.1
1418500	169200	13.5	1820858	402358	28.4
4305153	515207	13.6	5403576	1098424	25.5
413630	64534	18.5	588216	174587	42.2
4718782	579741	14.0	5991792	1273010	27.0
12508	12508	100.0	23780	11272	90.1
4731290	592249	14.3	6015572	1284282	27.1
761084	125314	19.7	1062779	301695	39.6
102716	13920	15.7	133944	31228	30.4
48607	9157	23.2	61570	12963	26.7
912407	148391	19.4	1258293	345886	37.9
8405	8405	100.0	14097	5692	67.7
920812	156796	20.5	1272390	351578	38.2
3806375	431349	12.8	4733499	927124	24.4
4103	4103	100.0	9683	5580	136.0
3810478	435452	12.9	4743182	932704	24.5
260600	27921	12.0	284055	23454	9.0
338783	44189	15.0	372661	33878	10.0
189603	15655	9.0	218044	28440	15.0
152090	23200	18.0	182508	30418	20.0
941077	110966	13.4	1057268	116191	12.3
2869401	324486	12.8	3685914	816513	28.5
80.7	-0.9	-1.1	79.0	-1.7	-2.1
80.5	-1.0	-1.2	78.8	-1.7	-2.1
60.6	-.8	-1.4	61.3	.6	1.0

Trading Account — March

	This month							Year to date		
	Actual	Budget	Var.	%	Last yr	Var.	%	Actual	Budget	Var.
Revenue										
Display	278516	283140	-4624	-1.6	214930	63586	29.6	477094	567452	-90358
Classified	114534	139464	-24930	-17.9	103850	10684	10.3	252599	277628	-25029
Total advert.	393050	422604	-29554	-7.0	318780	74270	23.3	729693	845080	-115387
Circulation	36235	36380	-145	-0.4	31270	4966	15.9	94680	89485	5195
Total publishing	429285	458984	-29699	-6.5	350050	79236	22.6	824373	934565	-110192
Other trading										
TOTAL	429285	458984	-29699	-6.5	350050	79236	22.6	824373	934565	-110192
Variable Costs										
Production	72971	73081	-110	-0.1	61177	11795	19.3	133178	139839	-6660
Distribution	8439	8747	-308	-3.5	7484	954	12.8	22729	22696	33
Editorial	4300	4400	-100	-2.3	4275	25	0.6	8125	8800	-675
Total publishing	85710	86228	-518	-0.6	72936	12774	17.5	164033	171335	-7302
Other trading										
TOTAL	85710	86228	-518	-0.6	72936	12774	17.5	164033	171335	-7302
Publish'g GM	343575	372757	-29181	-7.8	277114	66462	24.0	660340	763230	-102890
Other trad'g GM		.								
GROSS MARGIN	343575	372757	-29181	-7.8	277114	66462	24.0	660340	763230	-102890
Fixed Costs										
Advertising	20678	21449	-771	-3.6	16418	4260	26.0	54637	56188	-1551
Editorial	23354	25724	-2370	-9.2	16807	6547	39.0	66113	72519	-6406
Administration	14539	15143	-604	-4.0	11831	2708	22.9	42275	42864	-589
Promotion	15930	14215	1715	12.1	4093	11837	289.2	28436	26955	1481
TOTAL	74501	76531	-2030	-2.7	49149	25352	51.6	191461	198526	-7065
GPP	269075	296226	-27151	-9.2	227965	41110	18.0	468879	564704	-95825
Publish'g GM %	80.0	81.2	-1.2	-1.5	79.2	0.9	1.1	80.1	82.2	-2.1
Total GM %	80.0	81.2	-1.2	-1.5	79.2	0.9	1.1	80.1	82.2	-2.1
GPP %	62.7	64.5	-1.9	-2.9	65.1	-2.4	-3.8	56.9	63.7	-6.8

				Sheet 1						
			The full year — latest estimate							
%	Last yr	Var.	%	Estimate	Budget	Var.	%	Last yr	Var.	%
-15.9	486055	-8961	-1.8	2450288	2540646	-90358	-3.6	2111295	338993	16.1
-9.0	271819	-19220	-7.1	1224271	1249300	-25029	-2.0	1030317	193954	18.8
-13.7	757874	-28181	-3.7	3674559	3789946	-115387	-3.0	3141611	532948	17.0
5.8	80871	13809	17.1	354291	349095	5195	1.5	295855	58436	19.8
-11.8	838745	-14372	-1.7	4028850	4139041	-110192	-2.7	3437466	591383	17.2
-11.8	838745	-14372	-1.7	4028850	4139041	-110192	-2.7	3437466	591383	17.2
-4.8	117769	15409	13.1	629110	635770	-6660	-1.0	513826	115284	22.4
0.2	21411	1319	6.2	88829	88796	33	0.0	75610	13219	17.5
-7.7	7525	600	8.0	38775	39450	-675	-1.7	33681	5094	15.1
-4.3	146705	17328	11.8	756713	764016	-7302	-1.0	623116	133597	21.4
-4.3	146705	17328	11.8	756713	764016	-7302	-1.0	623116	133597	21.4
-13.5	692040	-31700	-4.6	3272136	3375026	-102890	-3.0	2814350	457786	16.3
-13.5	692040	-31700	-4.6	3272136	3375026	-102890	-3.0	2814350	457786	16.3
-2.8	40914	13723	33.5	231128	232679	-1551	-0.7	221045	10083	4.6
-8.8	49460	16654	33.7	288188	294594	-6406	-2.2	261749	26439	10.1
-1.4	32990	9285	28.1	173359	173948	-589	-.3	165251	8108	4.9
5.5	21542	6894	32.0	130373	128890	1483	1.2	110817	19556	17.6
-3.6	144906	46555	32.1	823048	830111	-7063	-0.9	758862	64186	8.5
-17.0	547134	-78254	-14.3	2449088	2544915	-95827	-3.8	2055489	393600	19.1
-2.5	82.5	-2.4	-2.9	81.2	81.5	-0.3	-0.4	81.9	-0.7	-0.8
-2.5	82.5	-2.4	-2.9	81.2	81.5	-0.3	-0.4	81.9	-0.7	-0.8
-10.7	65.2	-8.4	-12.8	60.8	61.5	-0.7	-1.1	59.8	1.0	1.7

Trading Account — March

	This month							Year to date		
	Actual	Budget	Var.	%	Last yr	Var.	%	Actual	Budget	Var.
Advertisement Volumes										
Inserts	6	8	-2	-25	4	2	50	13	16	-3
Mono	110	105	5	4.8	86	24	27.9	178	211	-33
Colour	76	83	-7	-8.4	77	-1	-1.3	136	166	-30
Classified	60	67	-7	-10.4	64	-4	-6.3	124	133	-9
Directory	54	53	1	1.9	50	4	8.0	97	106	-9
Total	300	308	-8	-2.6	277	23	8.3	535	616	-81
Ad/ed ratio	63.56	63.6	-0.1	-0.1	61.8	1.7	2.8	62.2	63.7	-1.5
Editorial pages	172	176	-4	-2.3	171	1	0.6	325	352	-27
Total pages	472	484	-12	-2.5	448	24	5.4	860	968	-108
No. of issues	5	5			5			13	13	
Advertisement Yields										
Inserts	1556	1750	-194	-11.1	1667	-111	-6.7	1690	1750	-60
Mono	1200	1172	28	2.4	1007	193	19.2	1190	1172	18
Colour	1805	1760	45	2.6	1580	225	14.2	1760	1760	29
Classified	1134	1300	-166	-12.8	1198	-64	-5.3	1265	1300	-35
Directory	987	988	-1	-0.1	879	108	12.3	987	988	-1
Ave. (ex ins)	1279	1327	-48	-3.6	1127	152	13.5	1323	1326	-3
Advertisement Revenue										
Inserts	9336	14000	-4664	-33.3	6668	2668	40.0	21970	28000	-6030
Mono	132000	123060	8940	7.3	86602	45398	52.4	211820	247292	-35472
Colour	137180	146080	-8900	-6.1	121660	15520	12.8	243304	292160	-48856
TOTAL (ex ins)	269180	269140	40		208262	60918	29.3	455124	539452	-84328
Classified	61236	87100	-25864	-29.7	59900	1336	2.2	156860	172900	-16040
Directory	53298	52364	934	1	43950	9348	21.3	95739	104728	-8989
TOTAL	393050	422604	-29554	-7.0	318780	74270	23.3	729693	845080	-115387

				Sheet 2						
			The full year — latest estimate							
%	Last yr	Var.	%	Estimate	Budget	Var.	%	Last yr	Var.	%
-18.8	14	-1	-7.1	68	71	-3	-4.2	65	3	4.6
-15.6	187	-9	-4.8	910	943	-33	-3.5	839	71	8.4
-18.1	159	-23	-14.5	715	745	-30	-4.0	663	52	7.8
-6.8	142	-18	-12.7	591	600	-9	-1.5	534	57	10.7
-8.5	103	-6	-5.8	466	475	-9	-1.9	423	43	10.2
-13.1	591	-56	-9.5	2682	2763	-81	-2.9	2459	223	9.1
-2.3	66.3	-4.0	-6.1	63.4	63.6	-.3	-.5	62.2	1.2	1.9
-7.7	301	24	8.0	1551	1578	-27	-1.7	1497	54	3.6
-11.2	892	-32	-3.6	4233	4341	-108	-2.5	3956	277	7.0
	13			50	50			50		
-3.4	1600	90	5.6	1739	1750	-11	-0.7	1617	122	7.5
1.5	1085	105	9.7	1176	1172	4	0.3	1093	82	7.5
1.6	1640	149	9.1	1766	1760	6	0.3	1642	124	7.5
-2.7	1207	58	4.8	1293	1300	-7	-0.6	1202	90	7.5
-0.1	975	12	1.2	988	988			919	69	7.5
-0.3	1244	78	6.3	1326	1327	-1	-0.1	1235	91	7.4
-21.5	22400	-430	-1.9	118220	124250	-6030	-4.9	105094	13126	12.5
-14.3	202895	8925	4.4	1069724	1105196	-35472	-3.2	917519	152205	16.6
-16.7	260760	-17456	-6.7	1262344	1311200	-48856	-3.7	1088682	173662	16.0
-15.6	463655	-8531	-1.8	2332068	2416396	-84328	-3.5	2006201	325867	16.2
-9.3	171394	-14534	-8.5	763960	780000	-16040	-2.1	641959	122001	19.0
-8.6	100425	-4686	-4.7	460311	469300	-8989	-1.9	388358	71953	18.5
-13.7	757874	-28181	-3.7	3674559	3789946	-115387	-3.0	3141611	532948	17.0

Trading Account — March

	This month							Year to date		
	Actual	Budget	Var.	%	Last yr	Var.	%	Actual	Budget	Var.
Circulation Volumes										
Trade	20087	19876	211	1.06	19560	527	2.7	19908	18260	1648
Subscriptions	4708	4903	-195	-4.0	4104	604	14.7	4900	4891	9
Frees	305	258	47	18.2	380	-75	-19.7	78	204	-126
Returns										
Print order	25100	25037	63	0.3	24044	1056	4.4	24886	23355	1531
Circulation Yields										
Trade	.26	.26			.24	.02	8.3	.26	.3	
Subscriptions	.43	.43			.38	.05	13.2	.43	.43	
Circulation Revenue										
Trade	26113	25839	274	1.1	23472	2641	11.3	67289	62139	5150
Subscriptions	10122	10541	-419	-4	7798	2325	29.8	27391	27346	45
TOTAL	36235	36380	-145	-0.4	31270	4966	15.9	94680	89485	5195

				Sheet 3						
			The full year — latest estimate							
%	Last yr	Var.	%	Estimate	Budget	Var.	%	Last yr	Var.	%
9.0	18670	1238	6.6	18733	18517	216	1.2	18005	728	4.0
0.2	4579	321	7.0	5008	4988	20	0.4	4890	118	2.4
-61.8	364	-286	-78.6	161	179	-18	-10.1	120	41	34.2
6.6	23613	1273	5.4	23902	23684	218	0.9	23015	887	3.9
	.24	.02	8.3	.26	.26			.22	.04	18.2
	.38	.05	13.2	.43	.43			.40	.03	7.5
8.3	58250	9039	15.5	247024	241874	5150	2.1	198055	48969	24.7
.2	22620	4771	21.1	107267	107222	45		97800	9467	9.7
5.8	80871	13809	17.1	354291	349095	5195	1.5	295855	58436	19.8

Trading Account — March

	This month							Year to date		
	Actual	Budget	Var.	%	Last yr	Var.	%	Actual	Budget	Var.
Production Costs										
Setting	6032	6318	-286	-4.5	5640	392	7.0	11674	12610	-936
Origination	3870	3960	-90	-2.3	3591	279	7.8	7313	7920	-608
Printing	32698	31022	1676	5.4	27252	5446	20.0	59069	58934	136
Paper	29618	30779	-1161	-3.8	24236	5382	22.2	53505	58473	-4968
Inserts	753	1001	-248	-24.8	457	296	64.8	1618	1902	-284
RS cards										
TOTAL	72971	73081	-110	-.1	61177	11795	19.3	133178	139839	-6660
Distribution Costs										
Carriage	1000	1000			1000			2600	2600	
Postage	6120	6374	-254	-4.0	5335	785	14.7	16562	16535	27
Wrapping	1318	1373	-55	-4.0	1149	169	14.7	3567	3561	6
TOTAL	8439	8747	-308	-3.5	7484	954	12.8	22729	22696	33
Editorial Costs										
Contributors	4300	4400	-100	-2.3	4275	25	0.6	8125	8800	-675
Author's corr.										
TOTAL	4300	4400	-100	-2.3	4275	25	0.6	8125	8800	-675
Statistics										
Print MCP	2.76	2.56	0.20	7.8	2.53	0.23	9.1	2.76	2.56	0.20
Paper MCP	2.50	2.54	-0.04	-1.6	2.25	0.25	11.1	2.50	2.54	-0.04

				Sheet 4						
				The full year — latest estimate						
%	Last yr	Var.	%	Estimate	Budget	Var.	%	Last yr	Var.	%
-7.4	9746	1928	19.8	55068	56004	-936	-1.7	44680	10388	23.2
-7.7	6773	540	8.0	34898	35505	-608	-1.7	29939	4959	16.6
0.2	53078	5991	11.3	269024	268888	136	0.1	227618	41406	18.2
-8.5	47181	6324	13.4	261819	266787	-4968	-1.9	204857	56963	27.8
-15.0	992	626	63.1	8301	8586	-284	-3.3	6732	1569	23.3
-4.8	117769	15409	13.1	629110	635770	-6660	-1.0	513826	115284	22.4
	2600			10000	10000			9350	650	7.0
0.2	15477	1085	7.0	64859	64832	27	0.0	53790	11069	20.6
0.2	3334	234	7.0	13970	13964	6	0.0	12470	1500	12.0
0.1	21411	1319	6.2	88829	88796	33	0.0	75610	13219	17.5
-7.7	7525	600	8.00	38775	39450	-675	-1.7	33681	5094	15.1
-7.7	7525	600	8.00	38775	39450	-675	-1.7	33681	5094	15.1
7.8	2.52	0.24	9.5	2.66	2.60	0.06	2.5	2.50	0.16	6.4
-1.6	2.24	0.26	11.6	2.59	2.6		0.5	2.3	0.34	15.0

Trading Account — March

	This month							Year to date		
	Actual	Budget	Var.	%	Last yr	Var.	%	Actual	Budget	Var.
Advertising Fixed Costs										
Salaries	11555	11555			10284	1271	12.4	34665	34665	
Pensions	1733	1733			1239	494	39.8	5199	5199	
Bonus	1393	1546	-153	-9.9	1075	318	29.6	2385	3092	-707
Travel	1200	1672	-472	-28.2	1000	200	20.0	2987	3344	-357
Entertaining	768	635	133	20.9	530	238	44.9	1160	1271	-111
Motor exp.	978	1217	-239	-19.6	800	178	22.3	2098	2434	-336
Recruitment	763	773	-10	1.3	467	296	63.4	1536	1546	-10
Training	2288	2318	-30	-1.3	1023	1265	123.7	4607	4637	-30
TOTAL	20678	21449	-771	-3.6	16418	4260	25.9	54637	56188	-1551
Editorial Fixed Costs										
Salaries	14444	15888	-1444	-9.1	12068	2376	19.7	43331	47664	-4333
Pensions	1444	1589	-144	-9.1	1209	236	19.5	4334	4767	-433
Bonus										
Travel	3059	3679	-620	-16.9	2167	892	41.2	5967	7258	-1391
Entertaining	879	974	-95	-9.8	603	276	45.8	1870	1948	-78
Motor cars	351	417	-66	-15.8	297	54	18.2	1080	1251	-171
Recruitment	794	794			367	427	116.3	2382	2382	
Training	2383	2383			96	2287	2382	7149	7149	
TOTAL	23354	25724	-2370	-9.2	16807	6547	39.0	66113	72519	-6406

Specimen trading accounts

Sheet 5

%	Last yr	Var.	%	Estimate	Budget	Var.	%	Last yr	Var.	%
				The full year — latest estimate						
	27732	6933	25.0	138660	138660			131727	6933	5.3
	2773	2426	87.5	20796	20796			19759	1040	5.6
-22.9	2430	-45	-1.8	13159	13866	-707	-5.1	13173	-13	-0.1
-10.7	2545	442	17.4	14644	15001	-357	-2.4	14251	393	2.8
-8.7	978	182	18.6	5590	5701	-111	-1.9	5416	111	3.2
-13.8	2004	94	4.7	10584	10920	-336	-3.1	10374	210	2.0
-0.6	367	1169	318.5	6925	6935	-10	-0.1	6588	337	5.1
-0.6	2085	2522	121.0	20770	20800	-30	-0.1	19760	1010	5.1
-2.8	40914	13723	33.5	231128	232679	-1550	-0.7	221045	10083	4.6
-9.1	36398	6933	19.1	186323	190653	-4333	-2.3	164657	21665	13.2
-9.1	3639	695	19.1	18635	19068	-433	-2.3	16465	2170	13.2
-18.9	4308	1659	38.5	31611	33002	-1391	-4.2	31352	259	0.8
-4.0	1276	594	46.6	8662	8740	-78	-0.9	8303	359	4.3
-13.7	743	337	45.4	4833	5004	-171	-3.4	4754	79	1.7
	947	1435	151.5	9528	9528			9052	476	5.3
	2149	5000	232.7	28596	28596			27166	1430	5.3
-8.8	49460	16653	33.7	288188	294594	-6406	-2.2	261749	26439	10.1

Trading Account — March

	This month							Year to date		
	Actual	Budget	Var.	%	Last yr	Var.	%	Actual	Budget	Var.
Administration Fixed Costs										
Salaries	5333	5333			3552	1781	50.2	15999	15999	
Pensions	533	533			355	178	50.1	1599	1599	
Bonus										
Travel	673	892	-219	-24.6	487	186	38.2	1360	1783	-423
Entertaining	994	1338	-344	-25.7	1500	-506	-33.7	2598	2676	-78
Motor exp.	293	334	-41	-12.3	276	17	6.2	580	668	-88
Recruitment	208	208			369	-161	-43.6	624	624	
Training	742	742			845	-103	-12.2	2226	2226	
Sundries	125	125			87	38	43.7	375	375	
Stationery	192	192			164	28	17.1	576	576	
Subscriptions	42	42			42		-0.8	126	126	
Telephones	667	667			576	91	15.8	2001	2001	
Computers										
Bad debts	4737	4737			3578	1159	32.4	14211	14211	
TOTAL	14539	15143	-604	-4.0	11831	2708	22.9	42275	42864	-589
Promotion										
Circulation	5194	4915	279	5.7	3520	1674	47.6	13600	13755	-155
Exhibitions	10436	9000	1436	16.0		10436		10436	9000	1436
Rate cards								3500	3200	300
Research										
Miscellaneous	300	300			573	-273	-47.6	900	1000	-100
TOTAL	15930	14215	1715	12.1	4093	11837	289.2	28436	26955	1481
FIXED COSTS	74501	76531	-2030	-2.7	49149	25352	51.6	191461	198526	-7065
Edit staff no.	10	11	-1	-9.1	9	1	11.1	10	11	-1
Advert staff no.	8	8			6	2	33.3	8	8	
Admin staff no.	3	3			2	1	50.0	3	3	
TOTAL STAFF	21	22	-1	-4.6	17	4	23.5	21	22	-1

				Sheet 6						
			The full year — latest estimate							
%	Last yr	Var.	%	Estimate	Budget	Var.	%	Last yr	Var.	%
	13759	2240	16.3	63996	63996			60796	3200	5.3
	1376	223	16.2	6396	6396			6076	320	5.3
-23.7	1200	160	13.3	7576	7999	-423	-5.3	7599	-23	-0.3
-2.9	1989	609	30.6	11922	12000	-78	-0.7	11400	522	4.6
-13.2	469	111	23.7	2913	3001	-88	-2.9	2851	62	2.2
	780	-156	-20.0	2496	2496			2371	125	5.3
	560	1666	297.5	8904	8904			8459	445	5.3
	150	225	150.0	1500	1500			1425	75	5.3
	400	176	44.0	2304	2304			2189	115	5.3
		126		504	504			479	25	5.3
	1740	261	15.0	8004	8004			7604	400	5.3
	10567	3644	34.5	56844	56844			54002	2842	5.3
-1.4	32990	9285	28.1	173359	173948	-589	-0.3	165251	8108	4.9
-1.1	9860	3740	37.9	55637	55790	-153		47291	8346	17.6
16.0	8790	1646	18.7	47936	46500	1436	3.1	40746	7190	17.7
9.4	2567	933	36.3	9500	9200	300	3.3	8075	1425	17.6
				13200	13200			11220	1980	17.7
-10.0	325	575	176.9	4100	4200	-100	-2.4	3485	615	17.6
5.5	21542	6894	32	130373	128890	1483	1.2	110817	19556	17.6
-3.6	144906	46555	32.1	823048	830111	-7063	-0.9	758862	64186	8.5
-9.1	9	1	11.1	11	11		-0.9	10	1	9.0
	7	1	14.3	8	8			8		
	3			3	3			3		
-4.6	19	2	10.5	22	22		-.45	21	1	4.3

Chapter 8

Production

Print and paper probably represent the largest single cost area for any magazine, yet this is likely to be the area the majority of people know least about. Most companies, very sensibly, employ a specialist print and paper buyer to oversee the whole area and advise everyone else. In fact, buying print is much like buying any other service by negotiation. The small print needs to be read and understood, and estimates from competing printers need to be analysed carefully.

To buy print effectively, it is important to know the magazine and its printing requirements well and to know the suppliers well, too. Know their plant and its capacities; know the different processes; know, for example, whether a 32-page eight-unit web press will suit your job or whether some other press configuration or type of press would be better.

There are three things publishers seek: service, quality and price.

Service essentially means delivering the right quantity, to the right place, at the right time.

Quality is concerned with registration (printing colour plates in the correct position), colour fidelity, strong, consistent blacks, no hickeys or blemishes on the printed or non-printed areas of a page, accurate binding and trimming, etc., in accordance with a quality specification.

Price is the most competitive quote, taking the first two criteria into account.

In the publication plan there should be at least a paragraph or two about the production of the magazine and what it should look like. Considerations such as the format, the quality and weight of the paper, method of binding, the amount of four colour advertising and editorial, and some comparative indication of the quality of print required.

They are the factors which are going to affect the reader's attitude to the publication. For example, an architect might expect a clean, well-designed A4 magazine using modern, if not fashionable, type-faces. Plenty of white space in the layout, high-quality colour photography, and a paper with good bulk (thickness) and an excellent surface. An architect lives in the world of design and expects a magazine about architecture to have the attributes of a beautiful and well-designed building, with maybe even a hint of the esoteric.

A builder, on the other hand, would expect something far more down to earth, yet still with good-quality colour photographs. Paper quality not so high. Good design, but workmanlike and with much less white space. Practical articles in plainer English. Format likely to be A4, but could be tabloid.

Print specification

The design and quality statements, along with the frequency, the issue pagination and the number of copies to be printed, enable the production manager to prepare a specification.

The next task is to find suitable suppliers to submit estimates. Most production managers tend to work with a number of printers on a regular basis and know their abilities well. Each of the suppliers will have advantages for particular types of work, due either to the skills of the work-force or the nature of the plant and equipment used.

For example, sheetfed offset presses are suitable for magazines with print orders up to 12 000 or 15 000 copies, depending on the number of pages and the amount of colour. Web-offset presses might be more suitable for runs above 15 000 copies, but are most economical for runs exceeding 100 000 copies. Some production specialists argue that web-offset is suitable up to about 1 000 000 copies. For very long runs involving at least 250 000 copies gravure presses may be more suitable. These are generalizations, of course, and each printing job must be judged on its merits, remembering that with the rate of technological change, the goal-posts are moving continually.

The specification itself covers six areas:

- typesetting and page make-up — editorial, classified advertisements and set display
- origination (sometimes called repro) — colour separations, halftones, completed film
- paper — sometimes purchased separately by the publisher, otherwise supplied by the printer
- printing — it is normal for binding and despatch to be

effected by the printer, but sometimes that work is placed separately by the publisher or is subcontracted by the printer

- binding
- despatch

and may involve one supplier for all or even one for each area. Very large circulation publications, where production time is a constraint, may use several printers . The more common situation is that two or three suppliers are used:

Supplier 1: Typesetting, page make-up and origination
Supplier 2: Printing, binding and despatch
or
Supplier 1: Typesetting and page make-up
Supplier 2: Origination
Supplier 3: Printing, binding and despatch.

Typesetting in today's context may refer to one of three methods:

Conventional typesetting: hard copy is supplied, re-keyed and supplied as galleys, which are pasted up by a member of the editorial team and then made up into camera-ready pages by the typesetter.

Half-and-half: the copy is supplied on computer disc and is set and made up into pages by the typesetter according to a layout supplied.

DTP: copy is supplied on computer disc or via modem as fully made-up pages with keylines or low resolution pictures to show where illustrations are to be stripped in.

The specifications which the production manager prepares may look similar to those on pages 192 and 193.

Paper wastage
Paper wastage is a key element in the production cost. It occurs in two ways. First, wastage is inevitable in setting up the press and, where colour is involved, in getting the registration correct. Two factors contribute: the facilities of the press itself and the skill of the press operators. Several hundred copies may be wasted in getting a sheetfed press running properly, and several thousand copies for a web press. Further wastage occurs during the production run. On a web press the web may break, because of a fault in the material itself, incorrect tension or some form of mishandling; when the reels have to be changed, some wastage can occur. On a sheetfed press, mishan-

Specification for setting and origination

Frequency: Weekly
Trimmed size: 297 x 210 mm (portrait)
Pagination: Overall: 32 to 76 pages
                      Editorial: 22 to 32 pages
Editorial colour: Approx 80% of pages with one mono picture,
                      33% of pages with second colour solids or
                      tints, 20% of pages with one four-colour
                      picture.
Advert colour: 33% with second colour, 20% full colour.
Editorial: Supplied on 3.5 in. Apple Mac discs as fully
                      made-up editorial pages with keylined
                      spaces for pictures, advertisements, etc.
Editorial pictures: Four-colour — 133 screen
                      Scanned mono — 120 screen
Display adverts: Most supplied as film. Remainder as repeats,
                      camera-ready artwork or setting.
Classified: Camera-ready artwork, film or setting.
                      Small number of repeats.
Proofs: Two sets proofs with overlays for second
                      colour. Chromalins for four-colour.
Prices: 1. Cover-to-cover basis, excluding classsi-
                      fied, for all editorial and advertisement
                      pages. Price to include all editorial four-
                      colour and mono pictures, plus extras for
                      additional originals or cut-outs, together
                      with tints and spot colour, up to and in-
                      cluding finished final positive film.
                      2. Classified as separate page price, includ-
                      ing page make-up and two sets of proofs.
                      Prices for renewals, key changes to repeats
                      and display make-up. Price to include all
                      tints and spot colour up to and including
                      finished final positive film.
                      3. Prices to include deliveries between
                      publisher and typesetter, disc handling
                      and delivery of final film to printer.
Publication day: Saturday
Despatch time: Thursday noon
Film must be with printer:
                      Early sections: Tuesday 6pm
                      Final section: Wednesday 6pm

Specification for web-offset printing

Frequency:	Weekly
Trimmed size:	297 x 210 mm
Print run:	35 000 copies
Paper:	Mechanical blade-coated 90gsm (self-cover). Supplied by the publisher.

Reader service card:
Pre-printed 230 micron card. Supplied flat by publisher, size 307 x 215 mm, to be folded and bound between sections.

Binding:	Saddle-stitched 2 wires
Inserts:	Bound and loose required
Pagination:	4, 8, 12 and 16-page sections, averaging from 32 to 76 pages. No mono only sections.
Colour:	Up to 33% of pages with second colour solids or tints, 20% of pages with one four colour picture.
Despatch:	Postal copies: 23 500 Copies flat wrapped in three-colour pre-printed polythene, labels supplied to be affixed to outside of wrapper. Balance: bulk to office

Materials supplied:
Final page, mono positive and spot colour film, plus separated film for four-colour (right reading, emulsion side down).

Paper:	State reel size required and estimated wastage figures for set-up and run.
Publication day:	Saturday
Despatch time:	Thursday noon
Film supplied:	Early sections: Tuesday 6pm Final section: Wednesday 6pm
Price:	For basic 35 000 copies plus 1000 run-on, in 1/1, 2/2, 2/4, 4/1, 4/4 configurations.

Note that in this instance the printer is not being asked to supply paper. The production manager will buy paper directly from a merchant or paper mill and will thus secure a keener price, particularly if paper is being bought for several magazines at once. The production manager will also arrange for the separate printing and delivery of the reader service card — it is more economically produced on a sheetfed press.

dling of the paper or misfeeding through the press can cause wastage. Under- or over-inking on either type of press results in wasted copies.

Further wastage can occur when printed sections are damaged while being moved from the press to the binding line and in the bindery itself.

Colour positions
The expression 1/1 ('one back one') in the reference to press config-uration denotes one-colour backing one-colour, in other words, a single colour (usually black) is available on both sides of the sheet on all pages. 2/2 denotes two-colour backing two-colour. 4/4 is four-colour backing four-colour. Depending on the press configuration and the number of pages being printed on the web, it is possible to have 4/4, 4/2, 4/1, 2/2, 2/1, and 1/1.

Typesetting costs
Whatever size the issue, only two figures have to be considered for typesetting: the cost of a standard page and the cost of a classified page. The arithmetic is then simple. For this example, standard pages will cost £25 each, and classified pages £60 each. The reader service card will cost £1295 for 35 000 copies.

Paper costs
Paper costs might be presented as shown on the facing page.

Printing and binding costs
Printing and binding prices are presented as a schedule of charges (see facing page) from which the production manager can calculate the costs for different issue sizes.

Using a price schedule

Armed with all this information, it is possible to cost any permutation of paging and mix of mono and colour, and with the run-back and run-on figures the cost of fewer or more copies within the range of about 30 000 to 40 000 may be calculated with reasonable accuracy.

To explain this last point: the run-on figure is the additional labour and materials cost for extra copies over and above the base print order, and the run-back figure is the reduction in labour and materials cost for fewer copies.

The base print cost and the run-on, run-back figures include ele-

Paper costs

8pp section	35 000 £	1000 run on £
1 or 2 colour	545.00	14.32
3 or 4 colour	558.00	14.32
16pp section		
1 or 2 colour	1089.00	28.11
3 or 4 colour	1116.00	28.11

24pp and 32pp twin web sections are pro rata to the 16pp prices

Price schedule for a web-offset printed magazine

Print and fold from final films:

2-colour:	35 000 £	1000 run on £	1000 run back £
8pp (2/2)	787.00	12.28	11.05
16pp (2/2)	898.00	14.26	12.83
24pp (2/2)	1034.00	16.29	14.66
32pp (2/2)	1123.00	18.27	16.44
4-colour:			
8pp (4/4)	903.00	12.84	11.56
16pp (4/4)	1060.00	15.36	13.82
Binding:			
1 section	377.00	9.33	8.40
2 sections	377.00	9.33	8.40
3 sections	494.00	12.00	10.80
4 sections	508.00	12.00	10.80
5 sections	637.00	14.66	13.19
6 sections	655.00	16.50	14.85
7 sections	797.00	19.50	17.55
8 sections	823.00	19.50	17.55
Inserts:			
1st	350.00	10.00	10.00
2nd	250.00	7.14	7.14
3rd	250.00	7.14	7.14

Bound inserts as extra section on binding.
Wrap for post and label:

	1400.00	40.00	40.00

ments for machine make-ready and machine running time, but the relationship between these elements is correct only when the print order is close to the base calculation figure, i.e. 35 000 copies in this case.

To show how the price schedules might be used, there is a breakdown for an issue of *Any Mag* on the facing page.

The calculated cost estimate can be used either to show in advance how much an issue is going to cost or to check the print invoice when it arrives.

Run-on cost
It's worth noting the difference between the cost of an 'average' copy and the cost of a 'run-on' copy.

The former is calculated like this:

$$\frac{\text{total cost}}{\text{print run}} = \frac{£12518}{35\ 000} = 36p$$

The latter is calculated like this:

$$\frac{(\text{print MCP} + \text{paper MCP}) \times \text{No. of pages}}{1000} = \frac{(2.24+1.97) \times 35}{1000} = 15p$$

This has particular importance in calculating the cost of promotional copies, or in assessing the benefits of sale or return (SOR).

(None of the figures quoted in these examples should be taken as representative of what would be charged in reality.)

Press configurations
Web-offset presses come in different sizes and consist of a number of units grouped together. Usually, a 'unit' is a 'perfector' — it prints one colour on each side of the web at the same time. Five units with two webs (and two reel stands) give 16 pages in four colours and 16 pages in mono. Depending on the system, an eight-unit press will give up to 64 pages in four colours throughout.

Of course, while colours do not have to be used merely because they are available, comparison of the figures for two-colour and four-colour in the price schedule above demonstrate that it is uneconomical to run two-colour on a four-colour machine.

Detailed planning of the imposition, including the possibility of

Cost estimate

Detail:

35 000 copies of a 56pp issue of *Any Mag*
Cover and 15 pages in four colour
5pp classified
51pp standard pages

    £

Typesetting and origination:

5pp classified @ £60	300.00	
51pp standard @ £25	1275.00	
Total		1575.00

	Printing	Paper	
First section:			
8pp 4-colour 1-4, 53-56	903.00	558.00	
Second section:			
16pp 2-colour, 5-12, 45-52	898.00	1089.00	
Third section:			
16pp 2-colour, 13-20, 37-44	898.00	1089.00	
Fourth section:			
16pp 4-colour, 21-36	1060.00	1116.00	
Total	3759.00	3852.00	7611.00

Reader service card	1295.00
Bind 5 sections (4 plus RS card)	637.00
Wrap for post and label	1400.00

TOTAL	12518.00

Cost per copy	0.32
Setting CCP — cost of setting an average page (1575/56)	28.13
Print MCP — cost to print and bind 1000 copies of one page ((3759+637)/35/56)	2.24
Paper MCP — cost of paper for 1000 copies of one page (3852/35/56)	1.97

Printing impositions

Imposition showing pages on which colour is to be printed and
the sections for the 56pp magazine *Any Mag*.

Section 1: 8pp 4/4	1cym	56cym
	2	55
	3cym	54
	4cym	53
Section 2: 16pp 2/2	5	52c
	6c	51c
	7	50c
	8	49
	9c	48
	10	47c
	11c	46c
	12	45
Section 3: 16pp 2/2	13	44
	14m	43m
	15m	42
	16	41
	17m	40
	18	39c
	19m	38
	20	37m
Section 4: 16pp 4/4	21cym	36
	22cym	35
	23cym	34
	24	33cym
	25cym	32cym
	26cym	31cym
	27cym	30
	28cym	29cym

Note: c = cyan y = yellow m = magenta
The fourth colour is black (k) which is available on all pages.

machining large sections and splitting them to bind as separate
sections in different parts of the magazine, can save considerably on
printing costs. It pays to liaise closely with the printer on the best
imposition for the magazine and the available plant.

Colour positions

The variety of colour printing combinations available on a five-unit press with two webs, printing to A4 size. One web is printed mono both sides (1/1), the second four-colour on both sides (4/4).

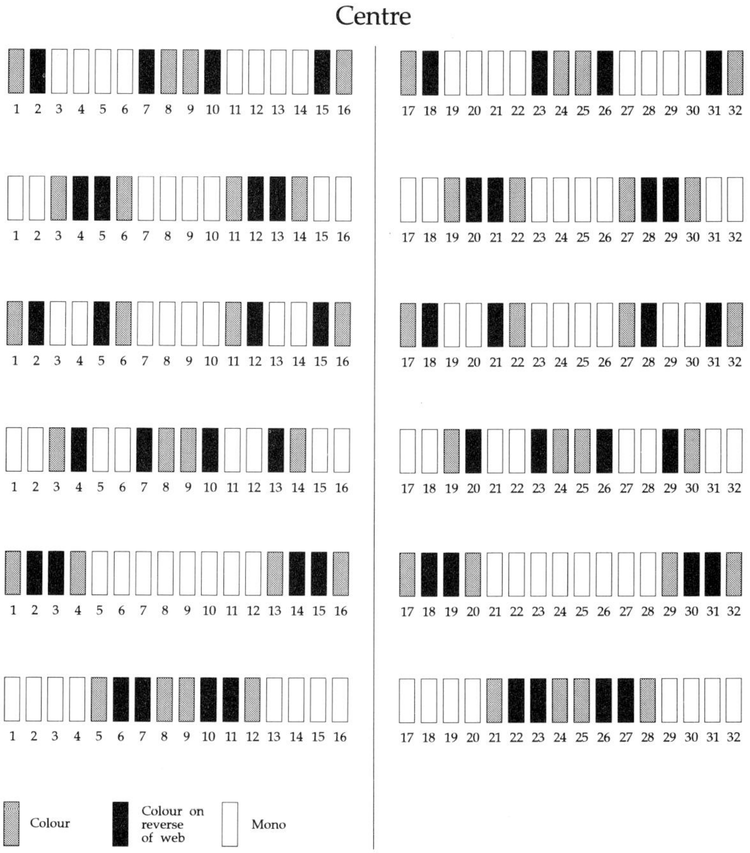

Centre

	Colour		Colour on reverse of web		Mono

Paper and board

Buying paper for a magazine is either merely a matter of negotiating the best price for a 'run of the mill' material where any one of a number of papers will do, or searching for a paper which meets a number of design or quality criteria.

Considerations in paper selection include:

Requirement	*Paper type*
Readability:	Uncoated paper, sometimes with a high surface roughness.
Picture quality:	Smooth surface, coated paper with a high gloss. Detailed pictures are best on art coated papers.
Readability and good pictures:	A compromise, a matt coated paper would probably be best.
Low issue weight:	Where postage costs are important, use a thinner paper with high opacity at low weights. Where weight is really critical special airmail paper could be used.
Durability:	A 'wood-free' paper is best — it's still made from wood, but from chemical pulp. It is free of mechanical pulp which discolours quickly.

Then other factors come into play, such as the type of press. Web-offset presses demand high tensile strength and tear resistance. Sheetfed presses need the two sides of the sheet to be similar, plus stiffness and squareness. Papers to be stapled must not be too brittle. Papers over 170 gsm need to be creased before folding.

It is important to consult with the printer about the most suitable paper characteristics for the press and the processes to be used. For example, adhesive binding works best with papers having high porosity and surface roughness.

The origination house should match separations to the characteristics of the paper. If possible, proofs should be made on the paper to be used for printing.

Whether or not to buy paper directly from a merchant or mill depends almost entirely on price, which in turn depends on quantity. The cost benefit on a relatively small amount of paper is probably not worth the time or expertise required to buy direct. Most printers will buy any paper specified by the customer.

If buying direct, it is essential to liaise with the printer over optimum reel sizes and the quantities to be stocked. The fewer the permutations, the less stock that has to be carried at the publisher's expense.

Environmental papers
As environmental pressures increase, more and more publishers will

wish to use recycled papers. It is widely accepted that for a paper to be classed as 'recycled' the minimum waste fibre content must be at least 50% of the total fibre used, although some sources claim it should be 75%.

'Green' paper facts

It takes 2.7kg of wood, 130g of calcium carbonate, 85g of sulphur, 40g of chlorine and 300 litres of water to make 1kg of paper.

Between 10 and 17 trees are needed to produce a tonne of paper – enough for about 7000 copies of a national newspaper.

The British paper and board industry circulates about 0.75 billion litres of water a day, and is one of the nation's largest industrial users of water. Some 86% is returned after treatment either at the paper mill or at a sewerage works.

Paper associated pollution is mostly caused by the bleaches used to whiten paper which may contaminate effluent discharged to rivers. To reduce this risk, the use of bleaches is gradually changing.

Recycling reduces the need for countries without large domestic sources of pulp wood to import pulp. Recycled material provides about 53% of the fibre used in the UK to make paper and board.

The type of waste used is classified by source and is often indicated in the technical description of a recycled paper. Broadly, there is high (A) or low (B) quality unprinted waste and high (C) or low (D) quality printed waste, although classifications from different sources do vary. A recycled paper may contain from 25% to 100% of one or more types of waste. A copier paper may consist of 10% A, 30% B, 30% C and 20% D. Waste paper does have limitations as a raw material for, unlike metal, it cannot be recycled indefinitely and fibre supply must be augmented by new fibres in the form of virgin wood pulp, or pulp-based papers. Moreover, not all papers and boards can be made from waste paper.

Production schedules

In the calendar of any magazine, there is a publication date for each issue. This might be a day of the week or of the month. It is the day on which copies must be available to the readership, and so the production schedule is worked back from that day.

There are many issues to consider. Preparation of editorial, selling

advertisements and collating advertising material, and the time
needed by the printer to produce and bind, then either wrap, label
and despatch, or bundle and distribute. Posted copies should arrive
on readers' desks or in their homes on publication day, and trade
sale copies should be on the newsagent's shelf first thing on the
same day.

Readers are creatures of habit and they expect their magazine to be
on time, particularly if they are calling into the local shop to collect
it. Advertising campaigns are often timed to coincide with publication dates and advertisers can be very upset if magazines are late.

Getting the schedule right is therefore very important. It is a matter
to be resolved with the printer during initial negotiations and sometimes a contract includes penalty clauses for late delivery. Of course,
the editorial staff and advertisement salespeople have to meet the
schedules as well.

On the next two pages are a couple of schedules for different kinds
of magazine.

With weekly magazines, in particular, the printer has a slot into
which a magazine's printing, binding, etc., must fit. One magazine
cannot be allowed to delay another, and so if a magazine is late, it
may have to go to the back of the queue. Then, instead of being only
a couple of hours late, it may end up ten or twelve hours late.

There are times when editorial deadlines are impractical. Budget
day is usually a Tuesday and the Chancellor doesn't get everything
off his chest until about 5pm or later. If a magazine is scheduled to
go to press at Tuesday noon and the budget news must be included,
some provision has to be made. Given adequate warning, most
printers can arrange for an extra-late page in an appropriate
section.

Saving money

In any area of high cost it is usually possible to economize. In
production, the obvious measures are:

Find a cheaper printer — this depends on whether it is a buyer's
(plenty of spare print capacity) or seller's (shortage of print
capacity) market. To go cheaper may mean lower quality
and service. To print abroad may be a possibility.

Change the process — depending on issue sizes and print runs,
it may be possible to go to a more cost-effective process
(from sheetfed to web, perhaps). Apart from printing cost

Schedule 1 — A weekly magazine using separate typesetters and printers

Standard weekly schedule (based on five sections)

	Cover	Section 1	Section 2	Section 3	Section 4	Section 5
Final copy	9 am Sat	12 noon Mon	11 am Tues	1 pm Tues	2 pm Tues	12 noon Wed
Final page make-up	9 am Sat	3 pm Mon	2pm Tues	4 pm Tues	5 pm Tues	3 pm Wed
Final OK for press	12 noon Mon	6 pm Mon	5 pm Tues	7 pm Tues	11 am Wed	6 pm Wed
Final film to printer	5 pm Mon	6 am Tues	6 pm Tues	6 am Wed	12 noon Wed	7 pm Wed

Covers to bindery	4 pm Wed
Press time final section	8 pm Wed
Binding commences	9.30 pm Wed
Subscription copies mailed by	12 noon Thurs
Copies to wholesalers	12 noon Thurs
Publication day	Saturday

and time, issues to be considered include the relative levels of paper wastage and the cost differences between paper on the reel and in sheet form.

Reduce paper thickness (weight) — thinner paper (of the same grade) costs less per square metre, but opacity will decrease and there may be more show-through.

Change paper type — different papers have different characteristics and prices vary widely. Surfaces have different textures and colouring, which in turn affects fidelity of colour reproduction and opacity.

Reduce editorial colour usage.

Change binding method — saddle stitching is cheaper than perfect binding.

The proportion of paper cost to total cost varies with the number of copies printed. For low print order (low run) magazines the paper cost element is less significant than on high run magazines.

Schedule 2 — A monthly magazine using separate typesetters and printers

Standard monthly production schedule
Working days prior to publication date

	Copy	Page proof	Page OK	Film to printer
Editorial				
Start	47	44	41	37
1st third completed	41	38	35	32
2nd third completed	35	32	29	25
Final third completed	28	25	22	18
Covers completed	35	32	29	25
Advertisements				
First			25	
Final new copy			20	
Supplied positives			18	
Classified film			18	
Final flat-plan			20	
Editorial Cromalins			24 to 15	
Advertisement Cromalins			21 to 16	
Band artwork			35	
Bound inserts			18	
Loose inserts			18	
Sections to printer			14 to 11	
Imposed proofs OK			11 to 9	
Print order / close date			15	
Press date — cover			11	
Press date — text			10 to 8	
Bind commence			7	
Subscription delivery			6	
Wholesalers delivery			5	
Publication date			0	

Notes: Flat-plan is an imposition showing position of advertisements and editorial.
Cromalin is a form of colour proof.
Band refers to a printed band encircling each issue, either promoting the issue or carrying an advertisment.

Monitoring quality and service

There are three things which should be monitored constantly: service, quality and cost.

Service to and from the printer during the production process can be monitored by keeping a simple log of items out and items in. Service in terms of final delivery to the reader can be monitored by having copies delivered to 'plants' as part of the normal circulation. The publisher, editor and sales manager can each have copies posted or delivered to their homes, for example. It's easy to run checks on availability on bookstalls, and so on.

Quality can be checked at each stage of the process and the published issue should be closely examined. Advertisers, quite rightly, are particularly sensitive about colour reproduction or anything which mars the effectiveness of an advertisement.

An assessment of quality is not subjective and for the issue overall there should be an agreed standard (perhaps a specimen issue). For colour, comparison can be made with the proofs supplied, for mono, with original photographs. Type is either crisp, clear and legible or it isn't. The editor's or designer's instructions have either been followed or they haven't.

Costs must be closely controlled. Invoices should be checked meticulously and suppliers should be paid only for work that was necessary and agreed in advance. Printers, for their own convenience, may print an issue in an uneconomic way (machining a 16-page section as two eights, for example) and try to charge accordingly.

The publisher should rightly refuse such a charge and pay for the less costly way.

It is a good idea to carry out a periodic price check. Get other suppliers to submit quotations, just to make sure that costs are in the right ball park. If it's found that the current printer is too expensive, give them a chance to reconsider. Changing printers frequently is not advisable, as the disruption can be considerable and can negate some of the apparent cost saving.

Other print buying
Most production departments also look after the general printing requirements of the magazine. Everything that is printed, in fact, from business cards and letterheads, through order forms, rate cards, brochures, to books, etc. The print and paper buyer can usually get the best price, quality and service.

Advertising production

An activity which is often carried out within the sales department, but sometimes comes under the control of the production manager, is that of advertising production. This involves gathering in material from advertisers, checking, logging and passing it to the origination house or printer, providing the advertiser with proofs where appropriate, ensuring corrections are made, and passing advertising pages for press.

Some production departments prepare the issue flat-plan, placing advertisements and allocating editorial pages. Both the sales manager and the editor are involved in approving the result.

Changing technology and the future

New technologies have been creeping into magazine publishing for several years. At one time feared, but now welcomed, they have resulted in the more efficient and effective use of magazine people, reduced costs, and the introduction of new products.

There are two distinct areas of interests for publishers: using technology to produce existing or new print-on-paper products, and using technology to produce new or existing products in other media. Although the two are very closely entwined, they will be discussed separately here. The first includes DTP (desktop publishing), the editorial system and advertising systems; the second is called electronic publishing.

DTP

A personal computer (pc), DOS or Apple Mac, can be used by journalists to write and sub-edit articles. The articles may then be set as galley or made up into pages on screen with blank areas for illustrations and output through an imagesetter as bromide or film. With slightly more sophisticated equipment, it is possible to scan in graphics, halftones and colour illustrations, to incorporate them on the page, cropping and modifying the images as required, and to output, through an imagesetter, complete colour-separated pages on film.

Personal computers can be networked together so that material can be passed from one journalist to another (writer to sub-editor to layout-sub to editor, and so on). Further links (modems) allow material to be sent from one office to another, and from magazine to typesetter.

A journalist working in Perth can write a story on a pc and send it over a public telephone line to virtually anywhere in the world, without it ever having to be printed out on paper.

A journalist using a pc can connect via the telephone line to any host database system to obtain information stored in it. This might be a database operated by the magazine for which the journalist writes and containing all that magazine's previously published material. It might be a database operated by a commercial database host and containing, for example, the fully-indexed contents of the world's leading newspapers. The range of information stored on such host systems is enormous and is growing at a considerable rate.

The editorial system

An editorial system includes DTP and a lot more besides. It should be tailored to the needs of the magazine and its budget, but typically might consist of a number of personal computers networked together and having common access to a number of services.

Perhaps the most important of the common services would be the magazine's databank containing text from past issues, plus information about the market being served, such as files on people, companies or subjects. If it is stored on a computer system, such information can be updated more easily and accessed very much more easily than by conventional methods. It can greatly improve the quality of information published because the data can be brought easily to hand.

Other common services would be electronic mail communications around the magazine, the company and externally; the editorial diary, a calendar of events, the editorial programme issue-by-issue; a customized thesaurus and customized dictionary and files holding material for coming issues.

Facilities such as facsimile transmission, scanning (optical character recognition or pictures) and indexing should also be part of such a network. Features of the system would be:

Centrally controlled editorial copy management

Text input
    Reporter/writer input with journal/section related
      formatting
    Tabular facilities
    Word and/or line counting
    Split screen functions
    Optical character recognition scanning
    Modem input

Sub-editing and layout
    Full text editing functions
    Hyphenation and justification
    WYSIWYG preview
    Graphics scanning
    Graphics creation and manipulation
    Halftone scanning
    Transparency scanning
    Colour separation
    Proofing devices (laser printers)
    Full page layout (interactive)

Communications
    Access to internal and external Email, external videotex, etc.
    Links to other in-company systems
    Modem links to typesetters/printers

Archiving
    On-line, fully cross-referenced index (index tagging at writ-
    ing and sub-editing stages)
    Off-line storage (magnetic tape or WORM optical discs) of
    all published text
    On-line access to published text and graphics
    On-line access to relevant background material or material
    published in other journals.

Editorial systems are developing quickly and while some of the
facilities mentioned above are not in use widely, often because of cost,
it will not be long before they are.

Other devices which are influencing journalists' work and the way
magazines are produced are cellnet telephones and still-video cameras.
The former mean that a journalist need never be out of touch, but perhaps
more important, that a journalist with a portable computer and portable
telephone can send in written copy with great speed and great ease.

The still-video camera enables a picture to be taken and sent
over a portable or other telephone within minutes and without the
need for any film or chemicals. At the time of writing, still-video
cameras are available but they are unlikely to be widely used until
the process has been refined.

Advertising systems
Many advertisement departments use commercial order processing
and invoicing systems, some of which also incorporate contact re-

ports and records. When an order is entered, the system automatically generates an order acknowledgement and might update a number of files, such as:

- the client file
- the representative's sales record
- the magazine's daily/weekly/monthly sales records
- forward bookings files by issue date

with appropriate details. At the end of the period, summary reports might be produced giving details of orders received classified by a variety of criteria and compared with budgets and targets.

Such a system might automatically call for advertising copy and the receipt and whereabouts of copy could be recorded. A list of those advertisers appearing in a particular issue could be created automatically. More sophisticated systems might also produce flat-plans. After publication, the system could produce invoices automatically and pass the relevant data to the accounts department electronically.

Sales contact reports might be recorded on the system, providing a comprehensive and accessible record of sales activity. Call-back reminders for the salespeople could be generated automatically.

Where telesales is part of the operation, a sales canvassing system is often used. This system is designed to help the canvasser optimize the sale. Customer records are maintained, showing a record of previous advertising and containing the copy for the most recent insertions. Also stored are 'prompt cards' for each classification of advertising the magazine publishes. These prompts come to the screen automatically as the canvasser types in the advertisement details.

For job advertising, there will be a set of questions designed to cover all the points normally contained in a recruitment advertisement — job title, qualifications required, salary, etc. The canvasser uses the prompts to obtain the right information from the advertiser. The prompts also remind the canvasser to ensure legal requirements are met.

Other prompts cover matters such as advertisement size, layout, number of insertions, payment terms, and so on.

The canvasser can type in the copy and set out the advertisement on screen. Some systems sort the advertisements into classifications and the page make-up is largely automatic. After an issue is published, such a system can generate invoices automatically.

Electronic publishing

Electronic publishing (ep) involves the use of electronic devices to capture, edit and disseminate information. It is the use of electronic devices to disseminate the information which distinquishes ep from the conventional form and which has created a wealth of new opportunities for magazine publishers.

Perhaps the first question to ask is: what is it that magazine publishers actually do? Is it putting information on paper, or disseminating information? If it seems to be the former, then the opportunities for development and increased profits are limited; if the latter, then the potential is far greater.

If you accept that publishing is about communicating information to people, why should the means of communication be restricted? If readers want the information in some medium other than print on paper, give it to them. If the magazine already uses computers, then to offer information in other forms is simple.

No one can predict with any certainty how computers and other electronic devices are going to be used in the future, but there are many indications that in some, if not all, fields they will be used widely.

Consider the devices, services and technology which might be utilized by a magazine publisher:

- computers
- CD-ROM discs
- video discs
- facsimile
- modems
- videotex
- TVs
- satellites
- cable TV networks
- public telephones, particularly special line services.

Consider the services which might be offered using one or more of the media:

- price and market information
- legal information
- recipes
- horoscopes
- holiday information
- travel data
- special offers
- sources of supply
- unpublished texts (full versions of published synopses)

- published texts from one or many publications
- tax information
- transactional services (buying and selling)
- situations vacant
- directories
- training material (business)
- instructional 'books' (consumer)
- 'filmed' reports of events, fashion shows, exhibitions, etc.
- specialist computer software.

It is not for this book to tell readers what to do or how to do it, but to suggest that a magazine publisher might well profit from using the technologies which are available.

Transactions then information
'Information follows transactions — if the terminal is being used for transactions then it will be used for information.'

Some magazines have the possibility of multi-media publishing — use of more than one medium to disseminate the same information — while others have the possibility of starting new profit-generating services, such as horoscope telephone lines where the caller pays.

And, of course, new technology can give birth to entirely new products.

Make things happen

As Manfred Lahnstein, executive vice president electronic media, Bertelsmann AG — one of the largest publishing companies in the world — said at an electronic publishing conference:

'Frequently enterprises categorize themselves into the following groups:

Those that wonder what happened,
Those that watch what happens,
Those that make things happen.

'In the face of these alternatives I wish that you and your company always belong to the last group.'

There will be no shortage of information to publish. The growth in magazines is well known, the growth in book publishing is well known, the development of technology is well known.

The rate of growth and development is increasing as well. From inception to stabilization, the telephone took 50 years; the personal computer first appeared in 1978.

The amount of new information produced each year is greater than the total volume of information that existed prior to the First World War (1914-1918).

Forecasters claim that by the year 2000, 60 per cent of the workforce will be engaged in or dependent upon information technology. Electronic information services for professional users alone will by then have a turnover of 50 to 100 billion dollars worldwide.

If you want a slice of that action, make things happen.

Chapter 9

Personnel

There have been many arguments over the role of personnel departments. One school of managers believes 'personnel' is merely a service function and should do as it is told. The other school claims it should have a positive directional role in the conduct of a business.

The truth lies somewhere in between. The best kind of personnel operation encourages the line manager to be part personnel manager, but to seek and listen to advice on all those many grey areas about which most of us know little.

A personnel manager or executive will have information immediately available on all the matters covered in this section, and can often prevent a molehill from turning into a mountain by anticipating potential problems that might not occur to the line manager. But this can happen only if line managers consider personnel people to be part of the team and involve them in discussions affecting the running of a magazine or department.

The message is: if there are personnel people in the company, use them. They have much to offer.

If there is no personnel department, then train yourself in the basics. The simplest way is to get hold of a good book on personnel management, either from a library or a bookseller. ACAS (Advisory, Conciliation and Arbitration Service, an independent statutory body) publishes a number of handbooks and leaflets, including *Employing people – a handbook for small firms*, which are all available free to employers. There are also several commercial loose-leaf and updatable manuals dealing with employment and particularly legislation.

Legislation

The amount of legislation generated over recent years — and there's probably a great deal more to come — cannot be absorbed and understood by any but the expert. There are likely to be in-company policies and procedures which must also be followed. Racial or sexual discrimination, employment protection, disciplinary procedures, safety at work, hours of work, holiday entitlements, sick leave, and so on, all present a nightmare to the manager who doesn't have time to study fine print and appreciate the implications of staff or manager's actions.

Again, advice is available from various external sources for those without a personnel department. ACAS will give free advice and help with many problems, particularly anything which could end up in an industrial tribunal. The PPA also has a legal helpline for members, which includes advice on matters relating to employment law.

Recruitment

The basic steps are:

- determine the need
- prepare a job description
- specify the person required — qualifications, experience, attitudes, interests, etc.
- attract some candidates, e.g. through advertising
- short-list and interview
- take up references
- make an offer
- meet and induct the new employee.

If the company has a personnel department, that can deal with most of the mechanics of recruitment. It can draft advertisements for the line manager's approval, suggest appropriate media in which to advertise, book advertisements, and receive and acknowledge applications.

It is the line manager's very clear responsibility to prepare the job description and decide what kind of person is required, and it is the line manager, perhaps with a lieutenant, who should short-list and interview applicants — taking care to avoid any form of discrimination that is not based solely on ability to do the job.

Interviewers should ensure they are familiar with the company's terms of employment. It is important to give an honest description of the job and its prospects — there's no point in bedazzling recruits with glowing promises which cannot be fulfilled. References must always be taken up, preferably by line managers and over the telephone. Most people are far more open in their opinions in a conversation and there is the opportunity to do a little probing.

Letters of appointment should de drafted by the personnel department if there is one, for they are legal documents and must be correct. If not signed by the line manager, that person should send an accompanying note of welcome. Unsuccessful applicants should be given the courtesy of a response as soon as possible.

Investor in People

To be recognized as an Investor in People an employing organization must measure up to a national standard which determines its attitudes to training and development. Recognition brings a number of benefits. Internally, it encourages managers and employees to take the right attitude to training and development. Externally, it serves as a quality standard and indicates to potential employees that a company is a good place for training. Ultimately, it is said, the better trained employees produce better work and staff turnover is reduced.

To gain recognition an organization must submit to a training and development audit carried out by one of the Training and Enterprise Councils (TECs) (Local Enterprise Companies, LECs, in Scotland).

The standard states that an Investor in People
- *makes a public commitment from the top to develop all employees to achieve its business objectives*
- *regularly reviews the training and development needs of all employees*
- *takes action to train and develop individuals on recruitment and throughout their employment*
- *evaluates the investment in training and development to assess achievement and improve future effectiveness.*

When new recruits start, it is vital to ensure they receive all the information and initial training necessary to make them effective quickly. Not only is this good business sense, but it makes the new employee feel comfortable in their new environment and satisfied with the decision they have made. It is not unknown for the investment in recruitment — time and money — to be wasted when a new employee leaves after a few days or hours because no one seemed to care or notice that they had arrived.

Salaries

In larger companies, salaries are usually administered by some arm of personnel, but where there is freedom of movement it should be the line manager's responsibility to fix individual salary levels. Any commission, bonus or other incentive scheme is also the line manager's responsibility. These should be very carefully evaluated to ensure they contain no pitfalls — for example, a bonus based on volume might encourage space selling at uneconomically low rates to achieve targets.

Personnel staff can provide the manager or individual with information about pensions and any other rights or benefits to which an individual employee is entitled. They may also be able to provide information about market rates for salaries and what is being paid elsewhere in the same company.

Staff records

All documents relating to individual staff should be kept in a single file, including copies of any reports, appraisals or assessments. If there is no personnel department, the confidentiality of such files must be ensured. Always remember that an employee is entitled to see what is in their own file, including any data held on a computer.

Appraisal and assessment

It is fairly common now for members of staff (including line managers) to be appraised and assessed at regular intervals of no longer than a year.

This is an essential and effective technique for determining and influencing an individual's level of job performance and job satisfaction. The purpose of the procedure is to discuss with the individual their performance against the standards and objectives set in their job description, to review results and highlight key areas of performance, to examine strengths and weaknesses, to identify training needs and areas for personal improvement, and to set objectives for the ensuing period.

An appraisal meeting is between an individual and the immediate line manager. The individual is expected to participate fully in the conversation and to discuss any problems there may be, or ways in which the job may be performed better. It's an opportunity for straight talking and honesty. It's also an opportunity to identify any shortcomings on the part of the individual and to institute change or training to improve the situation.

Should it be that the individual is failing to meet an agreed standard despite training and encouragement, then it may be that the appraisal discussion constitutes part of the disciplinary procedure and that warnings are given.

At each appraisal meeting, objectives for the ensuing period should be set, together with any training which may be required. The training may be for the present job or may prepare the individual for promotion. The substance and conclusions of the meeting are written in an appraisal document which is signed by the manager and the individual. The document is filed in the individual's personal file. If this is held by a personnel department, they will be in an excellent position to monitor the appraisal process and to remind line managers of their responsibilities.

Appraisals are not easy to institute or carry through. It is a testing time for the manager and the individual and so must not be treated in a cavalier fashion. The future career of an individual and, perhaps, the well-being of a magazine depend on the outcome.

The manager and the individual must prepare for the meeting. When an appointment has been fixed it shouldn't be broken, and plenty of time should be allowed. It is often better not to have any following appointments so that the meeting can run its full course.

The individual should come from the meeting knowing exactly what the manager thinks of them, and what is expected of them and by when.

If you are inexperienced in the techniques of appraisal, it may be a good idea to find out what courses are available.

Training

Where there is a personnel department, one of its major activities will be to organize and monitor training activities within the company. Following the appraisal procedure, the line manager should decide, in consultation with the training officer (if there is one), exactly which training course is appropriate for each individual. The training officer should then make the necessary arrangements.

As far as the trainee is concerned, the moving force should be the line manager. The latter tells the member of staff of the training arrangement (the need having been jointly identified in the appraisal and assessment procedure, as noted above), ensures that he or she is free to attend, and receives any feedback as part of the appraisal procedure. Some companies run in-house training courses, while others will have to rely on external training providers. Lists of publishing-oriented courses and training providers are available from the PTC.

Training courses are not the only solution to training needs, and very often it will be more appropriate to give 'on-the-job' training through one-to-one coaching. This would be arranged, supervised and assessed by the line manager.

Of course, all training must be appropriate to the training need.

National Vocational Qualifications

A National Vocational Qualification (NVQ) is, simply, a proof of competence — the holder not only has the skill and knowledge to do a job, but has actually done it to standards set by publishing professionals.

The system was born out of demands from a government working party in 1986 for a sensible, national training policy, based on qualifications that guaranteed basic competence for employment. NVQs are carefully drawn up sets of standards which describe accurately what a competent person (journalist, salesperson, production clerk, etc.) has to be able to do, and so what they must be trained to do, and against which they can be objectively assessed. When an individual achieves the NVQ standards and receives the qualification, it is proof that they are competent and also a validation that the training they have been given has worked.

The first NVQs in magazine publishing were introduced in 1992.

Health and safety

Although an office environment may seem considerably safer than a factory or building site, office workers run many risks and UK legislation is beginning to recognize these in more detail. For publishing companies, a main concern will be the new *Directive on working with display screen equipment*, which is of particular relevance to editorial staff using page make-up systems, as well as to other computer-intensive areas, such as accounts or order processing.

If there is a personnel department, it will provide advice and guidance, but line managers must realize that the law makes them personally responsible for the safety of their own staff, as well as of any visitors or contractors working in their offices.

Disciplinary matters

It is vitally important that the company's disciplinary procedures are followed to the letter. On the one hand, it is fair to the company and fair to the individual if procedures are followed, and on the other, it can avoid any unpleasant aftermath involving the courts. If there are no procedures, you will have to re-invent the wheel each time there is a problem, and you could well end up with a claim for unfair dismissal. ACAS has a helpful book, *Discipline at work*, which includes guidance on handling different problems and guide-line procedures to follow.

Where there is a personnel department, the line manager should use it as a kind of 'people consultancy' in all matters relating to disciplinary proceedings. It is a good idea to invite someone from personnel to sit in on formal disciplinary hearings to take notes and advise on procedure. This is particularly important if the employee is a member of a recognized trades union, as they will probably ask to be represented by a union official.

Job descriptions

Here is a selection of job descriptions culled from a number of sources, heavily sub-edited to obscure their origins, but otherwise unchanged. While these are typical of some of the many hundreds of job descriptions which exist, they are not typical of all.

Some companies produce a series of 'model' descriptions which are used for all similar posts in the company; others give considerable freedom to individual directors/publishers to use an appropriate style.

The purpose of job descriptions (or, as they are now sometimes called, 'job objectives') is to ensure that the incumbent and the company are agreed on:

- the line of command (superior and subordinate)
- what is expected of the incumbent
- the precise areas of responsibility
- working relationships
- targets/objectives
- performance criteria.

They can be used in assessing the worth of a job, in evaluating the performance of an individual, in defining training needs, in disciplinary proceedings, legal disputes and so on. They should be taken seriously and all members of staff should have one, so that there can be no arguments about an individual's responsibilities and duties.

There can be a sting in the tail: some people believe the job description defines both the minimum and maximum expected of the employee. It is an unfortunate belief, and may stem from a poorly worded description or the way in which it is presented to the individual concerned. Most managers expect that most staff will do that little bit more than the job description demands — indeed, that is what makes the individual stand out from the crowd. There is nothing more frustrating than hearing an otherwise valuable member of staff say, 'It isn't in my job description' — ergo 'I'm not going to do what you ask'.

If you decide to use these job descriptions as models for your magazine, then the companies which provided them will be flattered, but it might be better to write your own. You need to analyse your line management structure, identify the ideal responsibilities of the various levels of management, and take into account the abilities of the incumbents, the objectives for each magazine and the magazine's staffing.

Whatever the approach, consultation and agreement with the jobholder are vital. A side benefit can be the identification of training needs.

The other point to remember is that a job description should not be cast in stone. As an individual is trained and develops, the job description can be varied to reflect increased responsibility. And if you do decide to give someone increased responsibility, don't forget to update the job description.

Job title: Publisher

Basic function:
> To ensure optimum performance in all areas of the assigned publication/s and ancillary activity/ies.

Major responsibilities:

1. Prepares profit plan for each magazine and its ancillary activity/ies for agreement with the managing director:
> Studies current and future trends in the readership.
> Studies current and future trends among existing and potential advertisers.
> Constructs with editor and advertisement manager an annual editorial programme.
> Prepares advertisement paging forecast with advertisement manager.

Agrees annual ad/ed ratio.

Plans circulation and advertisement promotion.

Agrees projected print order and circulation sales and/or controlled circulation forecasts with Sales and Distribution.

2. Monitors the performance of each journal and directs policies to meet or exceed the profit plan contribution targets:

Carries out continual review of both the circulation and space sales programmes, and ensures that every opportunity created by the editorial content, publication's influence and circulation are fully exploited.

Ensures that sales results are monitored against plan, and against performance of opposition publications, and that all sales staff are adequately supported with market information and advertisement promotion material.

Carries out a continual review of editorial policy to ensure that it is properly geared to the changing needs of the industry/ies it serves.

Monitors editorial, advertisement, production, promotion and distribution costs against budget and previous years, taking corrective action when appropriate.

Prepares reports as required for his/her managing director on market prospects, editorial and advertisement plans, projected revenue and profit contribution for at least three months ahead.

Establishes and maintains personal contact with key people in the industry/ies served by his/her journal/s.

3. Innovates:

Encourages innovations at all levels, and reports to the managing director on all new business projects put forward.

Conceives and develops profitable ideas for his/her existing publication/s; new mainstream and spin-off publications; and other profit-generating activities (for example, exhibitions, conferences, seminars, package tours, direct mail, merchandising, books, reprints).

Receives ideas for new projects from the managing director, evaluates them or leads working groups to investigate them as required.

4. Controls the editorial and sales teams:

Ensures editor/s and advertisement manager/s, and any

other staff reporting to him/her, have written job descriptions and action programmes and are fully aware of their responsibilities, and that they in turn provide clear job descriptions for their staff.

Directs the editorial and sales staff structures, and ensures that manning levels are sufficient in quality and quantity to meet company and magazine objectives.

Monitors the performance of each member of his/her staff, either directly or through delegation, ensures that staff are properly trained and developed, advises on individual career potential, and recommends patterns of career development.

Formally reviews the performance of each member of his/her staff at least annually, either directly or through delegation and maintains written records of such reviews.

Makes recommendations regarding levels of salary and salary increases.

Recruits staff as necessary.

Ensures, within existing limitations, satisfactory working conditions for, and relationships with, all staff members.

Administers his/her staff in accordance with the rules and guide-lines laid down by the company.

Holds a quarterly meeting for each magazine, involving all its staff and appropriate senior management.

5. Undertakes special assignments as required by the managing director.

6. Reports on progress in all above areas to the managing director on at least a monthly basis.

7. Working relationships:
    Line — Reports to managing director. Directly supervises editor/s and advertisement manager/s.
    Other — Works closely with other publishers and directors.

8. Performance criteria:
    Profitability of publications assigned to him/her, measured against agreed revenue forecasts, control of costs, growth or retraction of market sectors concerned, and any other relevant influences outside his/her control.
    Ability to identify and generate new sources of revenue/profit.
    Improvement of performance of editor/s and advertise-

ment manager/s and others reporting to him/her.
Level of morale, communication and co-operative spirit
among staff under his/her control.
Assistance given to managing director.

Job title: Editor

Responsible to: Publisher

Responsible for:
Assisting in the development of an agreed editorial policy for the
magazine and thereafter to implement the editorial policy.
Recruiting, motivating and disciplining the editorial staff, communicating with them on all aspects of policy, supervising
their work, encouraging them to be innovative, responsible
and involved so that
(a) they produce the highest possible quality of work and
(b) they achieve maximum job satisfaction.
Preparing an editorial plan and budget based on advertisement
paging forecasts and thereafter ensuring costs conform to
the budget provisions.
Meeting production deadlines.
Liaising with advertising, marketing, circulation, production and
publicity departments. Liaising with clients and agencies and
helping to promote the magazine more aggressively.
Working in close partnership with the publisher to promote and
enhance the magazine in every way and make media/pub-
lic appearances to promote the title.
Developing ideas for profitable supplements and special publications.
Monitoring current events so that changes of mood, needs,
tastes, etc. may be reflected in the magazine. Searching for
new writers, illustrators and photographers and motivating
them to produce high-quality work.
Monitoring the content of competitive magazines.
Through contacts with readers and others, monitoring the
progress of the magazine, and, when necessary, proposing
changes in policy.
Staff training generally to NVQ standards and, in particular,
training the deputy editor and other senior staff to run the
magazine in your absence.

Your achievement will be measured by:
> The success of the magazine in terms of circulation, readership, profit and standing.

Personal goals:
> To make your magazine the best magazine in its field, with a strong brand image.
> To be involved in planning new magazines.
> To have more involvement in the operation of the company generally.

Job title: Advertisement sales manager

Responsible to: Publisher

Responsible for: Deputy sales manager, four sales executives and secretary

Responsibilities:
> Assisting the publisher with the planning and implementation of the annual budgets.
> Assisting the publisher in seeking additional profit opportunities.
> Advising the publisher of possible changes of editorial policy which could attract more, or different types, of advertising and promotions revenue and improve profits.
> Advising the publisher on new market trends and new research which might affect the magazine's particular market.
> Advising the publisher of any conflict between editorial and advertisement or circulation policies.
> Planning and implementation of the advertisement sales policies.
> Overall supervision of the advertisement staff. Working closely with immediate subordinates to ensure that the maximum efforts are directed to selling.
> Keeping in close and regular contact with senior executives in advertising agencies and clients to ensure that the overall editorial policies of the magazine are fully understood — and that they are fully acquainted with our latest sales information.
> Allocating the agreed space for house advertisements.
> Advising and supervising the giving of credits to advertis-

ers when the standards of reproduction have caused a complaint.

Ensuring that the make-up of the magazine is the most economic and effective.

Ensuring that the advertisements in the magazine are positioned according to the requirements of the advertisers and to the satisfaction of the editorial department.

Following the editorial/advertisement ratios advised by the publisher.

Keeping to advertisement production schedules.

Responsible directly for advertisement and miscellaneous revenue.

Liaising with the publisher for all costs shown on budgets for advertisement salaries, advertisement expenses, advertisement promotion costs, expenses and accommodation, if necessary reversing unfavourable budget variances on all these costs.

In the absence of the publisher, the signing of expenses for advertisement department.

Appraisal and training of staff for whom you are directly responsible.

Advising marketing department on market research required in conjunction with the publisher.

Providing accounts and production departments with regular monthly forecasts.

Advising the publisher when staff should be replaced and when additional staff or salary increases are required.

Ensuring the performance of regional offices measures up to the target set.

Success measured by:

The total advertisement/miscellaneous revenue on the magazine.

Favourable variances compared to budgets on revenue or costs for which you are directly responsible.

How good the overall liaison is with the advertisement/editorial/production teams.

Limitations:

The following should be referred to the publisher:

Employing additional staff.

Firing staff.

Salary increases.

Personal goals:
1. To achieve final advertisement revenue figures greater than budgets.
2. To achieve additional sources of revenue for the magazine.
3. To maintain good liaison between staff of all departments of the magazine.
4. To improve the overall performance of the advertisement sales team.

Job title: Circulation sales manager (newstrade)

Responsibility:
For managing the wholesale/newsagent sales of all the company's paid-for titles.
For maintaining and developing the effectiveness of the circulation sales force.
In conjunction with appropriate management, for implementing newsagent sales strategies and development plans.

Reporting:
To the director of circulation.

Functional relationships:
Commercial director
Subscription promotions manager
Controlled circulation manager
Circulation field sales manager
Publishers
Advertisement managers.

Key tasks:
1. To ensure territory responsibilities are maintained and developed.
2. To ensure objectives set at appraisal stage are achieved.
3. To establish new lines of responsibility for special tasks with the current sales force and improve office reporting procedures.
4. To identify and develop special promotions with newsagent multiples and to negotiate the same.
5. To assist publishers to achieve targeted readership audience in the most cost-effective manner.

6. To organize exhibition supplies and improve exhibition sales performance. Also to work closely with subscription department to ensure best possible circulation performance at outside events.
7. To manage within agreed budgets the circulation newsagent sales environment.
8. To constantly seek new opportunities for business development and to construct a comprehensive information database on opposition/competitor activities.
9. To produce reports as required by director of circulation by the agreed deadlines.
10. To assist the director of circulation in developing circulation plans for new products and acquisitions.
11. Other ad hoc tasks as instructed.

Job title: Controlled circulation manager

Reporting to: Publisher

Responsible for:
Maintaining the magazine's controlled circulation lists in accordance with the magazine's objectives.
Building and maintaining lists of prospective readers.
Initiating and overseeing circulation promotions to achieve reader registration targets.
Ensuring that labels and associated data are produced in good time for the despatch of each issue.
Monitoring the handling of reader service enquiries to ensure that turn-round times are achieved and that data is processed correctly.
Preparing reports on registered readers, promotions, reader enquiries, as required.
Liaises with:
Editor
Advertisement manager
Circulation department manager
Reader service department manager
Marketing executive
Production manager
Printer
External suppliers of mailing services.

Job title: Marketing manager

Reporting to: Publisher

Co-operation with:

Magazine editors

Advertisement managers

Group marketing department

Financial planner.

Main purpose of job:

To be responsible to the publisher for the provision of a marketing, planning, research and promotion service to the group. To evaluate, research and plan new product launches.

Nature and scope of job:

The role of the marketing manager will be to assist the publisher to develop the necessary strategies and tactics in all areas of the group to ensure its continued success and profitability.

The immediate priorities of this role are as follows:

To work with the appointed creative resources to produce a marketing platform and ensure its use in all forms of promotion above and below the line.

To provide guidance and support to display and classified sales teams in positioning the magazine, including development and interpretation of research as required.

To work with PR resources.

To work with the group circulation department in implementing the agreed tactics for both subscriptions and trade promotion.

To co-ordinate with the marketing department market research.

To organize greater reader involvement/value through editorial surveys and reader clubs, etc.

To work with the publisher in reseaching and evaluating new product development plans to extend the magazine's market position.

To assess the potential for European publishing.

To be part of the group senior management team responsible for all pre-launch planning for new projects, including working with the publishing director/publisher in the development of: sales and marketing strategy, circulation promotion strategy, editorial product plan, financial targets, production plan, personnel requirements.

Useful sources of information

Readers and readership

Several studies provide information about the effectiveness of magazines, copies of which may be obtained from PPA:

Media values
In 1992, Research Services Ltd set out to establish how magazine reading compares with other media consumption, and how magazines meet the needs and interests of their readers. Comparisons with the Media Involvement Study of 1983 show that the media explosion of the past decade has not eroded readers' close relationship with their magazines. The study provides qualitative information detailing consumer attitudes to various media and various types of magazine.

The complete relationship
In 1991, the British Market Research Bureau used the TGI database to explore the attributes of women's monthly magazines and the ways in which readers relate to their titles. The results provide comparative quality of reading data across all major women's titles. This qualitative readership information was combined with TGI product usage information to produce a database for media planning and buying purposes.

The media multiplier
In 1991, the International Federation of the Periodical Press (FIPP) published the findings of research covering over 100 advertising campaigns which demonstrated that the combination of print and television has a multiplying effect on communication effectiveness. The studies also confirmed that a mixed schedule using both print and television delivers better coverage and frequency against a target audience

than does a schedule using television alone. This media synergy was validated by market-place studies which demonstrated actual sales increases.

People love their magazines

In 1989, advertising agency WCRS MM examined 33 pieces of independent and sector research into magazine readership. The survey concluded that 'research into business and consumer publications indicates that magazines have a very close relationship with their readers'.

Business magazines readership

Some data sources (sponsor's name in brackets):

Agriculture

Agridata - Taylor Nelson 1991 (joint)

Farm Advisers' Readership Survey 1989 (Reed)

Aviation

Aviation Readership Research - TNA 1988 (Reed)

Building

CCMI/Building Centre Readership Survey 1991 (INDAL Omnibus)

National Architects Survey 1989 (Morgan-Grampian)

Catering

MIL Catering Industry Survey 1988 (Reed)

Mass Observation Commercial Catering Readership Survey 1991 (Morgan-Grampian)

Taylor Nelson Catering Industry Survey 1987 (Reed)

Computing

Banner Readership Survey 1991 (syndicated)

MIL Computer Market Survey 1989 (Reed)

Construction

Mass Observation 1990 (Morgan-Grampian)

Design engineering

EIRS/Mass Observation 1986 (Morgan-Grampian)

Electronics

INDAL Electronics Market Survey 1989 (Reed)

RSGB 1989 (Morgan-Grampian)

Farm trade

Farm Trade Readership Survey 1990 (Morgan-Grampian)

Finance

Insurance Monitor 1989 (joint)

Taylor Nelson Survey 1988 (joint)

Food manufacture
Eurofood Readersp Survey 1988 (Morgan-Grampian)
General business
Business Media Research Committee 1990 (joint)
Grocery
MIL Grocery Market Survey 1989 (Reed)
Laboratories
British Lab Week Survey 1988 (Morgan-Grampian and
Chemistry in Britain)
Medical
JICMARS twice yearly (joint)
Motor trade
Motor Show Survey/NOP 1990 (Morgan-Grampian)
Personnel
Personnel & Training Market Readership Survey 1988
(Reed)
Process and control
IPEE/Promecon Readership Survey 1987 (Morgan-Grampian)
Road transport
MIL Key Points 1989 (Reed)
MIL Road Transport Survey 1991 (Reed)
Social services
National Readership Survey of Social Workers 1986 (Reed)
Travel
MORI Omnibus 1991 (MORI Omnibus)
TATR 1989 (joint)

Useful addresses

Advertising Association
   15 Wilton Road, London SW1V 1NJ. 071-828 2771.
Advertising Standards Authority
   Brook House, Torrington Place, London WC1. 071-580 5555.
Association of Market Survey Organisations
   Millward Brown, Ince House, 60 Kenilworth Road,
   Leamington Spa, Warwicks CV32 6JY.
Audit Bureau of Circulations
   207-209 High Street, Berkhamsted, Herts HP4 1AD. 0442
   870800. (Non-profit company which certifies circulation

statistics based on professional auditors' reports. To be eligible as a member of ABC, publications must accept advertising.)

British Association of Picture Libraries
13 Woodberry Crescent, London N10 1PJ. 081-444 7913.

British Copyright Council
29-33 Berners Street, London W1P 4AA. 071-580 5544.

British Direct Marketing Association
Grosvenor Gardens House, Grosvenor Gardens, London SW1W 0BS. 071-630 7322.

British Printing Industries Federation (BPIF)
11 Bedford Row, London WC11 4DX. 071-242 6904.

British Rate & Data (BRAD)
1a Chalk Lane, Cockfosters, London EN4 0BU. 081-441 6644. (A monthly magazine listing all UK publications which carry advertising. Essentially it gives information of interest to advertisers.)

Copyright Receipt Office
2 Sheraton Street, London W1V 4BH. 071-323 7039. (Publishers fulfil their legal obligations to the British Library by sending one copy of each publication within one month of publication. The copyright legal deposit libraries are at Oxford, Cambridge, National Library of Scotland, National Library of Wales and Dublin. Send five copies of each publication to A.T. Smail, 100 Euston Street, London NW1 2HQ. 071-388 5061).

Current British Journals
British Library Document Supply Centre, Boston Spa, Wetherby, West Yorks IS23 7BQ. 0937 843434. (Holds details of approximately 10 000 journals).

Data Protection Registrar
Springfield House, Water Lane, Wilmslow, Cheshire SK9 5AX. 0625 535777.

Department of Trade & Industry, Business Monitor
1-19 Victoria Street, London SW1. 071-215 7877.

Information Industry Association
555 New Jersey Avenue NW, Suite 800, Washington, DC 20001, USA.

Institute of Journalists
2 Dock Offices, Surrey Quay, Lower Road, London SE16 2XD. 071-252 1187.

Institute of Practitioners in Advertising (IPA)
44 Belgrave Square, London SW1X 8QS. 071-235 7020.

International Federation of the Periodical Press (FIPP)
5 St Matthew Street, London SW1P 2JT. 071-873 8158.

JICNARS (Joint Industry Committee for National Readership
Surveys)
44 Belgrave Square, London SW1X 8QS. 071-235 7020.

National Readership Surveys Ltd (NRS)
11-15 Betterton Street, Covent Garden, London WC2H 9BP.
071-379 0344.

Market Research Society
15 Northburgh Street, London EC1V 0AH. 071-490 4911.

Media Expenditure Analysis Ltd (MEAL)
31-39 South Street, Reading, Berkshire RG1 4QU. 0734
585626.

Media Monitoring Services Ltd (MMS)
Madison House, High Street, Sunninghill, Ascot, Berkshire
SL5 9NP. 0990 27553.

National Federation of Retail Newsagents
Yeoman House, Sekforde Street, London EC1R 0HD. 071-
253 4225.

National Union of Journalists
314 Gray's Inn Road, London WC1. 071-278 7916.

Periodical Publishers Association (PPA)
Imperial House, 15-19 Kingsway, London WC2B 6UN. 071-
379 6268. (The trade association for magazine publishing
companies. Can provide circulation statistics, production
information, advertising guidelines, postal information, to
bona fide enquirers. *PPA review* available on request.)

Periodicals Training Council (PTC)
Imperial House, 15-19 Kingsway, London WC2B 6UN. 071-
836 8798.

Pira
Randalls Road, Leatherhead, Surrey KT22 7RU. 0372
376161. (Independent centre for research, consulting, training and information services for the paper, packaging,
printing and publishing industries. Extensive library facilities, normally limited to members.)

Press Research Council (PRC)
34 Southwark Bridge, London W1A 1AQ. 071-928 6928.

Publishers Association
19 Bedford Square, London WC1B 3HJ. 071-580 6321.
Symbol Services
The Baltic Centre, Great West Road, Brentford, Middx TW8
9BU. 081-847 4121. (Commercial suppliers of bar codes.)
UK National Serials Data Centre
2 Sheraton Street, London W1V 4BH. 071-323 7039. (Free
service supplying ISSNs. Send description and photocopy
of contents page.)
Willings Press Guide
Reed Information Services Ltd, Windsor Court, East Grinstead House, East Grinstead, West Sussex RH19 1XA. 0342
326972. (Annual guide to the press of the UK. Includes free
listing of periodicals with details of publisher, editorial and
advertising offices, plus price, frequency, circulation, key
personnel, editorial content, advertising rates, agency commission, mechanical data, target audience.)

Valuable information on methods of training sales staff can be found
in the PTC publication *Training guidelines for advertisement sales
managers.*

Glossary

acetate Thin, flexible sheet of transparent plastic used to make overlays for artwork.

achromatic colour Expressed as simply as possible, four-colour printing where the complementary element of tertiary colours is replaced with black. (This is effected when the colour separations are made, and so the actual printing process is unchanged.) The risk of colour contamination is reduced and colour fidelity is more accurate. The process uses less coloured ink but more black. Also known as polychromatic colour removal, complementary colour removal, integrated colour removal and programmed ink reduction. See *colour correction* and *undercolour removal*.

against the grain At right angles to the grain of the paper. Generally web presses print pages with the grain running from the top to the bottom of the page, or in an upright position when viewed from the end of the press. The alternative is a short grain press where pages are printed against the grain or 'sideways'. On such presses modifications allow pages to be planned across the cylinder to give greater flexibility in product format and page length. The grain runs across the width of the page.

airbrush Compressed-air device to spray mist of ink to create illustrations and retouch photos.

American Standard Code for Information Interchange ASCII A code which assigns a binary number to each alphanumeric character and the non-printing characters used to control printers and communications devices. Used to interface computers and peripherals. Pronounced 'asskey'.

analogue Representation by physical entities or measurements — provides signals of continuously variable frequency or intensity. Compared with digital, which provides 'on' or 'off' information, it provides information as 'more' or 'less'. A conventional clock face with hands is an analogue display.

area composition Pages are made up in sections or areas — thus, a particular story is made up into the shape available away from the page and is dropped into place when completed. The technique can reduce the time taken to complete a page as a number of people may work on it at once.

artificial intelligence Application of reasoning to computer systems to develop techniques akin to human intelligence in amassing and applying knowledge, particularly for problem solving.

ASA American Standards Association. Measure of photographic film speed. See *ISO*.

ascender Portion of a lower case letter rising above its x-height.

ASCII See *American Standard Code for Information Interchange*.

author's corrections The changes made to typeset material, e.g. on the galleys or page proofs, usually incurring extra composition charges.

author's proof A proof sent to the author for approval.

back-up copy Duplicate of original data, software, or printout made in case original is lost or damaged.

banner A main headline across the top of a page.

bar code Machine-readable International Standard Serial Number (ISSN) placed on the cover of a magazine for marketing and stock identification purposes.

baseline Imaginary rule under a line

of type touching the bottom of each character. As the name implies, tails of characters with a descender (g,q,y) go below the baseline.

baud Measure of signalling rate, usually bits transmitted per second, from one digital device (computer, modem) to another. A tenth of the baud figure equates approximately to the number of characters per second (cps); therefore, 300 baud would be equivalent to 30 cps and 1200 baud to 120 cps.

bibliographic database Database containing attributes of information about an item or source of information.

billion One thousand million (10^9).

binary number The form of notation used in computers, it is a system which has only two different digits, 0 or 1. Reading right to left, the first column represents 1, the second 2, the third 4, the fourth 8 and so on. The maximum decimal system value of a binary number of ten columns (with values of 1 to 512) is 1023. 0001 = 1, 0010 = 2, 0011 = 3, 0100 = 4, 1111 = 15.

bind To put sheets in order and secure them together.

bindery Department or separate business that carries out trimming, folding, and binding.

bit Contraction of a 'binary digit'; it is the smallest item of information a computer will recognize. A bit is always 0 or 1. A group of bits — usually eight — is a byte.

bit-map graphics Control of individual pixels on a printer or display screen to produce graphic elements of superior resolution, permitting accurate reproduction of arcs, circles or other curved images.

blanket Flexible rubber sheet wrapped around the blanket cylinder on an offset printing press. It receives the ink image from the printing plates and 'offsets' it on to the paper.

bleed/bled off Printing that extends to the edge of a sheet or page after trimming.

body copy The bulk of a story, not its headline or sub-heads.

bold Heavy or emboldened type.

bromide Photosensitive paper used in phototypesetters and imagesetters

to produce high-resolution positive images. Bromide is used in other devices to produce photoprints (PMT machines).

browser bar Display rack or counter of magazines and newspapers where potential purchasers may browse through the publications before buying.

bullet Bold dot used for typographic emphasis and often used in place of numerals in a list.

buster A headline which has too many letters for the specified measure.

by-line Writer's name or title at the head or foot of story.

byte Group of eight bits representing one letter, numeral, or other character in a computer memory. Pronounced 'bite', abbreviation 'b'.

calendered Paper which is smoothed by heated rollers (calenders).

camera-ready copy Mechanicals, photographs, and artwork fully prepared for printing.

cap height Height of the capital letters of a typeface, expressed in points. Usually about 2/3 of the type size.

caption Identifying or descriptive text accompanying a photograph or other visual element.

cast off Calculation of the space that copy will fill in a given type size.

catch-line A temporary heading on manuscripts or proofs for identification.

CCITT Comité Consultatif International Téléphonique et Télégraphique. Worldwide representative body of PTTs and telecommunications organizations.

CD-I Compact Disc Interactive. A CD containing computer data, audio and video, where the choice of what is displayed or played is controlled by the user.

CD-ROM Compact Disc Read Only Medium (or Memory). CD-ROM is part of a system for the storage and retrieval of data. Consists of a compact disc for information storage, a disc drive for information retrieval, and a computer for the application software and information display. CD-ROM is essentially the same as that originally designed for audio playback of music recorded digitally.

Ceefax UK teletext service operated by the BBC.

centre marks Lines of a mechanical, negative, printing plate, or press sheet indicating the centre of a page or press sheet.

centre spread Middle two pages of a centre-stitched (saddle-stitched) magazine.

character Any letter, numeral, symbol, punctuation mark, or space between words.

character count Total number of letters, numerals, punctuation marks, and symbols plus word spaces in a given width or length (pica, inch, cm., line, column, page or article).

chip Integrated circuit in which all the components are miniaturized and etched on a tiny piece of silicon or similar material.

Cicero A European unit of typographical measurement of 12 Didot points. See *em, en, Didot, pica* and *point.*

classified advertisements Small, semi-display or display advertisements which appear in classified order, e.g. cars, jobs, property.

clicker Foreman compositor.

clip art Copyright-free drawings on paper or stored on disc which can be used to produce finished artwork.

coated paper Paper given a coating of kaolin or other substance in order to give a smooth gloss finish suitable for high-quality printing.

col. cm. See *column centimetre.*

cold set Applied to a web-offset printing where the press has no dryer unit. Uses absorbent papers such as newsprint on which ink dries quickly.

collate To assemble sheets of paper into correct sequence.

colour correction Adjustment made to the values of colour separations to compensate for deficiencies in dyes and pigments of originals, filters, and printing inks used in colour reproduction and printing. See *achromatic colour* and *colour separation.*

colour matching system System of numbered samples showing how coloured inks print. Helps designers choose and specify colours.

colour separation Method by which the four process colours used in printing are separated from a colour original to produce cyan, magenta, yellow, and black films or plates. See *achromatic colour* and *colour correction.*

column centimetre A unit one column wide by one centimetre deep, used when referring to the size of a classified advertisement. Column widths vary according to the design style of a magazine.

column inch A unit one column wide by one inch deep.

column rule Thin vertical line that separates columns.

composite negative or photo Negative or photo made by combining two or more images.

composition The arrangement of various characters into galleys or pages of type to the required style.

compositor (comp) Person at a typesetters who sets copy and makes it up into pages.

computer graphics Charts, maps, and other pictorial representations generated by software.

condensed type Style of type in which characters are narrow in proportion to their height.

contact print Photographic print made by exposing negative directly on to paper, thus the image is the same size as on the negative.

continuous tone An illustration or photographic print where tones are continuous, i.e. not broken down into halftone dots. Such an illustration cannot be printed until it is converted to halftone.

contrast Gradation in tone between lightest white and darkest black in continuous tone material or the abrupt change between light and dark.

copy In editing and typesetting, all written material. In graphic design and printing, everything to be printed: art, photographs and graphics, as well as typematter.

copy preparation In typesetting, marking up a manuscript and specifying type. In paste-up and printing, assembling the final camera-ready material and giving instructions to ensure proper placement, printing, and finishing.

copyedit To check and correct a manuscript for spelling, grammar, punctuation, inconsistencies, inaccuracies, and style.

copyfit To edit copy and adjust type specifications so that the type fits the space allotted.

copyright Ownership of a creative work, usually held by the writer, photographer, or artist or by their employer.

copyright notice The symbol ©, name of copyright holder and date of publication which must appear in published material to secure protection under the Universal Copyright Convention.

copywriter Person who writes copy for advertising.

corner marks Lines on artwork, a mechanical, negative, plate, or press sheet showing the edges of a page or finished piece.

cps Characters per second.

crop To remove portions of an image from the side, top or bottom.

crop marks Lines near the edges of an image or area showing portions to be eliminated. See *trim marks.*

cross grain See *against the grain.*

crosshead Small heading between paragraphs in the text. See *sidehead.*

cursor Marker such as small block or line on a computer screen indicating the position at which the next keystroke will be placed.

cut Delete, from copy or type.

cut-out A halftone, monochrome or colour, with the background removed or 'cut out' around the main subject.

daisy wheel Print head shaped like a wheel with many spokes, with a letter, numeral or symbol at the end of each spoke.

database Collection of information organized in records and fields and stored on a computer disc or tape.

data compression Reduction of file size by removing repetitions and other data which can be reconstructed.

data conversion To convert digital information from one method of coding or storage to another.

default Action that computer program automatically performs unless instructed otherwise by operator.

delete To cut word or words from copy or proofs.

densitometer Instrument to measure light reflecting from or transmitted through copy. Used to ensure proper exposure for halftones and measure density of ink on paper.

density range Difference between darkest and lightest areas of copy.

density Relative darkness of copy, ink on paper, or emulsion on film, as measured by a densitometer.

descender Portion of a lower case letter falling below its baseline.

desktop publishing Process of writing, drawing, manipulating, and laying out type, graphics, and other visual elements using a personal computer, then printing out the assembled pages using a laser printer or imagesetter.

diacritic Sign used to indicate different phonetic sounds or semantic values of an alphabetic character.

Didot European type measurement system. 12 Didot points (a cicero) equals 4.512 mm. See *em, en, Cicero, pica* and *point.*

digital Characteristic of information in binary code.

digitize To transform information from any non-digital form to digital form.

dingbat Typographic symbol, such as a bullet, used for emphasis.

display advertisements Any advertisement which comprises more than 'straightforward' text setting. Generally refers to advertisements which are not classified.

display type Larger typeface used for headings, etc., as distinct from body type.

DOS Disc Operating System. Often used to refer specifically to operating system for IBM and compatible computers. Pronounced 'doss'.

dot matrix printer Computer printer that forms characters from dots made when points of pins strike a carbon ribbon or jets of ink strike directly on to the paper.

dot-for-dot Process of shooting (making film from) copy which is already screened, rather than using original continuous tone material to make a new halftone. Dot-for-dot generally implies that the reproduction will be the same size as the halftone being copied.

double page spread (DPS) A term used for an advertisement or editorial feature where pictures or artwork extend over facing pages.

download Transmission of information from one computer, usually a central storage device, to another. Upload is the reverse.

drop letter/cap The initial letter of a paragraph, usually at the beginning of an article, the depth of two or more lines of body type. The style is also used within articles to break up slabs of text as an alternative to crossheads.

drop out To lose halftone dots or fine lines due to over-exposure during camera work or platemaking. The lost area is said to have dropped out.

dummy (1) A layout of a publication to show, for example, type specification. (2) A complete set of page proofs by folio number. (3) Mock-up using dummy type, e.g. to show design of a new publication.

duotone Photograph reproduced from two halftone negatives and usually printed in black and one other colour.

duplicator Sometimes used to refer to press for quick printing. Not to be confused with spirit duplicator or photocopier.

EFT Electronic Funds Transfer.

electronic mail Use of computers and telecommunications to capture, store and deliver messages which may be of any sort, such as a letter, an engineering document or a price change or facsimile of a diagram. Messages may be sent to a specific address or to a mailbox. The principal UK mailbox host system is Telecom Gold.

electronic memory Disc, chip, tape, or other device that holds information in digital form.

electronic page assembly Assembly and manipulation on a computer screen of type, graphics, and other visual elements stored in memory.

elite type Smaller of the two standard typewriter typefaces, being ten point and usually set in 12 pitch.

em (1) The square of any typesize, e.g. the em for a 9 pt typeface measures 9 pt x 9 pt, and generally the space occupied by capital M. (2) The 12pt em (1/6 of an inch), or pica em, is the standard unit of type measurements for line or column widths. (Depths are measured either in millimetres, centimetres, inches, pica ems, points or the number of lines — the size of the body type, including leading, divided into the depth in points.) See *en*, *Cicero*, *Didot*, *pica* and *point*.

emulsion Chemical coating on papers, films, and printing plates that records an image when exposed to light.

en An en is half the width of an em. Copy is measured and expressed in multiples of ens as the en is the average width of a character in its own type size. See *em*, *Cicero*, *Didot*, *pica* and *point*.

equal spacing Typographic system of allocating the same amount of space to each character regardless of its width: 'i' gets the same space as 'p' and 'w' or a punctuation mark. The system used in simple typewriters.

etching Chemical treatment given to a printing plate after its exposure, removing either the image or non-image area (depending upon type of plate).

expanded type Style of type in which characters are wide in proportion to their height.

exposure Time required for light to record an image while striking photosensitive emulsion.

facing matter An advertisement position in a magazine where the advertisement faces editorial copy. There is usually a surcharge for such a position.

fax Short for 'facsimile'. Scanning and digital transmission of a document via the telephone system.

field One 'parcel' of information,

such as a name or post code, that is part of a record in a database.

fill pattern Tint or pattern of objects (bricks, leaves, etc.) used to fill an area of an illustration or to create a background. Now commonly associated with computer graphics programs.

film make-up Assembly of pieces of film (usually whole pages) into their required position so that a printing plate may be made. Also known as 'planning' or 'imposition'.

finish With regard to paper, its surface characteristics. With regard to printing, any process taking place in the bindery.

floating rule Rule, usually between columns, the ends of which do not touch other rules.

flush left/flush right Type set to range vertically to the left, or the right. The opposite side is ragged.

foil A plate-sized composite of page-sized films planned up to their positions ready for platemaking. One foil must be made for each colour to be printed. It consists of a large piece of acetate with negatives or positives attached in position.

fold marks Lines on a mechanical, negative, printing plate, or press sheet indicating where it is to be folded.

folio Page number. Even number is the left-hand page; odd number the right.

font/fount Originally, complete set of characters of one size of one typeface, now generally refers to a typeface of a particular design, e.g. Times New Roman.

footer Information, such as the magazine's name, that appears at bottom of each page.

format Size, shape, and style of a layout or printed piece.

forme A number pages arranged together in a metal frame for printing on one side of a sheet of paper. See *section*.

four-colour process Technique of printing that uses what are termed the process colours — cyan, magenta, yellow and black — to simulate colour photographs.

g/m^2 Grams per square metre. The weight or substance of paper, also known as 'gsm'. It is, of course, the weight in grams of one square metre of the particular paper.

galley Metal tray on which metal type was stored prior to make-up.

galley proof Proof of typeset copy held in a galley (hot metal).

gatefold Generally a facility offered to advertisers although sometimes used for editorial. The width of a page is extended by a flap which folds in against the page. The flap must be slightly less than the width of the page or must have more than one fold. Some magazines have gatefold covers. The position and number of gatefolds is limited by the format of the magazine and the method of production.

gathering The collection (usually mechanical) of sections of a magazine into their appropriate order just prior to stitching or glue-binding.

gloss Characteristic of paper, ink, or varnish that reflects relatively large amounts of light.

gone-to-bed Passed for press and too late to make corrections. (The bed is the area of a sheet fed letterpress machine on which the type, locked in a forme, is laid for printing.)

gothic type Type without serifs (e.g. Helvetica).

grain In paper, the direction in which fibres are aligned.

grain long or grain short Paper whose fibres run parallel to the long or short dimension of the sheet.

graphic arts film Film whose emulsion responds to light on an all-or-nothing principle to yield high-contrast images.

graphic arts The crafts, industries and professions related to designing and printing of graphic material.

graphic designer Professional who conceives the design for, plans how to produce, and may co-ordinate production of a printed piece.

graphics Rules, screens, charts, tables, photos, drawings, and other visual elements used in printed material.

gravure Intaglio printing process. The image is etched into the surface of the printing plate (a cylinder) so that it is lower than the non-image area. The cylinder turns through a trough of ink and the ink is drawn into the etched image areas. Surplus ink is removed from the surface by a blade. The image is printed directly on to the paper. Only one side of the paper can be printed at a time. The hard-wearing, rigid cylinders are expensive to originate and the process is uneconomical for runs below 100 000.

grid Pattern of non-printing guidelines on paste-up board or computer screen used to help align copy.

gsm See *g/m²*.

gutter (1) Space between two pairs of pages needed on a printed section for binding purposes once folding has taken place. The gutters are cut off when the complete magazine is trimmed (guillotined) square. (2) Space between columns on a page.

hair-line Line or gap about the width of a hair: 1/100th inch.

halftone An illustration or photograph which has been rendered into tiny dots of varying sizes to allow tonal variation in the printed result, when only one ink (usually black) is used.

halftone dots Thousands of dots that together create the illusion of shading or a continuous tone image. Dots vary in size according to the tonal value.

halftone screen Piece of film containing a grid of lines that breaks light into dots as it passes through. The number of dots in a given area, e.g. 120 lines per inch.

hard copy Copy on paper, thus permanent.

hardware Keyboard, CRT (cathode ray tube), terminal, chips, and other physical units of a computer system.

head Top margin of a page.

header Information, such as its name, that appears at top of every page of a magazine.

heat set When coated (non-absorbent) paper is printed by the web-offset method it must be passed through a heater unit or 'oven' in order to dry the ink.

hickey Doughnut-shaped spot or imperfection in printing, most visible in areas of heavy ink coverage.

high contrast Few or no tonal gradations between dark and light areas.

highlights Lightest areas in a photograph or halftone.

hold over Keeping a story out of a magazine with a view to using it later.

hyphenation A hyphen is inserted in a word just before a break at the end of a line to denote the word is continued. Hyphenation is the act of so doing. See *justification*.

icon Symbol for a file or command displayed on a computer screen.

image area Portion of a mechanical, negative, or plate corresponding to ink on paper. Portion of paper on which ink appears.

image Type, illustration, or other original scene as it has been reproduced on computer screen, film, printing plate, or paper.

imposition Arrangement of pages on mechanicals or plates so they will appear in proper sequence after press sheets are folded and bound.

imprint Information in small type giving the publisher's and printer's name and other information, some of which is required by law.

in pro Short for in proportion, used to describe material which must be reproduced so as to retain its original proportions. See *s/s*.

indent Setting where the width of the type is less than the usual measure. Indents provide white space at the start or end of a line, or both. Paragraph indent is the indent of the first line of a paragraph.

input/output Data imported into or exported from an electronic system such as a typesetter or computer. Hardware: keyboards, scanners, etc., are input devices and printers, plotters, etc., are output devices.

intaglio See *gravure*.

interface Communicating link between two or more electronic devices.

ISBN International Standard Book Number. Number assigned to individual books. Part of the number identifies the publisher and the rest the title.

ISO International Organization for Standardization. The abbreviation followed by a number is used as to denote photographic film speed. See *ASA*.

ISSN International Standard Serial Number. Number assigned to magazines and other serial publications, which identifies the publisher, the title and the issue.

italics Characters that slant to the right.

JICMARS Joint Industry Committee for Medical Readership Surveys.

justified Type set so that lines begin and end flush both left and right. There is an optimum spacing between words and characters which is adjusted within pre-fixed limits to achieve desired results. The process, when aided by hyphenation, is termed 'H&J'. See *hyphenation*.

k Letter symbolizing 1000. Used in computer terminology to represent 1024. A computer memory of 64k is in fact 65 536 bytes. See *binary number*.

kern To reduce space between letters. Most typesetting systems carry kerning tables for the various type families and sizes. The kerning can be adjusted for individual characters, words, lines paragraphs, stories, etc., to fit more characters in a given space or to improve the visual appearance.

key number Usually placed in the coupon of an advertisement to identify the name and issue date of the magazine in which it appears. Some advertisements ask respondents to quote a key number. Enables results to be monitored.

key To relate photographs or loose pieces of copy to their positions on a layout or mechanical using a system of numbers or letters.

keylines Lines on a bromide or negative showing the exact size, shape, and position of photographs or other graphic elements which are to be included later in the process of assembly.

laminating The application of thin film over printing to enhance the appearance and to give protection. See *varnish*.

landscape Horizontal format (greater width than depth) on a computer screen or printout. Origin is the conventional shape of a landscape picture. See *portrait*.

laser Acronym for 'light amplification by stimulated emission of radiation'.

laser printer Device using a laser beam to deposit a pattern of electrostatically charged dots on paper (usually). The dots attract toner which is 'sealed' under high temperature. Laser printers are used as output devices for personal computers. High-speed laser printers can be used to produce complete books, reports, etc., one at a time. They are ideal for short-run or on-demand printing.

layout Plan showing position and size of text and graphics.

leader (1) A magazine's leading or opinion article; also called the 'editorial'. (2) Lines of dots or other characters used in tabular setting, leading from one column to the next.

leading Extra space between lines of type, e.g. 9/10pt is 9pt type with one point of leading. The depth is measured from the baseline of one line of type to the baseline of the next. Pronounced 'ledding'.

letter spacing The space between letters. May be adjusted to occupy more or less space as an aid to justification or to improve the visual appearance of text.

letterpress printing Method of printing where raised type, held in a forme (frame), is given a coating of ink and brought into contact with paper under pressure. The type is composed either by hand from cases (partitioned trays) containing individual characters, or by machine. The latter process uses moulds to cast individual characters or lines of type (slugs) from a molten lead-like material. Hence the term 'hot metal'. Early presses used wooden type and this is still used today for very large sizes and very short runs, such as posters.

ligature Two or more letters joined

for grammatical reasons or to avoid unsightly spacing or juxtapositions of serifs, etc., e.g. ae, fi, ffi.

light table Translucent glass surface illuminated from below and used for layout and make-up.

line drawing An illustration composed of lines or mechanical tints as distinct from a halftone or continuous tone illustration.

line measure The width of a line of type.

line spacing Alternative term for leading.

lines per inch or **lpi** Measure of screen ruling expressing how many lines or rows of dots there are per inch in a screen tint or halftone.

literal An error in typing or typesetting where one letter, word or line has been substituted for another.

lithography Method of printing using a chemically coated plate, the non-image areas of which repel ink and the image areas attract ink.

logo Distinctive symbol unique to an organization, business, or product. Short for logostyle.

lower case Letters that are not capitals. Dates from the days of hand composition when capitals were kept in the 'upper' case and non-capitals were kept in the 'lower' case.

M Mega, meaning one million. m (lower case) is one thousandth. See *megabyte*.

m/f Abbreviation for 'more follows' placed at bottom of page of copy.

machine finished A paper on which the surface finish is applied during its making rather than as a separate operation. Also known as 'machine coated'.

machine-readable Either a stream of data or codes on paper or magnetic tape, magnetic disc, floppy disc, etc., which can be read by a machine, or a document which can be scanned and read by an optical character reader.

macro Frequently used phrase, paragraph, or other combination of keystrokes that can be input with a single key or a combination of a few keys.

makeready All activities required to set up a printing press before a production run begins.

manuscript Typed or handwritten copy.

margin Space forming border of a page or sheet.

mark up To write instructions on copy or proofs using standard symbols and proof correction marks.

mask out To cover selected copy or art so it will not appear on a photocopy, negative, or printing plate.

masking material Opaque paper or plastic used to prevent light from reaching selected areas of film or printing plate.

masthead Nowadays commonly used for the titlepiece of a magazine displayed on the front page, but more correctly the title when used with other information about the magazine or publishing house above the leader columns.

matt finish Slightly dull finish on coated paper.

measure The length of a line of type, usually expressed in (12pt) pica ems. Often abbreviated to 'picas' or 'ems'. See *em, en, Cicero, Didot, pica* and *point*.

mechanical Camera-ready assembly of type and graphics complete with instructions to the printer. Often called 'paste-up' or 'finished artwork'.

media pack A brochure or collection of printed material describing the merits of a magazine and its technical specification.

megabyte One million bytes (actually 1 024 000) or 1000 kb. Abbreviated as Mb.

menu List of possible computer functions displayed on a computer screen.

merge/purge To combine two or more mailing lists (merge), then eliminate duplicated addresses (purge), usually with the help of a computer.

middle tones Tones in a photograph or illustration about half as dark as its shadow areas and represented in halftones by dots between 30% and 70% of full size.

modem Acronym for 'modulator/demodulator'. Device that converts digital signals to analog tones and vice versa, so that electronic systems can interface over telephone lines.

moiré Undesirable pattern in halftones and screen tints made with improperly aligned screens.

monitor To scan publications (usually competitors) to count advertising space sold by category to calculate estimated revenue, and to calculate advertising spend by individual advertisers. Provides a measure of market share and sales lead information.

monochrome Single colour, generally meaning black ink printed on white paper.

mounting board Smooth card used for paste-ups or to mount photographs.

mouse Device connected to a computer which enables the screen cursor to be moved two-dimensionally.

multicolour printing Printing in more than one ink colour.

NRS National Readership Survey.

near-letter-quality Highest quality output (and the slowest) of a dot matrix printer.

negative Image on film or paper which has been reversed black to white. Also, piece of film having a negative image.

nlq See *near-letter-quality*.

non-repro blue Light blue colour to which graphic arts film is not sensitive, and may therefore be used to write instructions on artwork or bromide.

OCR Optical character recognition. Method of digitizing printed text by scanner and 'reading' it into a computer.

offset lithography A printing process where the image is transferred to a light-sensitive surface on a printing plate which is then chemically etched. The plate is prepared so that the image area attracts ink and rejects water, and the non-image area attracts water and rejects ink. This is possible because of the incompatibility of ink and water. Water is applied to the plate, ink is applied, the water is removed leaving the ink, which is transferred on to the paper via a rubber blanket cylinder. As the ink from the plate is not printed directly on to the paper, the process is termed 'offset'. There is also a lithography process which does not use an offset blanket and prints direct. It is called dilitho, but is not common.

offset litho, sheetfed Single sheets are printed one at a time by being lifted mechanically from a stack, fed through the press, printed and stacked. Both sides of the paper can be printed simultaneously and such presses are capable of 6000 to 10 000 impressions per hour.

offset litho, web Web presses print on a continuous web of paper fed from reels. The main advantage is speed. Disadvantages are greater paper wastage when setting up, and loss of time if the web breaks. Speeds vary between 20 000 and 30 000 impressions per hour printing on both sides of the paper.

opacity In this context, a characteristic of paper relating to its degree of transparency. With 'high opacity' paper the print on the reverse does not show through, but with 'low opacity' paper it does.

opaque Not transparent. Also used as a verb meaning to make opaque (paint or cover with non-transparent material).

originals Photographs or artwork to be used for publication.

orphan Last line of paragraph appearing as first line of a column or page (to be avoided). See *widow*.

output See *input/output*.

overlay Sheet of tissue or acetate taped to a piece of artwork to carry material to be stripped in or to be in another colour, to carry written instructions or simply for protection.

overmatter Copy which has been typeset but not used in the final printing.

overs Number of items that were printed in excess of the quantity specified.

page proof Proof of a completed page.

pagination Page numbering.

paper dummy Unprinted sample of

a proposed item, trimmed, and folded, using the paper specified for the job.

paste up To affix copy to mounting boards and, if necessary, overlays, so it is in a camera-ready form. The result is called a 'paste-up'.

perfect bound Method of binding where folded sections are collated side-by-side, and the binding edge is trimmed and glued. The process creates a square spine. Covers are usually then drawn on and glued in position. See *saddle stitch*.

perfecting press Press capable of printing both sides of the paper during a single pass.

peripherals Hardware connected to a computer system for additional or alternate input, output, or memory.

photogravure See *gravure*.

phototypesetting (photosetting) Typesetting by a photographic system with the output on bromide (photo-sensitive paper) or film.

pi font Font with mathematical symbols, dingbats, and other characters for special needs.

pica An old size of type equivalent to 12pt. A pica em is the square of the letter M in 12pt type, i.e. 12pt or 0.166 in. or 4.2 mm. The pica em is still used by many as the linear unit of typographical measurement, but is being replaced by the centimetre. See em, en, Cicero, Didot and point.

pitch Number of equally spaced characters per inch (cpi) that a typewriter or computer printer will produce. Standard pitches are 10, 12 and 15 cpi.

pixel Acronym for 'picture element'. Dot generated by a computer, scanner, or other digital device.

platemaker Machine to make printing plates automatically after the original material is photographed.

PMS or **Pantone Matching System**. Commonly used initials and name of a colour matching system.

PMT or **Photo Mechanical Transfer**. Kodak trade name for process used to make paper or film, negative or positive prints of line copy and halftones.

point A unit of typographical measurement. There are approximately 72 points to an inch and 28.35 points to a centimetre. 12pt equals 0.166in. Typesizes are expressed in points and refer to the depth from the top of the highest ascender to the bottom of the lowest descender. See *em, en, Cicero, Didot* and *pica*.

portrait mode Vertical format (depth greater than width) of a computer screen, printout or magazine, etc.

positive An image on paper or film which is 'right-reading' and where blacks are black or opaque and whites are white or clear.

pre-sort To sort by post codes before mailing.

prepress Camera work, stripping, platemaking, and other activities by the printer before press work begins.

preprint To print work in advance to be ready for inserting or overprinting.

press proof Proof made on press using the plates, paper, and ink specified for the job.

press run The number of copies printed.

Prestel Videotex service run by British Telecom. See *videotex* and *viewdata*.

price break Quantity level at which unit cost of paper or printing drops.

printing plate Surface that carries the image to be printed. Depending on the press, the image will be 'right-reading' or reversed.

process camera Graphic arts camera used to photograph mechanicals and other camera-ready copy.

program The US spelling of programme, adopted as the convention when used in the context of computer software (computer program).

progressive proofs (progressives) A series of proofs showing the build up of colours from separated film/plates. Each colour is proofed separately and also superimposed progressively in the correct printing sequence (usually): yellow, cyan, magenta, black.

proof correction marks Standard symbols and abbreviations used to mark up manuscripts and proofs. There are two British Standards, BS 1219 and BS 5261 part 2. The latter is best used when marking foreign set material.

proof Test sheet made for checking.
proof-read To examine a manuscript or proof for errors. Strictly speaking, the proof should be compared character-for-character with the original.
proportional scale Device used to calculate the percentage by which an original image must be reduced or enlarged to give a specific reproduction size.
proportional spacing Characters spaced according to their width: 'i' gets least space, 'M' or 'W' get most.

quad left/right See *flush left/flush right*.

ragged Type not justified. 'Ragged right' describes text that is 'flush left'.
RAM Random Access Memory. Computer memory used to perform functions on files in immediate use.
random (market research) A method of selecting people to take part in a survey, which ensures that everyone in the universe has an equal chance of being selected.
range left/right See *flush left/flush right*.
reader One who corrects proofs. Machine that 'reads', such as a barcode reader.
register marks Crossed hair-lines on mechanicals and negatives for ensuring registration. See *cut marks*.
register To position print correctly in relation to edges of paper and other printing on the same sheet, i.e. other colours. When accurately printed it is described as 'in register'.
research, qualitative Deals with people, their opinions and aspirations.
research, quantitative Deals with statistical and demographic matters, or how many and where.
retouch To enhance a photographic print or correct flaws using techniques such as spotting and airbrushing.
reverse/reverse out Type or graphic reversed black to white. For example, a black character on a white background is reversed and printed as a white character on a black background.
revise Proof taken after corrections

have been made.
river Annoying pattern of white space running like a river through text type.
ROM Read Only Memory. Permanent computer memory used to store basic operating instructions. It cannot be altered by the user.
roman type Upright type, not italic nor bold. Abbreviated to rom.
rough layout Sketch giving general idea of size and placement of text and graphics.
rule Line used as graphic.
ruling See *screen ruling*.
run Total number of copies ordered or printed.
runaround Type set to conform to part or all of the outline of a photograph or illustration.
running head or **running foot** Information appearing at the top or bottom of every page of a publication.
running sheets Sheets taken from the production run on the press.

s/s Same size.
saddle stitch To bind by stapling sheets together through the fold at the spine.
sans serif Type without serifs.
scale To calculate the percentage by which artwork should be enlarged or reduced.
scanner Device used to digitize type, illustrations, or photographs.
screamer Exclamation mark (!).
screen A fine grid on film or glass which breaks a continuous tone illustration into a series of dots for printing. Scanned or computer generated illustrations are 'screened' by the computer software. The interval between the dots, described as lines per inch or lines per cm, is the screen value.
screen clash See *moiré*.
screen density Amount of tone expressed as a percentage between white (0%) and the full colour (100%).
screen ruling The number of rows or lines of dots per inch in a screen for tint or halftone. See *screen*.
screen tint Area of printing broken with dots so ink coverage is less than 100%. Simulates shading or a lighter

colour.

scum Undesirable thin film of ink on non-image area of printed sheet.

section A complete printed sheet either flat (not yet folded) or folded which makes up part of a magazine or book. The smallest number of pages in a section is two (one sheet of page size), but normally sections are composed of multiples of four pages. Section size depends on the dimensions of press and paper and the page size. (A section printed on an A2 press could consist of eight A4 pages, four on each side.)

separations Film for making printing plates for colour printing, obtained by separating from the original. The original is photographed through additive colour filters — red, blue and green — or scanned, to produce separations in four subtractive colours — yellow, cyan, magenta and black. When printed, the illusion of full colour is created.

serif type Type with serifs — short lines protruding at a variety of angles from the ends of main strokes of characters.

set solid Type set with no leading between lines.

set-off Transfer of wet ink from one sheet to another.

sheetfed printing Printing on single cut sheets as distinct from reeled paper. See *offset litho, sheetfed.*

short grain See *against the grain.*

show-through Printing on one side of paper that can be seen on the other side. The higher the opacity of the paper, the less the show-through.

sidehead Small heading in the text which is flush left. See *crosshead.*

side stabbing See *side stitching.*

side stitching A method of binding which secures together the sections of a magazine or book by stitching from the side.

signature See *section.*

small caps Capital letters which are less than full height but usually taller than lower case letters.

software Instructions needed to control and operate a computer; in practice, the term refers to programs alone.

solid An area of 100% ink coverage.

specification In printing, complete and precise description of paper, ink, binding, quantity, and other features of a printing job. For type, instructions about typeface and size, line measure, indents, headlines, etc.

spread Two pages that face each other. Also the layout, especially of photos, on such pages.

standing matter/type Setting that is used in each issue of a magazine, such as publication details and office addresses.

stet Correction mark for 'let it stand', instructing a compositor or keyboard operator to ignore an indicated change and retain the original version.

straight copy Copy that contains no charts, tables, formulas, or other elements that complicate typesetting.

strapline Introductory line or phrase above the main headline.

style In copyediting, the house or magazine rules for treatment of such matters as optional spellings, use of capital letters, dates, modes of address, titles, numerals, etc.

subtitle Secondary title.

swatch book Book with samples of papers or ink colours.

synopsis publishing Distribution of a summary of a scientific paper (usually). Readers who are interested in the complete paper can then apply for it if needed. It is a means of reducing publishing costs and delays.

Teletel Name of the public videotex service in France.

teletext International service and set of standards operated by telecommunications authorities, enabling subscribers to exchange information between terminals and computers on an automatic memory-to-memory basis. It may be likened to an improved telex service operating at a higher speed and with a much larger character set.

thesaurus (1) Dictionary or encyclopaedia, usually of words and concepts, giving synonyms, antonyms and metaphors. (2) Structured collection of terms used in information retrieval which usually includes the relationships of indexing terms and synonyms.

tick marks Alternative term for corner or crop marks.

tint See *screen tint*.

tissue Thin, translucent paper used for overlays.

transparency 'Tranny' for short, usually a single frame of positive colour film, although it is possible to have black and white transparencies.

trichromatic Colour printed from three colours instead of the usual four (without black).

trim marks Lines on artwork which are carried through to the press sheet showing where to cut off edges of paper or cut paper apart after printing. See *crop marks*.

trim size Size of the finished product after last trim is made.

trimming The guillotining of printed and bound material on (usually) three edges after binding.

turnaround time Amount of time from the start to completion of a job.

type family Group of type styles with similar letterforms and a unique name (Times, Helvetica, etc.).

type Letters, numerals, punctuation marks, and other symbols to be reproduced by printing. Type was formerly always cut or moulded from wood or metal, either by hand or machine. Now, most type is generated by phototypesetters or imagesetters on bromide or film.

type size The height of a typeface measured from the top of its ascenders to the bottom of its descenders. Usually expressed in points.

type style Roman, italic, condensed, bold, and other variations of a typeface.

typescale A device for measuring type sizes and type leading (the space between lines of type). Usually has scales in the most commonly used text sizes from about 6pt to 12pt.

typesetter A device that produces type, whether metal or on bromide or film. Also, person who operates such a machine or business which offers a typesetting service.

typo Short for 'typographical error'.

typography The art and science of setting and arranging type in a readable and pleasing manner.

uncoated paper Paper that has not been clay coated.

undercolour removal The subtraction of an equal amount of each primary colour from beneath shadows and dark degraded coloured areas to reduce the weight of ink being printed on the paper. In UCR the black is increased in density but not to the same extent as in *achromatic* printing.

unders Number of printed items less than the quantity specified.

unjustified Text of uneven line length, either flush-left, ragged-right, centred, flush-right, ragged left, etc.

upper case Capital letters.

value-added network Network operated by a private company authorized by a government agency to lease basic communications services from common carriers and specialized common carriers, to augment the services through additional facilities, such as switching centres and store-and-forward devices, and to re-sell the enhanced service to end users.

varnish Clear liquid applied like solid ink over underlying printing. Makes the surface and ink more glossy and gives some protection. See *laminating*.

videotex Generic term used for interactive systems that often use a modified TV set to display computer-based information, organised in a way that is simple to use. Connection is usually achieved by telephone line. See *Prestel* and *viewdata*.

viewdata British generic term for interactive videotex systems.

vignette Illustration where edges are gradually faded to nothing.

web A continuous roll, or reel, of paper.

web-offset See *offset litho, web*.

weight For paper, thickness of paper is generally specified by the weight in grammes of one square metre. Text paper is generally between 60 and 115 gsm (grammes per square metre). In typography, characteristic of type determined by how light (thin) or dark (bold, thick, heavy) it appears when printed.

white space Designer term referring to non-image area that frames or sets off copy.

widow First line of a paragraph appearing at the bottom of a page or column (to be avoided!). See *orphan*.

with the grain Parallel to the grain direction of the paper.

wood-free A paper made from chemically treated wood pulp and free from the inferior 'mechanical' pulp.

word spacing Amount of space between words. Automatically adjusted by typesetting software when operating in justify mode. The operator may set maximum, minimum and optimum values.

word-wrapping Automatic movement of words from a line that is too long to the next line.

WYSIWYG 'What You See Is What You Get.' Term to describe the ability to represent type and graphics on a computer screen precisely as they will output on paper. In fact, few programs can do this exactly — you are more likely to experience 'What You See Might Be What You Get' or 'What You See Is Nearly What You Get'.

x-height Height of lower case letters without ascenders or descenders, typically an 'x'.

xerography Method of printing that transfers the image as an electrostatic charge on the surface of the paper and creates it with powder (toner) bonded to the paper by heat. Photocopy machines and laser printers use xerography.

Index